Knowing Who

Knowing Who

Steven E. Boër and William G. Lycan

A Bradford Book
The MIT Press
Cambridge, Massachusetts
London, England

This book was set in Palatino by Asco Trade Typesetting Limited, Hong Kong and printed and bound by Halliday Lithograph in the United States of America.

Library of Congress Cataloging in Publication Data

Boër, Steven E.
  Knowing who.

  "A Bradford book."
  Bibliography: p.
  Includes index.
  1. Identity—Addresses, essays, lectures. 2. Self (Philosophy)—Addresses, essays, lectures. 3. Individuation—Addresses, essays, lectures. 4. Knowledge, Theory of—Addresses, essays, lectures. 5. Logic—Addresses, essays, lectures. I. Lycan, William G. II. Title.
BD236.B64 1986   126   85-11337
ISBN 0-262-02228-1

Feebly hoping to avoid protective reaction by the Daughters of Xanthippe, we dedicate this book with love to Ann Boër, M.D., and Mary Lycan, J.D.

Contents

Preface

In 1975 we published an article, "Knowing who" (*Philosophical Studies* 28 (1975), 299–344), in which we explored the little-understood notion of "knowing who someone is," and offered a semantical theory of ascriptions of "knowing who." Our analysis has been cited variously in the literature, with gratifying approval, but to our knowledge not a single objection has been made against it. For some time we ascribed this absence of criticism to our theory's manifest plausibility and power, and we are still tempted to do so. But only rarely is a philosophical theory's ring of truth as clear and as strong as its creators fondly suppose; and in this book we are moved to expand and ramify the theory in a more comprehensive and provocative way, applying it to some more familiar philosophical issues, the bearing on which of our semantical concerns would not have been immediately apparent.

We begin by offering a revised analysis of "knowing who someone is," "knowing a person's identity," and the like. Our account is now set in the context of a general theory of believing and a semantical theory of belief and knowledge ascriptions. Our main contention is that what one knows when one knows who someone is, is not an *identity* in the numerical or logical sense of "a = b," at all, but rather a special sort of predication: To know who someone is is just to know that that person is F, where "F" is a predicate that is "important" (in a technical sense that we define) for the purposes determined by context. We go on in part II to offer a rigorous formal semantics for ascriptions of knowing and of "knowing who" in particular; this treatment solves some well-known problems and paradoxes, such as Kripke's puzzle and Quine's difficulties regarding *de re* belief. Once the analysis has been entirely developed and refined, we apply it in part III to each of several more traditional philosophical issues in which the previously unexamined notion of "knowing who" has loomed large: linguistic referring, the foundations of epistemic logic, self-knowledge and self-regarding belief, universalizabilty and "Golden Rule" arguments in ethics, and moral "personalism" versus "impartialism."

We owe thanks to many people for discussion and for their generous comments on our original article and related papers. With little hope of success, we try to acknowledge all our particular debts in notes, but we are especially grateful for the more general and extensive contributions of Michael T. Carlsen-Jones, Hector Castañeda, Max Cresswell, Dan Dennett, Richard Garner, Gilbert Harman, Charles Kielkopf, Murray Kiteley, Robert Kraut, Keith Lehrer, Michael McKinsey, John Pollock, Jay Rosenberg, George Schumm, Ernest Sosa, the late Gail Stine, and especially Michael Devitt. Finally, as if anyone had to ask *who* are Bradford Books, we thank Harry and Betty Stanton for their expert help in producing this essay.

Acknowledgments

Chapters 1 and 2 are based on Boër and Lycan, "Knowing who," *Philosophical Studies*, 28 (1975), 299–344; copyright © 1975 by D. Reidel Publishing Company, Dordrecht, Holland. Sections 1 and 2 of chapter 4 are based on section II of Lycan, "Toward a homuncular theory of believing," *Cognition and Brain Theory*, 4 (1981), 139–159; copyright © 1981 by Lawrence Erlbaum Associates. Material reprinted by permission. Some of the material in sections 1, 3, and 4 of chapter 5 was written, in a different form, for presentation by Lycan at the Arizona Colloquium in Cognition in February, 1984. Under the title "Thoughts about things," that essay will appear in M. Brand and R. M. Harnish (eds.), *Problems in the Representation of Knowledge and Belief* (Tucson: Univ. of Arizona Press).

"Have a cigarette, Mr. McFarlane," said he, . . . "I should be glad if you would sit down in that chair, and tell us very slowly and quietly who you are. . . . You mentioned your name, as if I should recognize it, but I assure you that, beyond the obvious facts that you are a bachelor, a solicitor, a Freemason, and an asthmatic, I know nothing whatever about you."

—Sherlock Holmes
in "The Adventure of the Norwood Builder"

As Holmes turned up the lamp the light fell upon a card on the table. He glanced at it, and then, with an ejaculation of disgust, threw it on the floor. I picked it up and read:

CHARLES AUGUSTUS MILVERTON,
Appledore Towers,
Hampstead.

Agent.

"Who is he?" I asked.
"The worst man in London," Holmes answered. . . .

—"The Adventure of Charles Augustus Milverton"

I

Chapter 1
Adequacy Conditions and a Prototheory

What is it to know who someone is? There should be some enlightening general answer to this question, however crude. Speakers of everyday English often claim to know who such-and-such a person is or ascribe such knowledge to others. Philosophers concerned with the logic of knowing, with the natural functions of singular terms, or with the nature of doxastic states appeal to the notion of "knowing who" as if it were sufficiently clear to go on with.[1] But until recently, the literature contained no more than a half-hearted discussion of the notion. In the 1975 pilot article on which this book is based, we tried to fill this lacuna; here we make a far more thorough attempt to explicate "knowing who" and related locutions. In later chapters we bring our analysis to bear on related philosophical issues.

Some obvious questions: Can we provide an interesting and useful taxonomy for the different sorts of answers that might, under various circumstances, be given to queries of the form "Who is N?"? Given the (much-conceded) multiplicity of tests for "knowing who" appropriate to different sorts of situations, is there any single canonical paraphrase appropriate to all instances of "S knows who N is"? In the end can we give a general theory of "knowing who" that illuminates the traditional issues that have been supposed to hang on the notion?

We concern ourselves mainly with expressions of the form "S knows who N is," though several cognate locutions deserve individual treatment ("S doesn't know who N is," "S remembers who N is," "S wonders who N is," "S told T who N is," etc.). It is important to bear in mind throughout than in such formulas "N" can be replaced by terms of several different sorts: proper names, demonstratives and other pronouns, and singular and plural definite descriptions.

1 Multiple Tests and Privileged Facts

It is a truism that a well-reasoned answer to the question "Does S know who N is?" may rest, in different situations, on widely disparate grounds; different circumstances demand different tests for knowing who someone is. Although such a test normally consists of eliciting an appropriate singular term from S in response to "Who is N?," the standard of "appropriateness" differs dramatically.

It is easy to imagine situations in which an informant S's response to "Who is N?" prompts a repetition of the question; that is, S might respond to our original query with "N is M," "M" being a singular term distinct from "N,"[2] and we might well pursue the matter by asking "But who is M?" So far as grammar is concerned, this process could continue indefinitely, were we sufficiently loath to credit S with knowledge of N's identity. However, it seems that if S really does know who N $(= M, = \ldots)$ is in the ordinary sense of that expression, the serial questioning would (from the epistemological point of view) have to stop; at some point in the chain of questions, S would have provided us with contextually conclusive evidence (whether or not we see fit to accept that evidence) that S does indeed know who N is. After all—surely—if S knows *enough* facts about someone, then S cannot fail to know who that person is.

This datum gives rise to the suspicion that there is some privileged group of identifying facts about a person such that to cite a member of that group is to provide one's audience with conclusive grounds for saying that one knows who that person is; more strongly, it is natural to suspect that the ability to cite a member of the privileged group *constitutes* knowing who that person is. Several candidates for privileged feature suggest themselves: It might be held that one knows who N is if one can produce N's name, address, and occupation; or that one knows who N is if one knows individuating details of N's physiognomy and/or has a record of N's fingerprints; or that one knows who N is if one can physically locate or lay hands on N on demand.

Even if such hopes as these are unrealistic, can some such group of identifying facts *carry more weight* in certifying that S knows who N is? It certainly seems so. We would be much more likely to proclaim that S knows who N is if S were able to give us N's physical description, address, and occupation than if S were merely to offer the (unique) number of hairs on N's head. And N's social security number is surely a better guide to N's identity than is the (also unique) number of hackberry trees visible from his maternal grandmother's billiard-room window. This much seems beyond doubt; but are these disparities formally significant? Can we distinguish logically or syntactically between facts that count vis-à-vis N's identity and facts that do not? (This seems far too much to hope for.) Or are these data merely epiphenomena of the passing interests and predilections of twentieth-century middle-class American academics? Or—to aim somewhere in between—do they reflect pervasive though contingent features of normal human endeavor in general?

Let us quickly assess our strongest hypothesis: that there is a type of individuating fact such that S's citing a fact of that type about N is conclusive grounds for saying that S knows who N is. (Alternatively, it might be said that a chain of questions of the form "Who is N?" must or can always terminate in the citing of such a fact.) It is fairly easy to see that no hypothesis of this strong sort will do. If "D" is an identifying description of the allegedly preferred type, it should not make sense (or at least it should be palpably pointless) to ask, "Who is D?" But given any candidate whatever, it makes perfect sense to ask the relevant question unless some specific feature of context makes it otiose. To see this, consider the three candidates mentioned above: name, address, and occupation; physiognomy-*cum*-fingerprints; and physical location. Anyone can imagine circumstances in which it would be not only sensible but vital to ask, "But who is this Irving Smedley, the office boy who lives at 851 Amalgam Lane?" or, "But who is the man whose photograph and fingerprints we have here?" or, "But who is this scruffy character that we have just heaved into the drunk tank?" If these questions make sense, as they surely do, then possession of identifying facts of any of the three sorts we have mentioned is insufficient to guarantee knowing who someone is. And if having received a convincing answer to these questions, one could further ask, "But who is ———?," where the blank is filled by the immediately preceding answer, then our chain of questions need not come to an end on meeting an answer of one of our three types. It seems, then, that no type of identifying description is autocratically privileged in the way we have tried to suppose and that chains of "Who is ———?" questions may terminate in different ways on different occasions—we expect or demand different sorts of answers to "Who is N?"

One might at this point suggest that "S knows who N is" is multiply ambiguous. If we are asked, "Who is that man cutting his toenails in the conservatory?," we might naturally respond, "What do you mean? Do you want to know what his name is? Or what he does? Or what he's doing at this party?" And if we are asked, "Do you know who that man is?," it is even more natural to reply, "In one sense I do, but in another sense I don't" (e.g., I can tell you his name and occupation but not what he did to earn an invitation to this exclusive affair).[3] But several considerations militate against conceding that "S knows who N is" has different *senses* on different occasions. (i) It would be hard to *locate* the difference. There is neither any apparent syntactic ambiguity nor any independent evidence that "know" itself is polysemous. The most plausible option would be to say that "who" is ambiguous, but ambiguity in an interrogative pronoun would be hard to spell out. (ii) The alleged ambiguity would be not merely multiple but monstrous. We illustrate its profusion and offer a catalog of cases in chapter 2. (iii) The putative ambiguities would be widely proliferated. They would infect all the cognate locutions, as well as others that are somewhat more loosely related, such as "S remembers who N is," "S revealed who N is," "S made a guess as to who N is," and so on. (iv) Ambiguities should not be multiplied beyond necessity in any case. Our only motive to date for positing ambiguity here is the diversity of tests, and no one but a crass verificationist would take that to signal semantic ambiguity without further examination.

There do seem to be cases in which it is simultaneously both true and false to say of a person that he knows who someone is, i.e., in which the most natural and nonmisleading reponse to "Does S know who N is?" is, "He does and he doesn't." Consider the plight of the copy boy at the *Daily Planet* who catches occasional glimpses of Clark Kent. It is true that the copy boy knows who Kent is, in that the boy can produce Kent's name, address, staff position, journalistic accomplishments, salient personal characteristics, preference in sandwich condiments, and the like, but in an obvious way the boy also does *not* know who Kent is; he does not know that Kent is really the Man of Steel, scion of Krypton, and savior of Truth, Justice, and the American Way. (Less imaginative examples suffice to make the point: In one way, plainly, we know who the Dalai Lama is; he is the exiled leader of Tibetan Buddhism. But we do not know where he came from and what he did before ascending to his present religious position.) Yet we can maintain the presumed univocity of "S knows who N is" by regarding it as elliptical and positing a *hidden parameter.* If we can find a plausible domain for such a parameter, we can account neatly for the "yes and no" cases without yielding to the ambiguity hypothesis and hold that "knowing who" is merely *relative.*

Fortunately there is a candidate, however vague and unilluminating, captured by a fairly colloquial idiom: S may know who N is for some purposes but not for others. (Or S may know who N is for all practical purposes.) The answer S would give to "Who is N?" (which would determine our verdict as to whether S knows who N is) depends not just on the state of S's knowledge about N but (over and above that) on his interest in N, his purposes at the time regarding N, or, we might say, his *project* vis-à-vis N. Thus our copy boy knows who Clark Kent is for the everyday purposes of getting about the newspaper business but not for the purpose of getting immediate help for Lois Lane (who is being eaten by a giant squid) or for that of reciting an honor roll of patriots, crime fighters, and heroes. And we know who the Dalai Lama is for the purpose of telling the recent history of Buddhism but not for the purpose of writing a book of success stories. These locutions seem natural enough; so let us say that our parameter is represented in each case as a *purpose* or *project*, typically (but not necessarily) that of S, the knower. Note that the purpose mentioned or presupposed in a knowing-who attribution need not be one that either S or the speaker is actually acting on, even tacitly so.

We say much more about "projects" in succeeding chapters. For now let us formulate our preliminary analysis of "S knows who N is," first having glanced at a few earlier ideas suggested by some philosophers' writings on related topics.

2 Adequacy Conditions

What should we expect from a formal analysis or regimentation of "S knows who N is"? On our view, the following.

Requirement 1   The theory should meet the demand with which this chapter began, viz., it should yield a general answer to the question of what it is to know who someone is. (We do not expect that the general answer will be terribly illuminating, since our notion of purpose or project is necessarily so inclusive, but our hypothesized regimentation should display whatever is nontrivially common to all cases, or all standard cases, of "knowing who.")

Requirement 2   Our proposal should do this by capturing all the felt implications of ordinary knowing-who locutions (and, needless to say, by officially neglecting all those sentences intuitively not implied by the ordinary locutions). Of course, we have to start by offering rough approximations, in the sense that we may have to accept some unobvious consequences and/or neglect some apparent consequences, so long as the respective consequences or nonconsequences are close to being "don't cares." Any such mildly counterintuitive results are refined away later.

Requirement 3   Our theory should show exactly where our posited parameter fits into the analysis of "knowing who," i.e., just how the parameter functions semantically in relation to the other basic ingredients of "S knows who N is."

Requirement 4   The theory should display any actual ambiguity that *may* turn up. (Our defense of univocity in section 1 above is presumptive only. Although we reject the claim that each test for "knowing who" determines a different sense of "S knows who N is," we later find grounds for admitting one source of syntactic and semantic ambiguity.)

Requirement 5   It is clear that, superficially, the position marked by "N" in "S knows who N is" is not purely referential. Substitution of coreferring singular terms into that position can change truth value. Consider a detective's best friend, Boris, who has (unbeknownst to the detective) committed the nasty murder that the detective happens to be investigating. In this case the expressions "Boris" and "the murderer" corefer. But they do not substitute salva veritate into the context "The detective knows who ——— is," since the detective (of course) knows who Boris is but does not know who the murderer is. This referential opacity may be purely superficial; but it is the task of a canonical regimentation to pinpoint its source and perhaps to relate it to the operation of the purpose parameter. We make an attempt at this in section 4 of this chapter.

Ideally, a philosophical proposal for the semantical analysis of a natural-language construction would have syntactic plausibility in that it could plausibly be incorporated into an independently motivated grammatical theory of that construction's syntactic formation and behavior and thereby illuminate its striking grammatical features. In practice this rarely happens, for the classical aim of regimentation is basically that of finding a philosophically useful paraphrase of the target construction, couched in a perspicuous symbolic idiom whose formulas wear their truth conditions on their sleeves. Once found, such regimentations are often hyperbolically characterized as expressing the target constructions' *logical forms*; but the association of target sentences with their alleged logical forms is justified only as a handy translation that preserves the sentences' most salient inferential properties— most are not even as impressive as Russell's theory of descriptions. What *makes* these symbolic paraphrases the logical forms *"of"* their respective target sentences, let alone what they have to do with anyone's actual production and interpretation of those target sentences in speech, is left unexplained.[4] In this and the next chapter, we avoid speaking of logical form, for our initial concern is simply that of finding perspicuous paraphrases that satisfy the five desiderata we have mentioned. If taken as proposals about logico*grammatical* form, our suggested regimentations would impose a heavy demand for syntactic apparatus that is (to say the least) unlikely to be met. However, it is a major task of chapters 3–5 to reduce our explanatory debt by showing how one might divide the work of our regimentations between the syntactic and the semantic components in a truth-theoretic account of propositional-attitude ascriptions so that the successor regimentations are sufficiently simple and similar to their English analysanda as to be at least prima facie plausible candidates for genuine logical forms. In thus diminishing the explanatory deficit and trying for enough equity to make the balloon payment acceptable, we do not, of course, eliminate the deficit entirely, nor do we wish to minimize the importance of eventually paying it off. On our view, a proposal about the logical form of an English sentence that makes even comparatively minimal demands on syntactic implementation, in the absence of an account of what the analysans actually contributes to the grammatical production of the sentence, is blind.

3 Hintikka's Proposal

To the best of our knowledge, the only theorist actually to have offered an analysis of "S knows who N is" before our 1975 article was Jaakko Hintikka in *Knowledge and Belief*.[5] (His main objective in making his proposal was to put his analysis to technical use in providing semantical foundations for quantification into epistemic contexts, but he also purported to be giving a canonical rendition of the ordinary notion of "knowing who" (see p. 132), and he says that he "cannot find any fault with" his analysis (p. 143).) Let us test Hintikka's proposal against the requirements we set out above and briefly examine a similar but more elaborate hypothesis suggested by some remarks of David Kaplan; then we proffer our own prototheory and discuss its merits.

Hintikka begins by offering a general explication of "S knows who is such that p," where "p" is an open sentence expressing an attribute presumed to individuate[6]

(1) $(\exists x)K_S p$.

Certainly this is a natural hypothesis. It is tempting to agree that S knows who is such that p just in case there is a person whom S knows to be such that p, i.e., just in case there is some particular person known by S to have the individuating attribute in question. Now, taking our attribute to be that of *being N* (letting our open sentence be "$x = N$"), we can give a more specific analysis of "S knows who N is" (= "S knows who it is that is N")[7]:

(2) $(\exists x)K_S(x = N)$.[7]

Appealing as (2) is, however, it has a fatal defect as it stands, apparently noticed by Hintikka on pp. 144–145. The truth of (2), at least on a naive understanding of its components, is readily conceded to be necessary for that of "S knows who N is," but it is hardly sufficient. For (2) is evidently implied by

(3) $K_S(N = N)$.

Presuming that S is a noncretin and knows that N exists, S knows that N is self-identical. But it does not follow that S knows who N is. Our detective knows that the murderer exists and (for what it is worth) that the murderer is self-identical, but does not know who the murderer is. If (2) is to be saved, we must find a way of interpreting (2) so that it is not implied by (3), and that means sacrificing some of our preanalytical trust in existential generalization.

Hintikka plausibly suggests restricting existential generalization of a name "N" occurring within the scope of an epistemic operator to cases in which the knower knows who "N"'s referent is. This restriction, Hintikka says, is no mere ad hoc evasion of what he takes to be nasty consequences of Quine's theory of opacity; he believes it captures a sound intuition to the effect that "a conclusion in which the identity of at least one individual is assumed to be known can be drawn only from premises at least one of which embodies the same assumption" (p. 150).[8] If the restriction is accepted, it neatly blocks the troublesome inference from (3) to (2); such an inference would be legitimate only if (3) were to be conjoined with a canonical representation of "S knows who N is"—but of course that representation is just (2) itself, and so the resulting argument would be (explicitly) question begging.

This response to our particular difficulty itself corresponds to an intuitive piece of ordinary reasoning, as Hintikka points out on pp. 148–149: S's ability to produce a true identity statement concerning N is plainly insufficient for saying that S knows who N is. S's knowledge that N is M (where "M" is some further singular term denoting N) does not constitute knowledge of who N is unless S (antecedently) *knows who M is*. (Our detective does not know who the murderer is, even if he knows that the murderer is the man whose footprints were found in the fishtank, unless he knows who the latter man is.)

There are, then (Hintikka urges against Quine), quantifiers that legitimately bind variables across epistemic operators such as "S knows that," but they range only over persons *known to* S (persons *x* such that S knows who *x* is) (pp. 155–156). An existential quantifier of this type is read as "Of some man known to S, S knows that" (p. 155). What, then, does Hintikka's analysis of "S knows who N is" come to? Expression (2) is evidently to be read as "Of some man known to S, S knows that that man is (identical with) N." But for a person to be "known to" S is just for S to know *who* that person is. So what (2) really says is, "Of some person such that S knows who that person is, S knows that that person is N." And since (2), thus understood, essentially contains an occurrence of a knowing-who locution, it is circular to offer (2) as a general analysis of "knowing who." This is not to deny that (2) is correctly said to be *equivalent* to our analysandum, but *qua* analysis, (2) does not meet our first requirement for a theory of knowing-who locutions—it fails to display whatever may be nontrivially common to all cases of knowing who someone is. (We do not mean to imply that Hintikka believes otherwise.)

It does seem that if we know who some person M is (for purpose P) and if we know that N = M, we know who N is (for purpose P); the converse of this is trivial. The circularity that vitiates (2) thus guarantees uninteresting satisfaction of requirement 2 (the demand that felt implications be captured). Requirement 3, however, is ignored. Because of the circularity of the proposed analysis, we are told nothing about our teleological parameter's role in the structure of "knowing who"—indeed, we are not even told that there is such a parameter—nor does Hintikka's discussion require (as it should) that there exist either a hidden parameter or an ambiguity.

Hintikka does remark on the multiplicity of tests for "knowing who" (p. 149n),[9] but he dismisses this phenomenon as being irrelevant to his theoretical purposes:

> No matter how the criteria for the truth of statements of the form
> '$(\exists x)K_S (x = N)$' are chosen (within the limits of our normal logic), the
> truth of the two statements '$(\exists x)K_S (x = M)$' and '$K_S (N = M)$' accord-

ing to these criteria entails the truth of $(\exists x)K_S (x = N)'$ according to the *same* criteria. . . .

As we have conceded, this claim seems unexceptionable, but it is totally unilluminating as regards the role of the varying "criteria" in the semantics of "knowing who."

Hintikka's system as a whole does not permit the derivation of "S knows who M is" from the conjunction of "S knows who N is" and "N = M," so it acknowledges the referential opacity of "knowing who." Hintikka also gives a compelling general account of opacity in terms of a person's idiolectic referring expressions' having different referents in different possible worlds. We are not yet persuaded by this account,[10] but we would not go so far as to insist that Hintikka's analysis cannot meet requirement 5.

4 Kaplan and Privileged Names

The failure of (2) to meet more than one of the preceding four requirements is certainly adequate grounds for looking further. Let us therefore turn to an analysis reconstructed from a hint given by Kaplan in "Quantifying in."[11] Kaplan writes:

> One might understand the assertion, "Ralph has an opinion as to who Ortcutt is" as a claim that Ralph can place Ortcutt among the leading characters of his inner story, thus that Ralph believes some sentence of the form $\ulcorner \alpha = \text{Ortcutt} \urcorner$ with α vivid. (p. 136)

Kaplan goes on to assimilate the view alluded to in the quotation to Hintikka's, though Kaplan's and Hintikka's respective ways of explaining their basic notions differ so widely that it is difficult to assess this remark. It is easy, however, to expand Kaplan's hint into an account of "knowing who" (albeit one that Kaplan himself might disavow) by replacing "has an opinion as to" and "believes" with "knows" and then spelling out the notion of *vividness* to some extent. Minimally, then, our new analysis of "S knows who N is" is: For some referring expression α which is a vivid name, S knows-true the result of concatenating α, " =," and "N" in that order" ("N" being a schematic letter here). (As we shall see, vivid names are not always public linguistic items; " =" and "N" may well be morphemes of the "language of thought" in which S's "inner story" is told.) Formally (using Kaplan's Quine quotes):

(4) $(\exists \alpha)K_S \ulcorner \alpha = N \urcorner$.

It is easy to see the superficial similarity of this formula to Hintikka's. And a vivid name turns out, as Kaplan seems to suggest on p. 137, to be *something like* a singular term which refers to an individual known to S, but we believe the differences here are more striking than the similarities.

The most important difference for our purposes is that (4), *qua* analysis of "S knows who N is," prima facie avoids the vitiating circularity of (modified) (2). Kaplan characterizes the notion of a vivid name without reference to "knowing who" (though we later argue that his characterization does not help solve our immediate problems). Actually, we think that in giving an analysis of "*knowing* who" (rather than of "having an opinion as to who") Kaplan (and we) would want to add at least two more conditions: (i) that our vivid name α actually denote N (that α have N as its semantic referent), and (ii) that S's use of α not be merely accidental—that there be some appropriate causal connection between N's in fact having the name α and S's mentally using α to refer to N. We can add these conditions to (4) simply by invoking Kaplan's defined predicate "**R**":

(5) $(\exists\alpha)(\mathbf{R}(\alpha, N, S) \ \& \ K_S \ulcorner\alpha = N\urcorner)$.

Kaplan explains "**R**" as follows:

> '**R** (α, N, S)' is true (read "α *represents* N to S") just in case (i) α denotes N, (ii) α is a name *of* N for S, and (iii) α is (sufficiently) vivid. (p. 138)

Clauses (i) and (ii) merely state the two conditions we have just added. But clause (iii) is obscure, and Kaplan's roundabout introduction of his term "vivid name" is by his own admission somewhat fanciful, despite the fact that the notion bears the whole weight of his final theory of quantifying in.[12] Let us try to get at what it comes to.

Kaplan introduces the notion of vividness by analogy with the vividness of a picture. The main ingredients of this more literal kind of vividness seem to be *clarity* and *detail* (p. 134), as opposed to blur, fuzziness, shadow, and obscurity. (The vividness of a picture may vary slightly, though not radically, according to the special interests of the person contemplating it.) Somewhat similarly, a vivid name is a "conglomeration of images, names, and partial descriptions which S employs to bring N before his mind" (p. 136). This conglomeration, we take it, plays the role of a singular term in S's "language of thought."[13] Since a vivid name is "made" partly of mental images and definite and indefinite descriptions, it is, like a picture, open to varying degrees of clarity and detail. A vivid name is, then, such a mental conglomeration of "sufficient" clarity and detail. The trick is to see how far we can go in treating a vivid name as we would a purely linguistic item. What sorts of properties can a vivid name have in common with an ordinary (linguistic) singular term?

A vivid name can *denote* a particular individual (p. 137). The following definition seems to capture what Kaplan has in mind here (though he does not offer it explicitly): A vivid name α denotes N iff (i) the (linguistic) names in α actually denote N in the ordinary sense, (ii) the descriptions in α are in fact true of N, and (iii) the eidetic part of α depicts N more or less accurately.

Obviously, a name's being vivid does not guarantee its denoting, as Kaplan points out (p. 137). In our formula (5), S is intended to have a name for N whose descriptive content is cautious enough to be accurate but still detailed enough to be vivid.

A vivid name can also bear the appropriate genetic relation to its putative referent; let us say that a vivid name α is a name *of* N for S iff there is an appropriate sort of causal chain connecting S's (mental) tokening of α (i) to the actual states of affairs depicted by the descriptive content of α and (ii) to the events of "dubbing" in which N acquires the (linguistic) names in α. If a mental name both denotes N and is a name *of* N for S and is still "sufficiently" vivid, it *represents* N for S and (Kaplan says) puts S "en rapport" with N as an individual (p. 138). According to Kaplan, S must thus be en rapport with N if we are truly to say of S that he knows or believes such-and-such of N, i.e., if we are to quantify in and proclaim a *relation* between S and N.[14]

Let us now try to plug all this back into our most recent proposed analysis of "knowing who." According to that proposal, S knows who N is just in case S has a name that represents N to him and he knows-true some (mental) sentence consisting of that name concatenated with the mental version of "$= N$."

This analysis seems to meet requirement 1; it provides a general answer to our original question. It also satisfies requirement 5: From "$(\exists\alpha)$ $(\mathbf{R}(\alpha, N, S)$ & K_S $\ulcorner\alpha = N\urcorner$" and "$N = M$" we cannot derive "$(\exists\alpha)$ $(\mathbf{R}(\alpha, M, S)$ & K_S $\ulcorner\alpha = m\urcorner)$," because the occurrences of "N" and "M" in our "K_S" clauses lie in effect inside quotation. It is alleged that S knows-true some *sentence* or at least some "sentence" of his language of thought; no (pure) reference is made in those clauses to N or to M.

An analysis based on (5), however, has serious failings as well. To begin with, it does not tell us much about our parameter or even about *any* approach to the "yes and no" cases described in section 1. The vividness of a name, we are told, is to some extent relative to special interests, but, understandably, not very drastically. Some pictures just *are* clearer and more detailed than others; Kaplan's own examples of relativity (p. 134) are, though certainly sound, a little contrived. The proponent of (5) fails to exhibit the *full-scale* relativity of "knowing who" to purposes, since the relativity evident in (5) is minimal.[15]

More important, the entailment relations of "S knows who N is" are not well represented by (5). Here are some of the disparities:

(i) Expression (5) asserts the existence of vivid names and entails the existence of *mental sentences.* It is not clear that these consequences are shared by "S knows who N is"; could S not know who N is even if there were no language, mental or otherwise? This objection is not serious, however. First, we should not easily grant that S *could* know who anyone was in such impoverished circumstances, lacking an internal system of representation.

Second, any faintly plausible analysis that we can think of makes reference to some such items, including that which we shall devise. Whether or not it is metaphysically wrong to saddle "knowing who" with such an ontology, it is indispensable for the present, at least as a heuristic device.

(ii) Suppose that S has a name α for N that both denotes N and is a name *of* N for S; suppose further that S knows N personally. Given what Kaplan has said on p. 136, it follows that α represents N for S and presumably that S knows-true $\ulcorner \alpha = N \urcorner$. In short, it follows (on the analysis under discussion) that S knows who N is. But that should not follow, for we sometimes have a representing name for someone whom we know personally, the name being as vivid as one might like, and still utterly fail to know who that person is for some key purposes (cf. the case of the copy boy and Clark Kent). It might be replied that, from the initial conditions hypothesized here, it does follow that S knows who N is *for some purpose or other*. This much seems to be true, but trivially so—for, given that we know that a particular person exists at all, we know who that person is for some boring purpose or other; stated categorically as it is, without any reference to the teleological parameter, the Kaplan-style analysis is at best misleading on this point.

(iii) It is not clear how we are to take the requirement that S's representing name for N "robustly and clearly delineate" N's nature or character. We know who Thomas Edison was, for standard purposes: He was the man who invented incandescent light bulbs. Does it follow that we have a representing name for Edison that robustly and clearly delineates him? In whatever intuitive sense we attach to this phrase (having to do, again, with detail and completeness in particular), it seems not—for all we know about him is that he invented incandescent light bulbs.

(iv) A related matter: Kaplan requires (see again p. 136) that N play a "major role" in S's inner story. We assume that this means S must have fairly intimate knowledge of N (cf. Kaplan's remark about Julius Caesar; he speaks of being "well acquainted" with Caesar) or at least that N has some prominence in S's thoughts from time to time. But neither of these conditions is really necessary for S's knowing who N is.

Unless we have misconstrued Kaplan, it looks as if vivid names are not exactly what we are after. His emphasis on detail and completeness of information seems misplaced for our purposes. Also, the notion of vividness itself is too vague. However, we provisionally exploit Hintikka's and Kaplan's practice of invoking privileged or preferred singular terms, as this still seems to be the most promising line to take in catching the intuitive appeal of (2) while blocking the trivial inference from (3). It might be objected at this point (e.g., by Quine) that such an inegalitarian attitude toward referring expressions drags in a metaphysically repugnant form of essentialism; but this is not so—we confess to an inegalitarian weighting of individuals' properties but only relative to someone's purpose or project, and not even Quine could object to so interest-bound a notion of "essence."

One further objectionable feature of (5) as an analysis of "S knows who N is" is that the privileged status of S's representation is made relative to the subject in particular. We want "knowing who" to be relative to projects, but in our Kaplan-style analysis it is also relative to the idiosyncrasies of S's personal inner story. On our view, these features of S should be irrelevant. Relative to a particular project, it is easy to frame a question-and-answer test for whether an *arbitrarily* chosen subject knows who some N is. For example, relative to the desirable task of throwing the murderer in jail, we can say in advance what test *anyone* would have to pass in order to count as knowing who the murderer is: A subject would have to be able to tell whether he had the right human body in handcuffs (name, address, and occupation have only contributory relevance in this case). It would be strange to say that, once we are holding our parameter fixed, different tests might still be required for different subjects—we can think of no reason why this could ever happen. We conclude that a name is privileged (in a way useful to us) relative to the teleological parameter but irrespective of the identity of S, the knower.

We now propose our own analysis of "S knows who N is," proceeding more or less along Kaplan's lines. We invent our own category of privileged names, making use of Kripke's notion of a rigid designator. In chapter 2 we introduce a key modification, one that we take to codify our most important insight about "knowing who"; then in chapter 4 we formulate the final version of our theory.

5   "Knowing Who" and Important Names

Let us bluntly begin by stating our preliminary analysis, explaining it subsequently:

(6) $(\exists \alpha)\,(\text{Impname}\,(\alpha, N, P) \ \& \ (\exists \beta)\,(\triangle(\beta, N) \ \& \ K_S \ulcorner \beta \text{ is } \alpha \urcorner))$.

The second clause of this formulation is intended to say roughly that S knows of N that he is identical with the referent of α; the first clause specifies α's status as a privileged name.

The clause "$\triangle(\beta, N)$" is to be read as "β referentially designates N." As we use that term, a referential designator is first a *rigid* designator. (According to Kripke, this is for it to "designate ... its referent wherever [at every possible world in which] the object exists."[16]) Even though the same singular term may be used rigidly on one occasion but nonrigidly or flaccidly on another, we need not explicitly relativize rigidity to a speaker at a time; because "β" in (6) ranges over expressions of S's language of thought, the requirement that β rigidly designate N *in that language* is already sufficient to ensure that β rigidly designate N "for S." We now add, in keeping with Kripke's views and with what we take to be the requirements of "knowing who," that a rigid term β designates N in S's language of thought only if there is an appropriate genetic connection of Kripke's and Kaplan's type between S's (implicit) use of β and the dubbing of N with β. The idea of the second clause of (6), then, is that S knows-true a superficial identity sentence, one term of which is used (in S's language of thought) to pick out N, regardless of N's contingent properties, whatever they may be.[17,18]

"Impname (α, N, P)" is read, "α is an important name of N for purpose P." As we have insisted, a name is privileged in our sense only relative to certain purposes; but when those purposes have been fixed, the name is privileged irrespective of the identity of S, the person using the name. Superficially, the intuitive content of "Impname" is something like this: "Impname (α, N, P)" is true just in case α denotes N and also is the sort of item that would be accepted as a reply by a person asking "Who is N?" with purpose P explicitly in mind. Saying this, of course, does not help explain how "Impname" is ultimately to be spelled out or how the use of an important name is related to the purpose or project. We address these matters in chapter 2.

Let us now check our preliminary analysis against the requirements we appealed to in section 2. Plainly, it satisfies requirement 1, as did the Kaplan-style proposal. It also satisfies requirement 3 by placing the teleological parameter explicitly. According to our analysis, "knowing who" is relative to project precisely because a singular term α, as a name of an individual N, is *important* to people variously, depending on their interests and aims. (That explanatory fact should not surprise anyone.)

What about felt implications (requirement 2)? Expression (6) is certainly sufficient for "knowing who." If S knows that N satisfies $\ulcorner$is $\alpha\urcorner$ (and appropriately answers $\ulcorner$N is $\alpha\urcorner$ to the question of who N is), when α is an important name in the sense we have less than adequately described, then surely S knows who N is. And S knows that N satisfies $\ulcorner$is $\alpha\urcorner$ if S has a *referential* designator β of N such that S knows-true $\ulcorner\beta$ is $\alpha\urcorner$. So our only remaining question is that of whether satisfying (6) is *necessary* for S's knowing who N is.

Like the Kaplan-style analysis, our own is committed to "names in one's language of thought"; we continue to live with that for now for the reasons originally mentioned. Happily, our analysis avoids saddling "knowing who" with some of the counterintuitive consequences to which the Kaplan-style theory succumbed. Expression (6) entails none of the following: (i) that S's important name for N provides any particular degree of detail or completeness considered in the abstract, (ii) that S has any particularly intimate knowledge of N and N's doings, (iii) that S is well acquainted with N (even in the sense in which a historian can be "well acquainted" with Caesar), (iv) that N has any special prominence in S's thoughts. As we shall see, having an important name of N may amount to knowing just one key fact about N—

possibly an obscure fact at that. We have also avoided another pitfall of the Kaplan-style analysis: Knowing someone personally does not guarantee knowing who that person is (for all practical purposes) in the sense of (6), although, depending on the actual workings of an important name, it may guarantee knowing who the person is for some easily specifiable purposes.

Finally, we can list a few intuitive theses about "knowing who" that have considerable preanalytical plausibility and show that (6) squares with them. (i) We have said that S's knowing or being acquainted with N should not in every situation suffice for S's knowing who N is, nor should it be required, and nothing in (6) does, in general, require it. Of course, some particular purposes P are such that one does need to know N personally in order to know who N is for P; this fact is accommodated by the concept of an important name. (ii) It is hard to maintain that elaborate factual knowledge is always required for "knowing who." In some cases, naturally, certain sorts of facts are required, such as those concerning N's occupation or N's social status or whatever. But in other cases, it is not clear that any fact other than the superficial $\ulcorner\beta$ is $\alpha\urcorner$ itself is needed (we have more to say about this in chapter 2). Our analysis saves all these intuitions too. (iii) If S is asked, "Who is N?," S's answer "N is M" gives us reason to say that S knows who N is if and only if it is clear that S knows who M is.[19] Our analysis preserves this fact. From "$K_S \ulcorner N = M\urcorner$" we cannot derive (6), since "$K_S \ulcorner N = M\urcorner$" does not guarantee that S has an important name of N for the relevant purpose(s). Expression (6) does follow, however, from the conjunction of "$K_S \ulcorner N = M\urcorner$" and

(7) $(\exists\alpha)(\text{Impname}(\alpha, M, P)$ & $(\exists\beta)(\triangle(\beta, M)$ & $K_S \ulcorner\beta$ is $\alpha\urcorner))$

("S knows who M is")—the proof is trivial. (iv) "If you know *who* does something, you ipso facto know *that* someone did it," Hintikka observes (p. 160). In our case, if you know who has the property of *being N*, you accordingly know that someone has that property, i.e., that N exists. This fact falls easily out of our analysis; if, for the relevant α and β, S knows-true $\ulcorner\alpha$ is $\beta\urcorner$, then presumably S also knows-true $\ulcorner(\exists x)(x = \beta)\urcorner$. (v) Finally, notice that (6) does not require S to have purpose P explicitly in mind, to act on or with P, or even to have thought about P, however vaguely. Purposes are mentioned independently of *whose* purposes they might be at any time.

6 Opacity and Referential/Attributive Ambiguity

All this is very encouraging. However, we have not measured our analysis against requirements 4 and 5, concerning possible ambiguities and opacity, respectively. And here a difficulty emerges. From (6) and "N = M" we can easily derive (7), since all positions containing "N" in (6) are plainly transparent. If (6) is an accurate analysis of "S knows who N is," then how can we save our intuition that "knowing who" is referentially opaque?

The answer to this is roundabout and requires some antecedent discussion of possible ambiguities. We believe, in fact, that "S knows who N is" is subject to one ambiguity that no one else has pointed out. It is most clearly perceptible when "N" is a definite description, say, "the murderer." Temporarily adopting Donnellan's referential/attributive distinction (see note 1) and assuming its syntactic/semantic reality, let us examine the consequences of reading this description first referentially and then attributively[20] in "S knows who the murderer is." On the referential reading, "the murderer" serves merely to pick out the individual we are talking about and not essentially to describe that individual in any way (thus, on such a reading, we can *nontrivially* say, "The murderer murdered someone," or wish that the murderer had not murdered anyone without desiring that the predicate calculus contain falsehoods). "The murderer" would be canonically represented either by a Russellized description taking wide scope or (on a more drastic understanding of Donnellan's distinction) by an unstructured referring expression, an individual constant. On the attributive reading, however, "the murderer" takes narrow scope; a sentence containing it thus construed is about *whoever* did the murder, whoever that might turn out to be. "The murderer" would be Russellized narrowly in the canonical representation, leaving behind a *general* statement with no variables bound from outside the relevant sentence operator. In an important way, therefore, attributive definite descriptions are not really singular terms (referring expressions) at all. We assume for purposes of this chapter and the next that the referential/attributive contrast is sufficiently familiar, hoping that our heuristic use of it will not be troubled by the various difficulties that have attended various attempts at refining it.[21]

On the referential reading, then, "S knows who the murderer is" is to be understood as saying that S knows who *that person*, the one whom we are picking out, is, for whatever purposes are in question, regardless of that person's having committed any murders. On the attributive reading, by contrast, "S knows who the murderer is" is equivalent to "S knows who did the murder," which says that there is some person whom S knows to have committed the murder. This latter (general) statement may well be false even when it is true that S knows who the murderer (referential use) is. It entails, for example, that S knows that someone did the murder; our referential reading does not.

In order to codify such facts, it appears that we must posit a second, alternative formal representation of "S knows who N is," where "N" is a definite description "the F." "S knows who N is" is then said to be syntactically and semantically ambiguous. We propose to Russellize the attributive description in the way suggested above:

(8) $(\exists!x)(Fx \ \& \ (\exists\alpha)(\triangle(\alpha, x) \ \& \ \mathrm{Impname}(\alpha, x, P) \ \& \ K_s \ulcorner F\alpha \urcorner))$.

(For a particular replacement of the schematic letter "F" such as "invented bifocals," $\ulcorner\alpha$ invented bifocals$\urcorner$ would be the result of concatenating α with whatever predicate translates "invented bifocals" in S's language of thought— i.e., a Mentalese · invented bifocals · in Wilfrid Sellars's sense.)

Expression (8) seems to us to capture the way in which the attributive sense of "S knows who the F is" differs from the referential sense explicated by (6). The added implications we have mentioned are present in (8); and the analysis captures the fact that knowing who the F is in the attributive sense is not, as it is in the referential sense, knowing an apparent *identity*—it is, rather, knowing a (unique) predication. To see this, imagine our familiar question-and-answer situation. To ask "Who is the murderer?" in the attributive sense is precisely to ask, "Who did the murder?" An identity statement would be an inappropriate response to such a question; what is called for is some claim of the form, "M did the murder." Accordingly, (8) ultimately ascribes to S knowledge of a predication rather than knowledge of an identity.

Notice that the teleological parameter functions even in the attributive case, which is, in a way, preanalytically much less mysterious than the referential sense. (On the face of things, the only mysterious feature of "knowing who" in the attributive sense is the quantification into an epistemic context—"S knows *of some particular person* that that person is (uniquely) F"). But S may know, and at the same time not know, who did the murder, depending on purposes. For the purpose of writing history books, S may know, in that he knows that the murderer is the man named Boris Flammenwerfer, a chicken-sexer who hails from Berlin; yet S may still not know who the latter individual is for the purpose of laying hands on his person, throwing him into a cell, bringing him to trial, and executing sentence. (Flammenwerfer may long since have decamped incognito.) Thus, even in the attributive sense, S knows who the F is (S knows which individual is F) only relative to a project.

One further detail should be mentioned:[22] Knowing-who ascriptions in which "N" is replaced by definite descriptions are typically ambivalent as to whether it is the speaker or the subject who is to take responsibility for the *uniqueness* of an F, implied by the descriptor. It is perfectly acceptable to say that S knows who the F is when S satisfies (8) and also knows (as does the speaker) that there is at most one F. But it is also usually acceptable to say that S knows who the F is even when S may not know that there is only one F. (For example, if S, a Nicaraguan communist, has discovered that our agent in Nicaragua is a CIA spy, we may well (and properly) say, "S knows who our agent in Nicaragua is," even though S does not know that we have only one agent in Nicaragua.) To allow for the latter possibility, we have stated our analysis (8) in a particularly weak form, by assigning the shriek wide scope. In some cases, however, a purist might insist that S does *not* know who *the* F is unless S actually knows that there is but one F; in such cases we might move (8)'s shriek inward, penetrating the knowledge clause, as in

(8*) $(\exists x)(Fx \ \& \ (\exists \alpha)(\triangle(\alpha, x) \ \& \ \text{Impname} \ (\alpha, x, P) \ \& \ K_S \ulcorner F!\alpha \urcorner))$.

We shall not commit ourselves on the question of whether this further distinction betokens a real semantic ambiguity. The only evidence for saying that (8*) captures a genuinely distinct sense of (attributive) "knowing who" is that some speakers of English sometimes feel uncomfortable in ascribing such knowledge to a subject when the subject does not know that there is but one F. We believe that English is not determinate on this point. A possible explanation for this is that (i) uniqueness is usually *presupposed* all around (as a matter of fact, the vast majority of murders are the work of individuals rather than of committees), and (ii) in any case, uniqueness does not usually *matter* to speakers nearly so much as does the existence claim. So we do not choose between saying that (8) is correct to the exclusion of (8*), that (8*) is correct to the exclusion of (8), or that (8) and (8*) are both correct readings of an ambiguous attributive "knowing who" construction.

Expression (8), and a fortiori (8*), seem much stronger than (6), in the sense that they appear to require more epistemic activity on S's part in order for S to know who N is. But this is what we would have expected. "Knowing who" in the attributive sense does require more of the subject. In order to know who the murderer is, referentially speaking, S need only have an important name of him (of that person, regardless of his murdering or any of his other contingent attributes), vis-a-vis whatever project is in queston. But attributively, S must know in addition some general facts about the world— e.g., that a murder took place and that whoever committed it fulfills such-and-such an identifying description—and only then go on to worry about knowing who the murderer is for practical purposes, such as locating and jailing him.

In expounding our referential/attributive ambiguity, we have thus far used only definite descriptions as examples. Demonstratives are by nature referential, or so it seems. Proper names are generally held to fare similarly, since the semantical function of a proper name is solely to pick out the appropriate referent (cf. note 16); but there are attributive uses of proper names,[23] and we reveal and examine further complexities in chapter 2.

It is time to return to requirement 5 and to explain the apparent opacity of "knowing who." In light of the ambiguity we brought out, we can do this fairly easily, for the most plausible cases in which truth value is not preserved through substitution of "coreferring singular terms" are those in which one of the alleged "singular terms" is actually a definite description (or possibly even an apparent proper name) *used attributively*. Since such expressions count superficially as singular terms, they give rise to opacity in the accordingly superficial way. But opacity of *this* sort is simply a case of amphiboly; the description is not really (semantically) a singular term at all; thus we would not expect opacity of this relatively trivial sort to be reflected in logical form.

Does this treatment succeed in handling all cases of apparent opacity? It seems not. Even stipulating that all replacements of "N" are referential singular terms, we can doubt the truth of "S knows who M is" even when that sentence is, in fact, the product of substituting "M" for a coreferring term "N" in a true instance of "S knows who N is." For example, one might contend that our detective would say (and an impartial observer might agree) that obviously he knows who Boris is but does not know who the murderer is, even though "the murderer" is being used referentially here. Why is this?

If there truly are such cases, we believe that they are products of quite natural *parameter shift*. Certain singular terms carry with them suggestions of particular projects. The name "Boris," as the detective uses it, brings to mind Boris in his capacity as neighbor, best friend, confidant, and fly-tying companion to the detective, whereas the term "the murderer," even when used referentially to pick out Boris himself, plainly connotes someone whose smudged fingerprints we have, who was seen by a near-eyewitness fleeing the fatal scene in a bloodstained anorak, etc. We submit (for now) that in any such cases of apparent opacity over and above the referential/attributive ambiguity, what is going on is simply that two different values of the teleological parameter are being rung in. Nothing more recondite than this parameter shift is required to account for a change of truth value on substitution. If S knows who Cicero is for purpose P, then S knows who Tully is for P, even if S himself has never heard the name "Tully." (To see this, notice that *we* are the utterers of "S knows who Tully is." "Tully" is a name in *our* language, serving solely to indicate that person, Tully or Cicero, whatever he is called; it is not required or even expected that S would express himself in that way.) Our position, then, is that the apparent opacity of "knowing who" is real enough superficially (it occurs in either of the two ways we have mentioned), but in neither case does it penetrate to the level of logical structure—so we should not be surprised if "N" occurs everywhere transparently in (6).[24]

This concludes the case in favor of our preliminary analysis. But the analysis still stands in need of modification, in light of a difficulty that first shows itself as merely technical but turns out to prompt a significant conceptual revision. We cannot discuss it until we say a bit more about important names in chapter 2, so we pass over it for now. Instead, let us note a few other prima facie drawbacks that we try to address later on.

First, we must provide our allusions to quasilinguistic items and "languages of thought" with some real substance; until we do so, these allusions are no more than a subterfuge designed to help us avoid commitment to the thesis that a knower must have and express himself in a natural language, such as English. Second, we have played fast and loose with the notion of a referential designator, which despite its currency and despite our quick attempt at definition, remains none too clear.

Third, our account so far is minimal, collapsing all the really difficult conceptual analysis into the allegedly primitive predicate "Impname," which is made to carry all the intuitive content of "knowing who." Toward giving the *meaning* of "S knows who N is," we have done relatively little. On the other hand, that is what one expects from a logical regimentation, and rightly so: It is better to have to deal with the meaning of an untidy primitive than with unknown logical grammar.[25]

Chapter 2
Important Names and Important Predicates:
Refining the Prototheory

We have made a tentative hypothesis as to the most perspicuous representation of referential and attributive knowing-who locutions and tested it against some general requirements. It is time to look at some more data. We first offer a brief overview of the sorts of conversational episodes that may properly be initiated by questions of the form, "Who is ———?," thereby providing a clearer picture of the role of our teleological parameter. We then attempt a characterization of the purposes underlying "who" questions that relates these purposes to the content of what one must know in order to know who someone is relative to those purposes, and we shape this characterization into a tentative explication of "Impname." Finally, we locate a conflict between two of our earlier results and resolve it by replacing the notion of an important name with that of an important *predicate*, producing our final informal theory of "knowing who."

1 "Who" Questions and Their Answers

We first consider the three specific forms that initial "who" questions might take: (A) "Who is N?," where "N" is a proper name; (B) "Who is the F?," where "the F" is a definite description functioning referentially or attributively; and (C) "Who is D?," where "D" is a demonstrative pronoun, accompanied perhaps by a pointing gesture and/or some indefinite description of the intended referent. Let us try to determine whether these questions prefer answers of certain syntactic types.

A question of form (A) typically receives a response of one of the following three forms:

(A1) "N is the G."

(A2) "N is M."   ["M" is yet another proper name.]

(A3) "D is N."   ["D" is a demonstrative pronoun.]

Since the initial question, "Who is N?," already contains a proper name, replies of type (A1) are most frequently forthcoming; as we argue, (A2) and (A3) require much more specialized stage setting. Form (A2) occurs only in those circumstances in which N (the referent of "N") has or is thought to have more than one proper name (Cicero is a favorite example). Form (A3) of course requires that N should be or be thought to be actually present at least by proxy to speaker and hearer. (Because a detailed discussion of "deferred ostension" would take us too far afield, we simply regard demonstratives used in this way as contextual ellipses of *attributive* descriptions containing "direct" demonstratives. For example, "That is Tom," accompanied by a gesture toward a portrait is treated as shorthand for something like "Tom is the person depicted by that portrait.")

We argue that for all but a tiny range of purposes, replies of forms (A2) and (A3) ultimately fail to stop a potential regress of "who" questions, whereas a suitably chosen reply of form (A1) does not permit such a regress and so can be used to plug the gap left by replies of the other two forms. We maintain that replies of forms (A2) and (A3) are importantly parasitic on replies of form (A1); (A1) provides what are for most purposes the only definitive (final) answers to "Who is N?"

Consider first a reply of form (A2). If S asks, "Who is Tully?," and we obligingly reply, "Tully is Cicero," then it may appear that our reply is final, since the question-and-answer game sometimes terminates at this point. But it is important to realize that, for any purpose other than the special one of finding another label for one's (possibly empty) "Tully" file, there is nothing *intrinsically* final about our reply; it is still *open* to the further question, "But who is Cicero (for purpose P)?" Our reply suffices for these other purposes, if it does so at all, simply because S antecedently knows who the referent of "Cicero" is (for that purpose), i.e., S antecedently possesses an appropriately stocked "Cicero" file. In the absence of such specific prior knowledge, our response "Tully is Cicero" generates yet another legitimate question on S's part, viz., "But who is Cicero?" So long as we reply with another proper name, we must continue to rely on S's background knowledge of the identity of its referent. The illusion of finality in this sort of case derives from the fact that common knowledge is taken for granted so automatically that we are prone to forget its contingency.

The illusion of finality attaching to (A2) can have a second source as well, and at this point an important qualification is needed. When we say that for normal purposes a reply of form (A2) cannot by itself stop the potential regress of "who" questions, we are assuming that the superficial form "N is M" is logically an identity statement; we are assuming that "N" and "M" are both referential designators. But not all sentences having the superficial form "N is M" are genuine identity statements, for it is possible that an ostensible proper name is functioning attributively—as mere shorthand for some attributive definite description. If the name "M" thus abbreviates the description "the F" occurring attributively, then the superficial form "N is M" would logically amount to a subject–predicate construction, viz., "N alone is F."

Thus the notion of an attributive name can explain some more of the cases in which we are inclined to say that a reply superficially of form (A2) provides an independent way of stopping the regress of "who" questions. When such a reply is truly final, it is so because the "name" "M" is shorthand for an attributive description that conveys precisely the information sought by the questioner.[1]

Incidentally, it should be clear that in the initial question, "Who is N?," the name "N" might itself be attributive, in which case the question would amount to something of the form, "Who is the F?," with "the F" taken attributively. Since questions of the latter sort are attended to below, we take it for granted in the present discussion that "N" in "Who is N?" is being used referentially.

We can say, then, that no *referential* reply of form (A2) is intrinsically or independently capable of stopping the potential regress of legitimate "who" questions (unless the operative purpose is mere label-seeking). An attributive reply of form (A2), i.e., one in which "M" is an attributive name, may stop the regress for some more demanding purpose (so far as has been shown), but only because it is in reality a disguised answer of form (A1). More on this below.

We now turn to replies of form (A3), involving demonstrative pronouns. There does not seem to be any referential/attributive ambiguity in this case; demonstrative pronouns are paradigmatically referential designators. It must be admitted that a reply of the form "N is D" is final in our sense at least for certain specialized purposes. One such purpose that comes immediately to mind is that of locating N in one's perceptual field. If N is successfully pointed out—i.e., if "N is D" is *understood*—then for this purpose, the issue is settled: One could not go on to ask, "But who is D?" without changing the subject, i.e., without introducing some new project into the proceedings. But it is equally obvious that there are many purposes for which demonstrative replies—even if available—are unsatisfactory. For example, a stranger may introduce himself to S, saying "Hello, I'm Fulbert Cipher!" and shortly thereafter S may turn to a friend and whisper "Who the hell is Fulbert Cipher?" The demonstrative reply *"That* man is Fulbert Cipher" just does not do, for S responds "Yes, I know that already, but *who is* that man?" What S wants is some salient biographical information for his newly opened "Fulbert Cipher" file, and one must have recourse to an attributive reply of form (A1) in order to stop the regress.

It seems, then, that answers of form (A1) are the only hope of stopping the regress of "who" questions driven by information-seeking (dossier-filling) purposes (though we have not as yet provided grounds for thinking that *they* are final in our sense either). In particular, as we have noted, the onus of terminating the regress where such purposes are concerned devolves on answers of form (A1) in which the description is used attributively. Since the regress of "who" questions should stop somewhere and since it cannot, save in special cases, stop anywhere else, it presumably stops here.[2] What is needed now is some direct evidence of this and some explanation of *why* attributive answers of form (A1) enjoy this privileged status.

2 *The Primacy of Definite Attributive Responses*

The purposes that underlie "who" questions normally inspire attempts to learn some subjectively pertinent fact(s) about N, and various purposes, of course, variously determine which facts are required. Attributive answers of form (A1), being equivalent to subject–predicate sentences, provide such factual information; and so they can, if they convey the *right* sort of information, stop the regress of "who" questions, which threatened virtually all referential answers. The regress began because the apparent finality of "N is M," where "M" is a referential name or description, is upheld only by the questioner's prior knowledge of N's identity under the title "M."

Such is not the case, however, with an attributive answer. If the definite description introduced is indeed an important name in our sense, it attributively *conveys* just the information about N that the questioner needs in order to carry out his project. It is therefore no longer open to him to ask, "But who is the G?" (= "But who G's?") relative to the same purpose P, since that question would necessarily be pointless—its very form indicates that the questioner already possesses the information he purports to be requesting (compare: "What color is Sheila's green coat?"). These considerations are illustrated by the following examples.

Suppose that at the party we ask, "Who is Jean-Claude Killy?," wishing to walk over to him, introduce ourselves, and say how much we have enjoyed watching him ski. Our informant replies, "Killy is the man drinking the Brandy Alexander alone in the laundry room." The latter description is an important name for our purpose; used attributively, it conveys to us just the facts we need to know in order to locate and approach Killy. Therefore we cannot properly go on to ask our informant, "But who is the man drinking. . . ?," unless a shift of purposes occurs.

When N is known to be a famous personage, one's purpose in asking "Who is N?" is often to determine *which* famous personage N is, and doing so is a matter of obtaining information about those traits or accomplishments of N that *made* N famous. The schoolgirl who asks her teacher, "Who was Ghengis Khan?," would understandably be annoyed by the reply, "My Aunt Alice's favorite historical character," accuracy of the latter notwithstanding. What is called for is something of the form, "Ghengis Khan was the Mongol conqueror who. . . ," in which one or more noteworthy exploits of Ghengis are enumerated. Taken attributively, such a reply tells the student what she wanted to know: She cannot, relative to the same purpose, ask, "But who was the Mongol conqueror who. . .?," although she could say, "So that's who he was; tell me more about him."

Public figures have private lives too, and sometimes the only appropriate answer to "Who is N?" is an attributive description pertaining to N's private life. This is especially evident when the underlying purpose has to do with N's origins, as in our earlier case of the Dalai Lama. For another example, when Spiro Agnew was first introduced to the public as the Republican Vice-Presidential nominee, even people who were aware that Agnew used to be Governor of Maryland found themselves asking, "Who *is* Spiro Agnew anyway?" The most appropriate reply would be an attributive description mentioning salient features of Agnew's pregubernatorial career. Being so informed, one who was curious about Agnew's origins could not go on to ask *who* did those things, since (unless there has been a shift of purposes) this would amount to asking about the origins of the man whose origins have just been recounted. As before, one could request additional information, but not in the form of a "who" question.

These constraints on replies of form (A1) operate by no means only in cases involving the famous and the notorious; similar things happen when N is an ordinary person. Often these constraints derive from an interest in N's role or position in society. If we see in the newspaper that a mathematician of our acquaintance has just married one Waldo Dobbs, we are likely to ask, "Who on earth is Waldo Dobbs?," with just such an interest in mind. Uniquely individuating information as to the number of warts on his nose, his ownership of a certain Maserati, or even his social security number is greeted with disdain. On the other hand, if we are told, "Waldo is a marine biologist at Woods Hole," we feel that we are learning *who* Waldo Dobbs is. That descriptions couched in terms of social role are often the most appropriate responses to "Who is N?" is explained by the simple fact that much of the importance of other people to us derives from the influence they exert, or are in a position to exert, on our lives by way of the interconnected social structure(s) to which we belong. Of course, a person can be important to us in other ways as well, e.g., by possessing an ability or having performed a deed that is of special interest. If S is an aspiring young logician who knows Frege only as a German thinker who held some odd views about concepts and objects, we could justifiably say to him, "You evidently don't know who Frege really is: Why, he's the father of modern symbolic logic [= your passion in life]!"

We have made much of the fact that attributive responses convey crucial information; so in order to forestall misunderstanding, let us say a few words about our use of the term "conveys." When we say that an intrinsically final answer is one that *conveys* a certain sort of information or (in the demonstrative case) a certain recognition ability, we mean that if a speaker gives that answer and *succeeds* in getting the hearer to *understand* it as a relevant response to "Who is N?," then, under normal circumstances, the hearer ipso facto has come to possess that information or ability. What an answer "conveys" in this idealized sense thus includes what its utterer would normally be deemed to have literally *stated* in its production (as opposed to what the speaker might thereby have suggested or conversationally implicated). But it also includes the perceptual "fix" necessary for determining what was stated in the production of an answer of form (A3), as well as certain local linguistic presumptions which, though not part of what is literally stated, must be triggered in the hearer if he or she is to understand answers of form (A2) as formally germane to the question "Who is N?"— e.g., the presumption that "Cicero" in an utterance of "Tully is Cicero" is used as a label, the acceptance of which is part of understanding that utterance as a relevant response to "Who is Tully?" for label-seeking purposes.

There is a residual point to be made about the (A) forms. In stressing the primacy of definite attributive answers to "Who is N?," we have deliberately ignored a fourth possible form:

(A4) "N is *an* H."

It is far from evident to us that an indefinite reply of that sort is ever an adequate answer to "Who is N?" If someone asks, "Who is Cicero?," the reply "Cicero was a famous Roman orator," though relevant and informative, does not seem to settle the question of *who* Cicero was. As against this, Saul Kripke contends that "you *do* know who Cicero is if you just can answer that he's a famous Roman orator" ("Naming and necessity," 293); but he offers no direct argument for this (indeed, he precedes it by saying that he "won't go into the question of knowing who someone is," which he admits to be "very puzzling"). Kripke is clearly right to point out that people do often accept indefinite replies of form (A4) as apparent answers to their "who" questions. Nevertheless we think that datum can be accommodated without the admission of (A4) to our list of appropriate response forms.

Briefly, our answer to Kripke is to point out that "who" questions for which replies of form (A4) seem appropriate are only superficially questions of form (A): They are really ellipses of related but importantly different questions. Suppose that it is S's first day in the army, and S is still unclear about rank and the meanings of insignia. N, an officer, approaches S and says, "Clean up the barracks!" On N's departure, S turns to a comrade and says, "Who is *he* to give me orders?" The comrade replies, "He's a *captain*, stupid!" This indefinite reply is perfectly adequate. But notice that "Who is N that he can give me orders?" is not the same question as "Who is N?" The difference is obscured by the fact that the latter is sometimes used elliptically to do the job of the former; but in such cases the stress would normally fall on "N" rather than on "is." In general, when someone asks a question of the superficial form "Who is N?" that *can* be adequately answered by something of form (A4), it is really an ellipsis of something like "Who is N *that he is F?*," which in turn amounts to "What property of N makes him F?" [4]

The foregoing remarks can be generalized to cover cases in which the pseudo–"who" questions do not initiate conversation but instead follow someone else's use of an unfamiliar name (the latter being closer to what Kripke probably had in mind). Pseudo–"who" questions are sometimes the first step toward a real query as to N's identity. "Who is Cicero?," asked by one who has just encountered the name "Cicero" for the first time, is frequently an ellipsis of something like "Who is Cicero that I should care about him?" or "Who is Cicero that he should matter to me?," whereby the audience is invited to give the questioner some interesting fact or other about the Roman. If "Cicero was a famous orator" happens to be of interest, then the questioner may well go on to inquire after Cicero's identity: "Tell me more—who exactly was he?"

Of course, these indefinite replies to pseudo–"who" questions do not always, or even often, lead to genuine "who" questions. The fact that people usually accept such replies without further ado owes merely to the fact that the indefinite reply (taken to be the best that the informant cares to supply) does not usually pique their interest sufficiently to prompt further inquiry on their part. If S has no particular interest in oratory or in Roman history, then the reply "Cicero was a famous Roman orator" is greeted with a casual "That's nice," and that is the end of the conversation. Since questions of form (A), when they are genuine questions about N's identity, do not tolerate replies of form (A4) and since "who" questions that do tolerate such replies are not really questions about N's identity, we feel justified in eliminating (A4) from further consideration (though Nuel Belnap protests to us in correspondence that we are missing a generalization here).

3 "Who" Questions Involving Definite Descriptions and "Who" Questions Involving Demonstratives

What about questions of form (B): "Who is the F?" Cases in which "the F" is used referentially introduce nothing new. Referential descriptions, like referential proper names on our view, serve to pick out an individual regardless of that individual's contingent attributes. Consequently, cases involving referential descriptions simply parallel those discussed in connection with questions of form (A).

However, it is worth noting that genuinely referential questions of form (B) are rare in ordinary discourse, occurring chiefly in connection with such "frozen" descriptions as "The Father of Our Country" and "The Great Emancipator." This is not surprising, since frozen descriptions do function in effect as names: The very temptation to capitalize and/or to hyphenate them and the feeling that "is" in "Who is the F?" should be stressed is a typographical or phonological symptom of this status. For reasons that are not entirely clear, questions of form (B) are almost always heard attributively by the audience.[5]

In any event, attributive uses of "the F" figure much more prominently in questions of the form "Who is the F?" Since on our Russellian view of attributive descriptions, the question "Who is the F?" amounts to "Who (uniquely) F's?," we can say that such questions request information as to *which* person F's. There are three verbal forms in which that information might be supplied, viz.:

(B1) "The F is the G."

(B2) "The F is M."   ["M" is a proper name.]

(B3) "D is the F."   ["D" is a demonstrative pronoun.]

Since our remarks about the limitations of demonstratives carry over mutatis mutandis from (A3) to (B3), we concentrate here on (B1) and (B2).

Consider first replies of form (B2). If the name "M" is employed referentially here, then "The F is M" (= "M alone F's") does not suffice as an intrinsically final answer to "Who is the F?" (= "Who F's?") for any purpose beyond mere label seeking. This is for the same reason as that given regarding (A2), viz., that "The F is M" always invites the further question, "But who is M?," unless the questioner antecedently knows for those very purposes) who bears the name "M." And if we answer this further question with yet another referential designator, the problem breaks out again. Cases in which replies of form (B2) do nontrivially appear to be intrinsically final are, like similar cases involving replies of form (A2), accounted for in terms of "M"'s being an attributive name—in which instance we are really dealing with an attributive version of (B1).

Since replies of form (B2) are easily the most common responses to "Who is the F?," it might seem odd that they should fail to be independently final answers to that question—especially in light of the fact that the questioner is almost always satisfied by such an answer. But the oddity is only apparent. For most of us know the names of a large number of persons, and most of our everyday discourse about persons concerns persons known to us by name. Consequently, most of us possess the kind of background knowledge that makes a reply of form (B2) appropriate. But it is this special background knowledge and not the reply itself that ensures success. We could, and sometimes do, ask, "But who is M?"; that we generally are not forced to do so is a propitious but thoroughly contingent matter of fact. The most common sort of reply is only extrinsically final.

Thus we are left with (B1) as the only candidate for the general form of an intrinsically final reply to "Who is the F?" for any information-seeking purpose. We can at once eliminate referential cases, for given our view of referential descriptions, these do not differ from referential instances of (B2): In the absence of antecedent knowledge of the identity of the G, the further question "But who is the G [i.e., *that* person]?" is always in order. Just as "N is the G" with "the G" attributive proved to be the form for intrinsically final answers to "Who is N?," so too it appears that "The F is the G" with "the G" attributive is the form for intrinsically final answers to "Who is the F?"

Unlike the attributive version of (A1), the attributive version of (B1) is a completely general statement, amounting to "Whoever F's G's." Despite this difference, the special status of attributive (B1) has exactly the same ground as that of attributive (A1), viz., that only an attributive answer can describe the F in the way seemingly demanded by information-seeking purposes underlying questions of form (B). Once the desired description is provided, no further "who" question is in order unless it is asked from the standpoint of some new purpose—in which event there is no regress but only a change of topic. The following examples illustrate these points as they apply to (B1).

When we ask "Who is the F?," what is at issue is *which* person F's. But the questioner is likely to frown on any answer of the form "The F is the G" (= "He who is F is he who is G") that fails to present the culprit in the right light. The policeman who asks, "Who is the murderer?" can be given an answer of the form, "The murderer is the G," but is not satisfied unless "the G" attributes properties to the murderer (whoever he or she may be) that are relevant to his desire to apprehend the criminal—e.g., personal appearance, place of residence, previous criminal record, etc. Given the policeman's obvious concerns, he can justifiably claim not to know who the murderer is until he is given such information. (The murderer's name may or may not be relevant, depending on just how useful such a datum would be; many criminals have so many aliases that the police are indifferent to their current sobriquets.) If, after receiving this information by means of the description "the G," the policeman still insists that he does not know who the murderer is, we can only suppose that he has come to entertain some new purpose. Nor could he complain that, relative to his original purpose, he does not know who *the* G is (i.e., who G's), for the question "But who G's?" is utterly pointless in relation to that purpose: It would be akin to asking "What is the address of the person currently residing at 10 Park Place?"

Again, the historian who seeks to know who (is the person who) led the Israelites out of bondage in Egypt is not likely to be satisfied with the stock reply, "Moses did." What the historian clearly wants and needs is an answer of the form, "The person who led ... is the person who is G," where the attributive description "the person who is G" conveys information that is both uniquely true of whoever led the Israelites out of bondage *and* historically pertinent in the sense of giving some picture of the leader's origins and later career. The historian desires to put the leader in historical perspective, and only information of the sort just mentioned suffices for that project.

Whatever the historian's particular interests, a sufficiently detailed answer of that kind satisfies them and renders further "who" questions pointless.

There are situations, however, in which the questioner who has been given an appropriate answer of the form "The F is the G" nonetheless goes on to ask, "But who is the G?" For reasons now familiar, this cannot be a question about someone's identity unless a new purpose has been introduced; it may be a pseudo–"who" question. An interesting feature of questions of the form "Who is the F?" (= "Who F's?") is that they are sometimes asked from the standpoint of curiosity about the culprit's *being F*. When the F has been appropriately identified as the G, the questioner may still be curious as to how the G came to be F, in which case he might pose the pseudo–"who" question, "Who is the G?"—which amounts to "Who is the G that he is F?" In terms of the foregoing example, one who has been given an appropriate account of the origins and career of the person who led the Israelites out of bondage—hence one who has been told *who* that leader was—may still wonder about that person's motivation for undertaking the exodus. What concerns the questioner now is not the person's identity but merely certain further attributes of the person thus identified. So his question "But who was that person (viz., the G)?" is plausibly construed as an ellipsis of "But who was the G that he lead the Israelites out of bondage?," i.e., as a request for an explanation, not an identification. The possibility of further questions of *this* kind is quite compatible with our claim about intrinsically final answers to questions of form (B).

We turn, finally, to questions of form (C): "Who is D?" Given the battery of distinctions already made regarding (A) and (B) questions and their answers, little remains to be said about (C). Of the three possible reply forms

(C1) "D is the G,"

(C2) "D is M" ["M" being a proper name],

(C3) "D is E" ["E" being a demonstrative pronoun],

we can give (C3) short shrift. Even for the limited purposes involving perceptual identification, an answer of this sort suffices only in specialized settings. Since the questioner has demonstrated D already, yet another linguistically mediated perceptual fix on D is pointless vis-a-vis the question, unless the questioner had some problem with "tracking" D (as in a fun-house mirror set-up, or when D shot by too quickly for the questioner to get a good look at him or her). (This case should not be confused with that of deferred ostension, which we have assimilated to the use of attributive descriptions with direct demonstrative components: For example, hearing a noise outside, a man might ask aloud, "Who is that?" and get his answer a second later when his wife throws open the door and says, "It's me, stupid! You were maybe expecting Liz Taylor?" We treat this not as a type (C3) response but rather as one along the lines of "Who is (making) that (noise)?"/"It is I (who am making that noise)!" Note too that an answer superficially of form (C3) might appear to be final for some other purpose simply because the pronoun replacing "E" is not really deictic but is instead either a "pronoun of laziness," going proxy for an attributive name or description, or part of an anaphoric discourse chain with suitable descriptive antecedents.)[6]

As regards (C1) and (C2), no reply of one of these forms can be intrinsically final for normal purposes if its right-hand side ("the G" or "M," respectively) is functioning referentially. The reason for this exclusion of referential answers is just as before. If the name "M" in (C2) is attributive, then we are dealing with a disguised version of (C1) involving an attributive description. So it is (C1) that on its attributive reading promises to yield intrinsically final answers to information-seeking (C) questions. As usual, the finality of the answer "D is the G" depends on the attributive description's conveying the sort of information about D that the questioner needs in order to carry out his (actual or hypothetical) project regarding D. Since the relevant ground has been covered extensively already, we content ourselves with a single example.

In most instances, a reply to "Who is D?" mentions D's name along with various salient properties of D. But not every sort of information about D is relevant to the purpose at hand. If the snobbish hostess of a posh party asks her husband (who invited many of the guests without consulting her), "Who (the hell) is *that*?," pointing to a strangely dressed man wearing grotesquely oversized shoes, it would not necessarily be satisfactory for her husband to respond, "That man is named Omar Faflik and is the only man alive with seven toes on each foot." We can still picture her then approaching Mr. Faflik and saying, "My husband has told me some remarkable things about you, Mr. Faflik, but I'm afraid I still don't quite know who you are." She will not be content until she learns how Faflik fits in with the other guests. Assuming that the party is not part freak show, what is in question is Faflik's social role: his job, major achievements, and so on—his claim to fame that earns him admission to such an exclusive gathering. An attributive reply of form (C1), such as "That is the UN ambassador from the new nation of Faflikistan" would have done the trick nicely.

4 The Aim of "Who" Questions

We have seen that attributive descriptions often have a favored status in replies to questions of the forms (A)–(C), since for purposes other than labeling and perceptual locating they alone serve as a general vehicle for conveying the sort of purpose-relative information that can stop the potential regress of "who" questions.[7] Moreover, we have seen that purposes that seek a specific kind of information constrain the way in which this information is conveyed. What remains to be seen is whether we can come up with any useful characterization of the purposes underlying "who" questions, a characterization that will enable us to give a general account of the relation of such a purpose to what one must know in order to count as "knowing who" someone is relative to that purpose. We offer a tentative sketch.

Considerable light can be shed on the matter at hand by thinking of the knower as a clerk in the Filing Department of the Ministry of Personal Records. The clerk's general responsibilities are to keep the Ministry's master files accurate and up to date, to economize on storage space by detecting and collapsing redundant files, and to catalog files under various headings as the need arises. The Ministry's spies continually bring in juicy data—written surveillance reports, photographs, tapes, etc.—and deposit them in the clerk's "In" tray for sorting and filing. The Ministry has strict rules for proper filing: No item may leave the "In" tray for the master files until it has been inserted into a folder whose cover has been labeled with at least one name and/or mug-shot of that item's putative owner. Sometimes the clerk's job is easy: The spies have thoughtfully included names or pictures with their other data, and the clerk need only search the cabinets for correspondingly labeled files to receive that data, or, finding no such files, he can simply open a new file on the spot. Sometimes, however, his task is more difficult: What he finds in his "In" tray is, e.g., an fragment of a wire-service printout on the doings of an unnamed individual. The best he can do pending further input is to keep his "In" tray organized by provisionally sorting its contents into unlabeled "protofiles" on the basis of internal evidence suggesting cotopicality.

Now like any good bureaucracy, the Ministry has forms that must be filled out by those seeking information from the Filing Department. (For the rest of this and the following section we shall continue to pretend that the Ministry's working language is English.) To set the clerk in motion on his or her behalf, a supplicant must fill out Form W.

The point of our fable is simple: H's asking a "who" question of S is functionally equivalent to H's treating S as the filing clerk and submitting to S an *incomplete* copy of Form W in which one of the lines A–C has been filled in but *none* of the boxes 1–3 has been checked. S's job, should he choose to accept it, is to make an educated guess as to which box H "meant" to check (and, in the case of box 3, how H meant to fill in the blanks) and then to proceed accordingly. If S does not feel like guessing, he can either "round-file" the request or return the copy of Form W with some suitable notation (say, a large question mark next to the boxes). The vaunted *purposes* underlying "who" questions simply correspond to the various clerical tasks that H could specify by checking boxes and filling blanks on Form W. Looked at in this way, there is no mystery about how a purpose, once specified, determines the form of an appropriate response to a "who"

FORM W

Supplicant hereby requests a check of Master Files and "In" tray for match with following (supplicant supply one):

    A. A name of victim: [_____].

    B. Mug-shot (attach here).

    C. Description of victim: [_____].

If no match is found, open new master file or protofile. If a match *is* found, please return following (supplicant check one) along with this form to supplicant:

    ☐1. A name of victim (distinct from any entry used on line A or mentioned on line C as a name of victim).
    ☐2. Recent mug-shot of victim (different from any supplied under B).
    ☐3. Descriptive catalog entry on victim under "_____" (supplicant supply heading) which (a) conforms to format of type _____(to be specified by supplicant); (b) contains no items entered on lines A or B; and (c) is noncircular with respect to content of any entry on line C.

---

question. If we momentarily indulge in the pretense that S is an "ideal" clerk who never misfiles data or miscatalogs files—an assumption about which we shall say more shortly—then we can equate S's "knowing who" so-and-so is for purpose P with S's having the resources (in his "inner Ministry") to complete and return copies of Form W on which the appropriate boxes and blanks corresponding to P have been respectively checked and filled by a hypothetical supplicant H. And we can equate a person's *learning* from S *who* so-and-so is for purpose P with S's returning to that person a completed copy of Form W on which the appropriate boxes and blanks corresponding to P have been respectively checked and filled (by someone or other).

The structural correspondence between asking/answering referential and attributive "who" questions (for given purposes) on the one hand and submitting/returning copies of Form W on the other is for the most part sufficiently obvious so that we need not belabor the analogy any further. One case, however, deserves further attention—viz., that involving purposes corresponding to box 3, where a certain kind of specially formatted "catalog-entry" is required. Suppose, e.g., that we have been asked by a fellow philosopher from ESU (Enormous State University), "Who is Fulbert Cipher?" and, not caring to guess at the inquirer's purpose in asking, we respond, "Why do you ask?", effectively returning her incomplete Form W for task specification. Suppose she replies "Oh, someone mentioned his name in connection with the job we have going in our department, and I'm wondering whether to get in touch with him." Then our course is charted: We try to provide biographical data about the potential candiate that bears on his suitability for the academic position—training, technical accomplishments, connections, and reputation as a teacher and colleague. We have been asked in effect for a "catalog-entry" in the ESU-job-application format, some data from our "Fulbert Cipher" file that identifies that individual relative to a cataloging of files under some heading in which the questioner has a special interest—in the case at hand, under the heading "philosopher"—and which conforms to the indicated format. The canonical form for such a catalog entry is accordingly "Fulbert Cipher is the (philosopher who is) F," where "F" spells out facts about the candidate salient to the job-application format. In one way, the questioner already knows who Fulbert Cipher is, viz., he is the person whose name was mentioned in connection with the job opening. But with respect to the current project of placing that individual in the profession *qua* potential employee, the questioner does not know who Fulbert Cipher is and will not know until she obtains the sort of information mentioned above.

What the foregoing example illustrates is that the "information-seeking" purposes corresponding to box 3 have built-in constraints: the requested catalog entry must not only locate the victim in a certain pertinent category but also do so according to a prescribed format. Where the category heading has to do with someone's *social role* ("job seeker in philosophy," "teacher of Classics," "policeman," "entertainer," etc.), the admissible subheadings under which an answer to a "who" question may classify the victim are restricted to predicates that can identify someone vis-a-vis the qualifications required for, and "duties" inherent in, playing that role. Relative, e.g., to the purpose of classifying under the heading "entertainers," no answer to "Who is Liberace?" is admissible unless it conveys information about Liberace's unique status in the entertainment profession.

What makes the "social-role" cases tractable is just that they are *institutional*: We have reasonably clear conventional criteria for what is involved in playing such roles. Of course, there are many institutional catalog headings besides the social-role variety, for people are sometimes classified in terms of their relation *to* an institution rather than by reference to their position within it: "Reformer," "heretic," and "apostate" pertain to one's actions *against* an institution and only incidentally, if at all, to one's status within it. Such a catalog heading as "reformer" delimits an obvious range of subheadings relevant to answering such questions as "Reforms of what practice?," "What reforms in particular?," "Why were the reforms proposed?"

By restricting "cataloging" purposes to those that include a format specification, we do not mean to suggest that every admissible category heading must *conventionally* determine a format for classification within that category. Clearly there can be idiosyncratic or "invented" cataloging purposes involving nonstandard category headings or bizarre formatting constraints: e.g., a sadist might stipulate the idiosyncratic category "good candidate for the torture chamber" and an equally bizarre format for sorting potential victims within this category. We mean only to capture the idea that a genuine information-seeking purpose must put *some* constraints (other than mere noncircularity) on what would satisfy it. For the questioner H to be on a pure fact-finding expedition, willing to stop asking "Who?" at the first sign of an individuating fact, is for H to be operating without any particular purpose at all regarding the victim: Bare individuative curiosity, in other words, is not a purpose in our sense. Although it is true that for every noncircular claim of the form "N is the F" there is some (standard or contrived) purpose in our sense relative to which S's knowing-true "N is the F" would suffice for S's knowing who N is, it is false that there is any purpose P (in our sense) such that, for every noncircular claim of the form "N is the F," S's knowing-true "N is the F" would suffice for S's knowing who N is relative to P. One purely practical reason for insisting that purposes be minimally discriminating is provided by the problem of false opinions about a person's identity, to which we now belatedly turn.

5 "Knowing Who" and False Beliefs

We have tentatively proposed equating S's "knowing who" so-and-so is for purpose P with S's being an ideal filing clerk with the resources (in his "inner Ministry") to complete and return copies of Form W on which the appropriate boxes and blanks corresponding to P have been respectively checked and filled by a hypothetical supplicant H. But we deliberately suppressed the obvious fact that normal humans are *not* "ideal" filing clerks; ordinary mortals, who suffer from false beliefs, are prone to misfiling and miscataloging. So the question arises as to the effect of false beliefs on someone's candidacy for "knowing who" so-and-so is.

If, e.g., it is stipulated that S *knows* that George Washington was the first President of the United States, some sorts of false beliefs are automatically ruled out—viz., any on which S *bases* his belief that George Washington was the first President of the United States. But what about false beliefs regarding Washington that are independent of S's justification for his target belief? Could false beliefs of this sort (which do not prevent S from knowing *that* George Washington was the first President of the U.S.) prevent S from knowing *who* George Washington was for some purpose P? The answer is, "It all depends on *what sort* of false beliefs S entertains regarding Washington."

Piddling little errors about the Father of Our Country intuitively do not count; knowing who Washington was does not require one to be an infallible source of information about him. What does seem to be required for "knowing who" in this case is that S should, so to speak, have no *importantly* false beliefs about Washington. But what is an "importantly" false belief? The answer lies in what we said earlier about purposes. Knowing who N is for purpose P requires, inter alia, having a correct opinion about who N is relative to P, i.e., a true belief about N of the P-specified sort. Positive and negative beliefs of the P-specified sort, regardless of their truth value, are the "important" ones relative to P. So, relative to P, an "importantly false" belief about George Washington would simply be a false positive or negative belief of the P-specified sort, i.e., an incorrect opinion regarding who (for purpose P) George Washington is *or isn't*. Because we require purposes to involve at least minimal constraints on what would satisfy them, the exclusion of incorrect opinions (modulo P) as to who George Washington is or isn't does not prohibit all possible errors about the man.

Suppose P is the purpose of locating Washington under the heading "heads of State" according to some standard historical format (e.g., one requiring at least some of the following: name of State, office title, and dates of service). Then a false belief would be ruled out if it potentially would lead to S's providing *in*correct catalog entries of the relevant sort. For S to believe that George Washington became Emperor of Mexico would obviously be fatal to his knowing who George Washington was for purpose P, for even though S might not include "Emperor of Mexico" on a particular occasion when he returns Form W, the existence of this item in his "George Washington" file is a ticking time bomb: Had he been a bit more thorough in working up his catalog entry according to the indicated format, a false catalog entry of the required sort would have emerged. In contrast, it would be *harmless relative to the purpose at hand* if S were falsely to believe, say, that George Washington chopped down his father's favorite cherry tree, since this alleged exploit of the youthful Washington is irrelevant to the kind of catalog entry called for. By the same token, it would be fatal to S's knowing who George Washington was for this purpose P if S were to believe that George Washington was never a head of State, since this would lead him to *misfile* all the desired data about Washington's political career under some other label, or perhaps to leave it idle in his "In" tray.

Continuing for a moment longer our official blindness to languages other than English, let us summarize the upshot of our latest exploration of the filing-clerk analogy. Taking "N" as schematic for a referentially employed term, we can say that S knows who N is for purpose P if and only if S has an "N"-file that enables him to complete accurately a copy of Form W (with "N" on line A or B) filled out in accordance with P and to file accurately related (but unused) data and that is so labeled and internally structured that (within his total system of files) no inaccurate completion of *that* copy of

Form W can be supported. Similarly, where "the F" is attributive, we can say that S knows who the F is for purpose P if and only if S has antecedently filed "the F" in a master file or protofile that is so labeled and/or internally structured as to enable S to complete accurately a copy of Form W (with "the F" on line C) filled out in accordance with P and to file accurately related (but unused) data but that does not support (within his total system of files) any inaccurate completion of *that* copy of Form W.

6 Fiction and Legend

Before getting on to the analysis of important names, we must address a residual difficulty occasioned by fictional characters. It is natural to suppose that S knows who (say) Sherlock Holmes is just in case S knows some of the Conan Doyle stories. But this appears to be independent of any teleological considerations. Worse still, there are no genuine facts about Sherlock Holmes to be known, since he never existed. We propose to sidestep this difficulty by emphasizing the distinction between knowing who N is and knowing who N is *supposed to be*. We maintain that one does not know *who* a fictional character *is*, strictly, since a fictional character is not really anything at all; rather one knows who a fictional character is supposed to be by knowing what is supposed in fiction about that character.[8] The point could be put by saying that there is no such thing as knowing who Sherlock Holmes (really) is and no such thing as (really) knowing who he is.

Our analysis handles in a natural way *legendary* figures, i.e., real people who are known to us only through totally or largely inaccurate stories. For example, most of us know who Moses was: He is the man of whom the Bible says so-and-so (it is irrelevant whether we believe the Bible stories). We know which legendary figure Moses was, which amounts to knowing who he was for purposes relating to his place in the semihistorical Judeo-Christian frame of reference. But for other purposes, such as dealing with history apart from legend, probably no one knows who Moses was. For such purposes, we might say, no one knows who Moses *really* was, and no one really knows who Moses was.

The contrast between fiction and legend reveals an ambiguity in "really" as attached to knowing-who locutions. When we speak or write of *knowing who N really is* or of *really knowing who N is*, we may be doing one of two things: (i) distinguishing between genuine "knowing who" and mere "knowing who N is supposed to be," or (ii) distinguishing *within* the realm of genuine "knowing who" between knowing who N is for a casual purpose and knowing who N is for a currently much more important purpose. Our final remark about Sherlock Holmes illustrates (i); our final remark about Moses illustrates (ii).

7 Important Names Again

We are now in a position to carry out the unfinished business of chapter 1. In our discussion of canonical representations of referential and attributive versions of "S knows who N is", viz.,

(1) $(\exists \alpha)(\text{Impname}(\alpha, N, P) \ \& \ (\exists \beta)(\triangle(\beta, N) \ \& \ K_S(\ulcorner \beta \text{ is } \alpha \urcorner)))$

and

(2) $(\exists!x)(Fx \ \& \ (\exists \alpha)(\triangle(\alpha, x) \ \& \ \text{Impname}(\alpha, x, P) \ \& \ K_S(\ulcorner F\alpha \urcorner)))$,

respectively, most of the weight was borne by the requirement that S have in his language of thought an important name α of N relative to the assumed purpose P, i.e., an expression that picks out N in a way especially appropriate to P. Given our reflections in sections 4 and 5 and switching from English to Mentalese as S's working language *qua* filing clerk, it is natural to analyse "Impname(α, N, P)" at least in part in terms of the Mentalese equivalents of the items requested by a P-appropriate filling out of Form W (or Form W(P) for short).

Let us first introduce the notion of the *nomenclature* NOM(P, T) *suitable to a purpose* P *with respect to a Mentalese term* T:

(3) NOM(P, T) = def. the set of Mentalese expressions corresponding to the *kinds* of items requested by a copy of (Mentalese) Form W(P) on which T occupies one of the lines A–C.

If it occurred on line A, T would be a Mentalese name or title; on line B, a Mentalese demonstrative-in-use; and on line C, a Mentalese definite description. (Thus to treat T in the third case is to commit ourselves to the idea that the "sentences" of Mentalese in which T appears may have surface structures that do not reflect their logical analyses. A more natural conception is that in which the "sentences" are "written" in a neutral, disambiguated logical idiom and wear their truth conditions on their sleeves; in such a language there would be no definite descriptions or other constructions subject to further semantical analysis.[9] But for now let us swallow the former conception, think of T in the third case as consisting of expressions of the superficial form $\ulcorner \imath x \phi x \urcorner$ in Mentalese, and see where this supposition leads.)

Relative to checking box 1, NOM(P, T) consists of Mentalese counterparts (other than T) of ordinary proper names and titles; and relative to checking box 2, NOM(P, T) consists of Mentalese demonstratives (coordinated with recognition abilities distinct from that mobilized by T, should the latter be demonstrative). What of NOM(P, T) when box 3 is checked and filled out? In light of our discussion above, it is natural to say that NOM(P, T) would consist of P-appropriate Mentalese definite descriptions (appropriately independent of T).

Now important names must be so defined that their invocation in (1) and (2) rules out the possibility of *circularity*, as when α and β in (1) are the same expression or when α in (2) is $\ulcorner \imath z F z \urcorner$. Since noncircularity with respect to T is built into definition (3), we can avail ourselves of its resources in defining "Impname" simply by further relativizing "Impname" to some Mentalese term T. Moreover, since forms (1) and (2) saying nothing about S's lacking "importantly false" beliefs, it is natural to relativize "Impname" still further to the subject S, defining important names in such a way that S's having one for N depends on his lacking such beliefs about N. All these strands are brought together in the following definition:

(4) $\mathrm{Impname}(\alpha, N, S, P, T) =$ def. $\alpha \in \mathrm{NOM}(P, T)$ & α denotes N & $\sim (\exists \beta)(\exists \tau)\,[\beta$ denotes N & τ does not denote N & $\tau \in \mathrm{NOM}(P, T)$ & $B_S(\ulcorner \beta$ is $\tau \urcorner)]$ & $\sim (\exists \beta)(\exists \tau)[\beta$ denotes N & τ denotes N & $\tau \in \mathrm{NOM}(P, T)$ & $B_S(\ulcorner \beta$ is not $\tau \urcorner)]$.

Suitably rewritten to accommodate the new parameters in (4), (1) and (2) respectively become (1*) and (2*):

(1*) $(\exists \beta)[\triangle(\beta, N)$ & $(\exists \alpha)[\mathrm{Impname}(\alpha, N, S, P, \beta)$ & $K_S(\ulcorner \beta$ is $\alpha \urcorner)]]$

and

(2*) $(\exists ! x)[Fx$ & $(\exists \alpha)[\triangle(\alpha, x)$ & $\mathrm{Impname}(\alpha, x, S, P, \ulcorner \imath y F y \urcorner)$ & $K_S(\ulcorner F \alpha \urcorner)]]$.

In our opinion, representations (1*) and (2*) together with the supporting definitions (3) and (4) carry the analysis of knowing who someone is in terms of the possession of purpose-relative important names as far as it can profitably be carried. It would be nice to announce that we are finished, but there is a nasty problem lurking just ahead. In the next section, we explore this difficulty and propose a way of accommodating it that does minimal violence to our overall picture.

8 From Important Names to Important Predicates—The Revised Prototheory

The account given in the previous section originated in our reflections in chapter 1 on the Hintikka-Kaplan tradition. These reflections motivated (i) the idea that knowing who someone is involves having an "important name" of the victim, a special sort of singular term that picks out the victim in a teleologically salient way, and (ii) the inclusion of the respective clauses "$\triangle(\beta, N)$" and "$\triangle(\alpha, x)$" in (1) and (2) to ensure some "real" epistemic connection between S, who has the term in question in his language of thought, and the mentioned or quantified-over victim.[10] Further reflections about the bearing of (a strong form of) the referential/attributive distinction on "who" question-and-answer episodes led us to the distinction between referential and attributive "who" questions and to the idea that (iii) a question of one of these kinds might for some purposes require an answer of the opposite sort and for other purposes an answer of the same sort. We then unpacked question-and-answer considerations by means of the model of the "inner filing clerk" dutifully complying with copies of Form W, and concluded that (iv) knowing who someone is for purpose P involves knowing a P-adequate answer to the question of who that person is, i.e., knowing-true something that enables one to comply accurately with a copy of Form W(P).

Now the problem is that, although each of (i)–(iv) sounds plausible by itself, the result of combining them, as we did in the previous section, creates internal tensions that threaten the viability of our project. To appreciate the tension, we need only remind ourselves that we have done nothing to preclude application of (our strong form of) the referential/attributive distinction *to the language of thought itself*. Indeed, our earlier talk of Mentalese definite descriptions seems to invite such application. But then $\ulcorner \beta$ is $\alpha \urcorner$ in (1*) would be *ambiguous* with respect to how S *employs* the "important" Mentalese term α.

Suppose, e.g., that the operative purpose P is an information-seeking one for which an important name α must be a descriptive term $\ulcorner \imath y \theta y \urcorner$. *Qua* important name, $\ulcorner \imath y \theta y \urcorner$ must, by definition (4), denote the victim N, i.e., be such that its descriptive content applies to N alone. But nothing so far forces S to employ $\ulcorner \imath y \theta y \urcorner$ in such a way that his acceptance of $\ulcorner \beta$ is $\imath y \theta y \urcorner$ would compel him to accept $\ulcorner \theta! \beta \urcorner$ (just as the fact that "the inventor of bifocals" denotes Benjamin Franklin does not preclude a speaker from using it in such a way—viz., referentially—that his utterance of "Benjamin Franklin is the inventor of bifocals" need not commit him to accepting "Benjamin Franklin (really) invented bifocals"). As (1*) stands, S can know who N is for this information-seeking purpose P even though he does not regard his use of the important name $\ulcorner \imath y \theta y \urcorner$ of N as in any way dependent on its literal denotation conditions! Surely this is wrong: What we want S to accept is something the knowing-true of which ensures that S knows-true $\ulcorner \theta! \beta \urcorner$, since what is at issue is the analog of knowing a correct *attributive* answer to a referential "who" question.

Matters are no better with (2*). Indeed, (2*) has a clause that actually *stipulates* that the important name function referentially. With or without that clause, (2*) is equally impotent to record the fact that knowing who the F is (= who F'd) requires, for certain purposes, knowing something that is the analog of an *attributive* answer to an attributive "who" question. Once again, what we want S to accept is something the knowing-true of which ensures that S apply to the victim some teleologically salient predicate—which, for many purposes, must be *other* than just S's Mentalese analog of "F" or "F!".

Something has to give. Of our four desiderata (i)–(iv), it seems in retrospect easiest to give up part of (i), viz., that part that commits us to *singular terms* ("names") as the teleologically "important" expressions. For it was that commitment that led us to speak of Mentalese definite descriptions as important names for purposes requiring attributive answers, hence to allow that the "sentences" of Mentalese in which important names appear may have surface structures that do not reflect their logical analyses. And the latter concession opens the door to referential/attributive ambiguity in the language of thought. But if we are to abandon important names, we must not only find a new vehicle for the teleological relativity of "knowing who" but also provide for those special purposes relative to which "knowing who" *is* something like being able to refer to the victim by name or being able to demonstrate the victim, i.e., the analogs of "who" questions that solicit merely *referential* answers. Fortunately, there is a fairly natural way of doing all this.

Let us now understand languages of thought as *fully disambiguated* in a way that until now we have (following Harman) eschewed;[11] let us suppose, therefore, that what answers to a natural-language sentence containing a referentially employed superficial "term" is a Mentalese sentence containing a rigidly co-designative individual constant or demonstrative of Mentalese and that what answers to a natural-language sentence containing an attributively employed superficial "term" (identical to or abbreviating the likes of "the F") is a Russellian paraphrase of that sentence in which the term disappears in the usual way, leaving behind a contribution to quantificational and predicative content. An immediate consequence of this proposal is that Mentalese has nothing of the troublesome sort $\ulcorner \beta = \imath y \phi y \urcorner$ but only its predicative cousin $\ulcorner \phi! \beta \urcorner$, which is just the sort of thing we want S to know-true in cases where the operative purpose requires a descriptive catalog entry (i.e., where box 3 is checked on Form W(P)). But what about the analogs of acceptable referential answers to "who" questions (i.e., where box 1 or 2 is checked on Form W(P)?). Here what is wanted is a naming or demonstration by means of the likes of $\ulcorner \beta = \alpha \urcorner$, not a new predication of the sort $\ulcorner \phi! \beta \urcorner$. This fact can be accommodated within our Russellian picture of languages of thought simply by supposing them to contain the Frege-Russell device of *predicate abstraction*, whereby open sentences can be converted into predicates. Thus, e.g., $\ulcorner \beta = \alpha \urcorner$ can, if desired, be equivalently rewritten as $\ulcorner (\hat{x} = \alpha)(\beta) \urcorner$; and so the requirement for a naming or demonstration can be assimilated to the demand for a "predication" of this "derived" variety.

What the foregoing suggests, as a way of escaping from the lately encountered difficulties, is a switch from important names to important *predicates* as the vehicle of teleological relativity. Formally, the required changes are minimal. First, we replace definition (3) with (5):

(5) NOM(P, E) = def. the set of (monadic) Mentalese *predicates* of the kind requested by a copy of (Mentalese) Form W(P) on which E is an appropriate entry on one of the lines A–C,

where the "predicates" in question are now understood potentially to include items of the form $\ulcorner (\hat{x} = \alpha) \urcorner$ and E is required (for lines A or B) to be a Mentalese term or (for line C) a Mentalese primitive predicate or predicate abstract (other than the sort $\ulcorner \hat{x} = \alpha \urcorner$). (Thus, where previously something of the form $\ulcorner \imath y \theta y \urcorner$ would have appeared on line C of Form W, we now envisage it supplanted by $\ulcorner (\theta!\hat{x}) \urcorner$ (θ containing no subformula of the sort $\ulcorner x = \alpha \urcorner$), and likewise for responses to box 3.) The case in which E is a line C entry will prove to be of interest in chapter 4, but for reasons that emerge below, the only cases of current interest are those in which E is a Mentalese *term* β on line A or B. Second, we replace definition (4) with (6), which captures the new notion of an "important predicate" relative to a purpose P:

(6) Imppred $(\phi, S, P, \beta) =$ def. $\phi \in$ NOM(P, β) and $(\theta)((\theta \in$ NOM(P, β) & B$_S(\ulcorner \theta(\beta) \urcorner)) \rightarrow \ulcorner \theta(\beta) \urcorner$ is True-in-Mentalese) and $(\theta)((\theta \in$ NOM(P, β) & B$_S(\ulcorner \sim \theta(\beta) \urcorner) \rightarrow \ulcorner \sim \theta(\beta) \urcorner$ is True-in-Mentalese).

And third, we accordingly rewrite (1*) and (2*) as (1**) and (2**):

(1**) $(\exists \beta)(\triangle(\beta, N)$ & $(\exists \phi)[$Imppred(ϕ, S, P, β) & K$_S(\ulcorner \phi!\beta \urcorner)))$

and

(2**) $(\exists!x)[Fx$ & $(\exists \alpha)(\exists \phi)[\triangle(\alpha, x)$ & Imppred(ϕ, S, P, α) & K$_S(\ulcorner F\alpha$ & $\phi!\alpha \urcorner)]]$.

Things are happening pretty quickly, so let us stand back and see what has been accomplished.

To begin with, "Imppred," unlike its recently decreased ancestor "Imp-name," is a four-place predicate. Within the current framework there is no need to relativize important predicates to individuals that satisfy them. In determining a nomenclature relative to a term or predicate as "request" entry, a purpose simply fixes a generic system of predicates (in our broad sense) for use in *potentially* suitable answers: What matters is their satisfaction conditions not the obtaining of those conditions. (The entries on lines A–C only put noncircularity constraints on relevant predicates; it is the checking of boxes 1–3 that determines *which* noncircular predicates are relevant.) Thus, e.g., "discovered penicillin" counts as an important predicate relative to a box 3 request specifying the catalog heading "makers of famous medical discoveries" and a standard, achievement-listing format, even if the entry on line A of Form W is "Dr. Jonas Salk" (or, for that matter, "Napoleon"), for "discovered penicillin" is a *relevant* subclassification in *that* format, regardless of who (if anyone) satisfies it. To know who Dr. Jonas Salk is for this particular purpose, one must be able to attach some such important predicate to him; but it is redundant to require separately that he satisfy the predicate, since this is already ensured by the stipulation in (1**) and (2**) that the subject must *know*-true the predication in question. "Discovered penicillin," though of the right *sort* for the purpose at hand, won't do where Salk is concerned: too bad, but another of the same sort (e.g., "developer of the first poliomyelitis vaccine") does do nicely. (Prospects for Napoleon are less bright: Presumably it is impossible to know who Napoleon was for the purpose at issue, since he fails to fall under the general heading; we do not require that purposes be viable in order to be purposes. By the same token, a nameless wanderer with no job, special talents, or socially interesting connections would be such that for *most* garden-variety purposes no one could know who he is—not because his "identity" is a metaphysical mystery but simply because he has no "identity" of the garden-variety sort (he is for all practical purposes (as we say) a "nobody.")

Where (2^*) had "Impname$(\alpha, x, S, P, \ulcorner \imath y F y \urcorner)$," (2^{**}) has "Imppred(ϕ, S, P, α)." Why not "Imppred$(\phi, S, P, \ulcorner F! \hat{x} \urcorner)$" instead? The reason is simple: In "S knows who the F is," "the F" is an attributive description in the hypothetical *ascriber's* mouth. But for S to know who the F is ($=$ who (uniquely) F'd), S need only know the required sort of thing about whoever F'd in a way which is noncircular with respect to S's *own* way α of referentially designating the F. In other words, S is required to be *both* sender and receiver of a Form W(P) with α on line A or B when the question-and-answer game is moved inside S's head. What matters for S's knowing who F'd is S's ability to comply with such a Form W(P) by finding an α-file that contains $\ulcorner F \hat{x} \urcorner$ together with whatever additional predicate $\ulcorner \phi ! \hat{x} \urcorner$ (if any) is reqired by P. This is what we have recorded in (2^{**}) by expanding the knowledge clause to $\ulcorner F\alpha$ & $\phi ! \alpha \urcorner$.

Let us now consider the intuitive content of (1^{**}) and (2^{**}) as applied to some concrete cases. According to (1^{**}), to know who, say, Tully is (for given purpose P) is just to know-true a mental sentence $\ulcorner \phi ! \beta \urcorner$ whose subject term β referentially designates Tully and whose predicate ϕ is noncircular with respect to β and characterizes Tully in a P-salient way, while lacking any P-important false beliefs about Tully. For certain limited purposes, ϕ might just be $\ulcorner (\hat{x} = \text{Cicero}) \urcorner$; but ϕ could never be $\ulcorner (\hat{x} = \beta) \urcorner$, since $\ulcorner (\hat{x} = \beta) \urcorner$ is never in NOM(P, β). For other purposes, ϕ would have to be a salient catalog entry—perhaps $\ulcorner \hat{x}$ authored *De Fato* $\urcorner$. If, for β suitably designating Tully, S knows-true $\ulcorner \beta = \text{Cicero} \urcorner$ (strictly, $\ulcorner (\hat{x} = \text{Cicero})!(\beta) \urcorner$) and if $\ulcorner (\hat{x} = \text{Cicero}) \urcorner$ is an important predicate with respect to β for S under P, then S knows who Tully is (for P), provided that S believes-true no P-important falsehoods, such as $\ulcorner \beta = \text{Socrates} \urcorner$ or $\ulcorner \sim (\beta = \text{Tully}) \urcorner$. Similarly, if S knows-true $\ulcorner \beta$ (alone) authored *De Fato* $\urcorner$ and if $\ulcorner \hat{x}$ authored *De Fato* $\urcorner$ is important with respect to β for S under P, then S knows who Tully is (for P), provided that S believes-true no P-important falsehood $\ulcorner \theta(\beta) \urcorner$ or $\ulcorner \sim \theta(\beta) \urcorner$ for other $\theta \in \text{NOM}(P, \beta)$.

According to (2^{**}), to know who, say, Lincoln's assassin was (for given purpose P)—i.e., who (alone) assassinated Lincoln—is just to know-true a mental sentence $\ulcorner \alpha$ assassinated Lincoln & $\phi ! \alpha \urcorner$, in which α referentially designates the assassin (viz., John Wilkes Booth) and ϕ characterizes him in a P-salient way (noncircular with respect to α) while lacking any P-important false beliefs about John Wilkes Booth. Once again, ϕ might for certain limited purposes be $\ulcorner \hat{x} =$ John Wilkes Booth$\urcorner$; for other purposes, ϕ might be $\ulcorner \hat{x}$ assassinated Lincoln$\urcorner$ (in which case we might as well drop the first conjunct from the knowledge clause because $\ulcorner \phi!\alpha \urcorner$ is doing all the work). For still further purposes, however, ϕ would have to be a saliently novel catalog entry—perhaps $\ulcorner \hat{x}$ was a son of Junius Brutus Booth (1796–1852) and brother of Edwin Thomas Booth (1833–93) who became an actor and Confederate sympathizer$\urcorner$.

Let us summarize the main results of this section. We have seen that failure to disambiguate the language of thought along referential/attributive lines set our initial program—embodied in (1*), (2*), (3), and (4)—at odds with our conversational data described in referential/attributive terms. The required disambiguation amounts simply to the formal recognition of the potentially *predicative* character of what we had been calling an "important name." This formal recognition is implemented by the shift from "Impname" to "Imppred" as the key ingredient. The resulting renditions (1**) and (2**)—backed by definitions (5) and (6)—are now in accord with our observations about teleologically final replies to "who" questions. Our current theory thus inherits all the advantages of its predecessor but lacks the incongruity that flawed it.

The shift from "Impname" to "Imppred" also represents a significant reconception of "knowing who" itself. Common sense sees "knowing who" as knowledge of *identity*, and the objects of such knowledge are uniformly taken to be identity statements. But as we have shown, this appearance is largely superficial, both grammatically and ontologically. The mental sentence to be known-true by our subject S is only (equivalent to) an equation relative to special purposes; for a vastly wider range of purposes it is a singular predication. For the latter purposes, knowing who someone is involves knowing saliently individuating contingent facts about the person in question; and for the former purposes, it involves knowing something the grasp of which enables one saliently to label or to demonstrate that person. In neither case does it involve grasping a metaphysical essence (which, incidentally, is why it is perfectly acceptable, both to common sense and in our theory, to speak of "degrees" of "knowing who" (relative to a given purpose P), e.g., of A's knowing *better than B does* who N is, of A's *barely* knowing who N is, etc.) We elaborate on this reconception in chapter 4.

II

3

A Theory of *Oratio Obliqua*

The analysis of "knowing who" offered in part I still requires considerable refinement. In our zeal to find appropriate necessary and sufficient conditions for "knowing who," we were driven by our provisional acceptance of a tendentiously strong view of the referential/attributive distinction to proliferate formal paraphrases in order to account for the transparent versus opaque "senses" of "knowing who." In the process we have attended insufficiently to the desirable aim that the rough-and-ready account thus obtained should mesh with a plausible syntactic and semantic theory of attitude *ascriptions* in general. But when viewed from this standpoint, the complicated analysis formulated in chapter 2 does not look very attractive, for two reasons.

Heretofore, we have regarded our prototheory merely as an account of the *truth conditions* of knowing-who ascriptions. But this leaves the question of a strict logical form and/or an underlying syntactic structure for "X knows who N/the F is" and how a plausible semantic theory could link sentences having such forms with their truth conditions. It would be fanciful at best to suppose that the highly complex paraphrases we have provided so far are really mirrored in strict logical form.

Second, even meeting the latter problem would still not give us the required degree of generality. For "X knows who N/the F is" is but a special case of the general form "X knows who————," in which the blank can be filled by a wide variety of verb phrases, some of which contain several "who" terms. The deliverances of part I do not offer any immediate help with the likes of (1a–c):

(1) a. John knows who bought tickets.

b. John knows who is conspiring against whom.

c. John knows who insulted whom in whose presence.

For example, we cannot assimilate (1a) to (2):

(2) John knows who the ticket-buyers are,

for (2) is ambiguous in a way that (1a) is not: If "the ticket-buyers" is taken referentially (like a plural demonstrative), then (2) does not entail that John thinks of the people in question *as* ticket-buyers, whereas (1a) ineluctably does carry this implication.

In the next three chapters we attempt to work out precisely such a general theory of ascriptions of "knowing who," adequate at least for nonembedded cases—i.e., where "X knows who————" is completed by a verb phrase containing no verbs of propositional attitude—and incorporating the basic insights of chapter 2 while dispensing with some of its more tendentious underpinnings. This project requires fairly extensive backtracking. In this chapter we examine *oratio obliqua* constructions, propose a modified paratactic account of their structure, and develop the formal apparatus for their semantic interpretation in a highly general way that extends to a whole family of related paratactic constructions. In chapter 4 we urge a similar paratactic treatment of *de dicto* belief and knowledge ascriptions, showing how the antecedently developed apparatus applies to these and how it can be extended to apply to knowledge ascriptions in the "who"-clause format, both the special case of "X knows who N is" and the general case of ascriptions such as (1a–c). The final account of the logical form and semantic interpretation of (*de dicto*) knowing-who ascriptions, which emerges in chapter 4, constitutes our official theory, differing in some details from the prototheory of chapter 2 but capturing all the latter's essential insights within a linguistically more plausible framework. We then proceed in chapter 5 to tackle the vexed question of the *aboutness* of thoughts and its bearing on the analysis of *de re* attitude ascriptions; after surveying various notions of the *de re*, we propose a generalization of our formal apparatus to accommodate *de re* attitude ascriptions (in both the "that"-clause and the "who"-clause formats) that maintains a reasonable neutrality between those ostensibly rival notions (yet we also defend one of them as most properly contrasting with the *de dicto*).

1   Parataxis, Deferred Ostension, and Pragmatic Ambiguity

Our background theory of attitude ascriptions takes its cue from Donald Davidson's paratactic account of indirect discourse constructions.[1] Davidson proposes that the superficially unitary construction "X says that p" splits at the level of logical form into two paratactically related sentences, "X says that" and "p", where the complementizer "that" functions as a *demonstrative* and the complement "p" as its referent. Suppose that someone assertively utters

(3) John says that Tom is a fool.

Then the utterer is to be regarded as having produced *two* separate utterances: first, an assertive utterance of "John says that"; second, a *non*assertive, purely "illustrative" utterance of "Tom is a fool," lacking illocutionary force and intended solely to serve as the object to which the demonstrative "that" in the assertive component refers. It is as if one asserted "John says that" while pointing to a placard on which one had inscribed a token of "Tom is a fool":

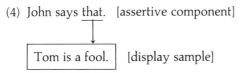

(4) John says that.   [assertive component]

Tom is a fool.   [display sample]

An immediate advantage of this proposal is that it explains the opacity of "says that" complements without the need for any further apparatus. We cannot automatically replace "Tom" in (3) by a coreferring singular term salva veritate, simply because "Tom" is part of what is displayed as the referent of "that": Replacing "Tom" by any other term, coreferential or not, changes the identity of the referent of "that," with obvious peril to the truth value of the assertive component. This economical account of opacity still comes at a price. For since (3) can clearly be true even though John speaks no English and has never uttered an English sentence, we are now prevented from paraphrasing "says" in (3) by anything like "assertively utters." To escape this problem, Davidson glosses "John says that" with

(5) Some utterance of John's and my next utterance make us samesayers.

Nor is this new, unexplicated notion of "being made to be samesayers" the only price demanded. We must also accept the dubious entailment of the existence of English sentences.[2] Rather than engaging in further tinkering to save Davidson's original proposal, we suggest a different but obviously related paratactic construal.

Instead of treating the demonstrative "that" (or its surrogate, "my next utterance" in (5)) as having direct reference to the displayed sentence, let us treat the displayed sentence as the vehicle of a *deferred* ostension: The displayed sentence serves merely as a *sample* of a kind or class of sentences which is the deferred referent of "that." What class is this? We might noncommittally describe it as the class of sentences which "play the same role as" the displayed sentence, i.e., which resemble it in some key linguistic respect. The force of "John says that," concatenated with display of a sentence, is to attribute to John a saying of one of those "resembling" sentences. Accordingly, we might think of "John says that" as having the simple logical form[3]

(6) **SAY(John,THAT₁)**,

where **THAT₁** refers in context to the aforementioned class of sentences and **SAY** is glossed as "assertively utters one of." (This may seem to break the link with direct quotation and to proliferate senses of "say." In fact it does not, since quotation names themselves can plausibly be viewed as referring to sets of types. Where *written* utterances are concerned, this should be obvious: Certain English script characters bear so little resemblance to their block-letter counterparts that they might as well be counted as being of different types, and the need to type-differentiate longhand and printed inscriptions from those in shorthand or Morse is even greater.)

Since the burden of indirect discourse now lies with the nature of what is said and since this nature is relational, our question becomes: What respect of resemblance is operative? There is no need to expect any single, global answer to this question, for every deferred ostension is *pragmatically ambiguous* as regards just how closely and in what respects something must "resemble" its display sample.[4] For example, when John points to a passing Rolls Royce and says "That's what I want!," he is (normally) engaging in deferred ostension; the passing automobile is a sample of the *kind* of thing he wants. Yet his utterance is pragmatically ambiguous in that it provides no intrinsic criterion for individuating that kind. Must things of that kind be Rolls Royces, or would any expensive, hand-made automobile suffice? What about color, model, equipment, and the like? It is up to the audience, using whatever contextual clues and collateral information they possess, to sort matters out for themselves.

The same is true when linguistic objects are at issue. The situation depicted in (4), construed now in terms of deferred ostension, provides no criterion for individuating the linguistic role-kind in question. There are various sorts of roles that sentences can have, each with its own criterion of sameness. So we cannot continue to speak, as we did above, of "the" role of the displayed sentence; we should speak instead of its "M-role," for various values of "M" yet to be specified. Then, as a rough first approximation, we could say that what **THAT**$_1$ in (6) refers to (as homing on a particular display sentence) is the class of sentences playing the same M-role as the display sentence, where M is the *salient* role-kind. But what sorts of roles are at issue, and what makes one rather than another "salient" on a particular occasion?

2 *Sentential Roles and Contextual Salience*

Two major sorts of sentential roles have occupied philosophers' attention. Those who, like Davidson, take as their basic goal the provision of formal truth theories for natural languages have emphasized the *truth-theoretic* role of (declarative) sentences, their systematic association with truth conditions. For such theorists, to play the same role is (roughly) to have the same truth condition. Those who, like Sellars, emphasize the connection of language *use* with human cognition and behavior have focused on what might be called the *conceptual* role that a sentence plays within a speaker's public language,

"language game," "conceptual scheme," or behavioral economy. (In this last case, it is natural to speak of the sentence's *computational* or simply *functional* role, though it is no trivial task to spell out what it means to attribute a psychological role of this sort to a sentence of a public natural language.) Again very roughly, a sentence S plays for a speaker x the same conceptual role that a sentence S' plays for a speaker y just in case x and y mobilize S and S', respectively, in closely similar ways in practical and theoretical reasoning (i.e., the pattern of "moves" associated with S in x's public or internal language game is functionally equivalent to that associated with S' in y's language game). So we might alternatively characterize the reference of $THAT_1$ in (6) as follows: When it ostends a token of S, $THAT_1$ refers to the class of sentences that play the same "conceptual" or functional role for their utterers as S plays (for the tokener).

Before addressing the salience issue, we hasten to note that our two sorts of sentential role vary independently of each other. That is to say, sameness of semantical (truth-theoretic) role is not entailed by sameness of conceptual or functional role, and vice versa. In the course of defending his views about reference, Hilary Putnam[5] provided some nice examples of how agreement in one of these dimensions can be accompanied by difference in the other.

Consider Twin Earth, a planet indistinguishable to the unaided senses from our Earth but which differs slightly in its underlying physical makeup. Every macro-object on Earth has a counterpart on Twin Earth, and conversely, but at the microlevel there is the following difference: The liquid that is the Twin Earth counterpart of water—which is of course called water by speakers of Twin English—is composed not of H_2O molecules but of XYZ molecules (even though phenomenologically water and Twin-water are indiscernible). Now suppose that John utters "Water is wet" here on Earth and that Twin John utters "Water is wet" in Twin English on Twin Earth. Given reasonable assumptions about how words such as water were introduced on Earth and on Twin Earth, respectively (with *local* stuff as paradigms in each case), it seems tolerably clear that the two sentences do not have the same truth condition (play the same semantical role); the former is true (in English) iff water is wet, whereas the latter is true (in Twin English) iff Twin-water is wet; and water and its twin are distinct stuffs. Yet it is plausible to think of these sentences as playing the *same* conceptual role for John and Twin John, for the hypothesized isomorphism of Earth with Twin Earth obviously carries over to the *use* of English and Twin English by John and Twin John, respectively. Anything that John would utter or otherwise do in connection with his sentence is exactly matched by Twin John with respect to his (Twin John's) sentence. Every motivational, evidential, and inferential feature that the English sentence has in John's language game is paralleled by the features of the Twin English sentence in Twin John's language game. Prescientific Twin Earthers, we might say, have the same internal concept of water as we; they lack only the substance. (Please note a key assumption: that "conceptual" or functional role in our sense is what has come to be called a "narrow," "autonomous," or "solipsistic" notion in the sense that if S has such-and-such a conceptual role for x then S has that same conceptual role for any molecular duplicate of x. Thus it satisfies Putnam and Fodor's constraint of "methodological solipsism." [6])

Examples of the converse—same semantical role but different conceptual roles—abound in Putnam's discussions of the preservation of meaning (truth-conditionally construed) across theory-change. Perhaps the most striking case is that in which a sentence once regarded as virtually analytic (necessary relative to a given conceptual scheme) comes, as a result of a "conceptual revolution," to be regarded as contingent and perhaps even as false. Putnam writes, [7]

> The principles of geometry are a case in point. Before the development of non-Euclidean geometry by Riemann and Lobachevski, the best philosophic minds regarded them as virtually analytic. The human mind could not conceive their falsity. Hume would certainly not have been impressed by the claim that "straight line" means "path of a light ray" and that the meeting of two light rays mutually perpendicular to a third light ray could show, if it ever occurred, that the Parallels Postulate of Euclidean geometry is false. He would have contended that it rather showed that light does not travel in straight lines. Thus he would not have admitted that, since we can visualize light rays behaving in the manner described, it follows that we can "visualize non-Euclidean space."

Interpreted as a claim about the physical universe and stated in English, the conceptual role played for Hume by the Parallels Postulate is vastly different from that played for a contemporary Riemannian physicist. But, Putnam argues, the postulate's truth condition (*qua* physical claim) has not changed at all; whatever states of affairs would count for or against the truth of the claim in Hume's mouth would equally count for or against the claim in the mouth of the Riemannian physicist. What has changed is our internal concept of those states of affairs.

If these two examples, of Twin Earth and of sameness of reference through drastic theoretical change, are too arcane to persuade, consider the lowly indexical pronoun. "I am underpaid" as uttered by John has the same conceptual role as the same sequence of morphemes as uttered by Twin John—the two utterances have exactly parallel circumstantial causes, inferential properties, and behavioral effects—but they manifestly differ in truth condition, for John and Twin John are two different people, and there are possible worlds in which one is underpaid but the other is not. Conversely, "I am underpaid but you are not" said by Lois Lane to Clark Kent and "You are underpaid but I am not" said by Clark Kent to Lois Lane have the same truth condition but hardly the same conceptual role: Lois is spurred to pound on Perry White's door, demanding a raise, whereas Clark slinks off to a phone booth. As before, truth condition depends on conceptual role only in conjunction with historical and contextual factors; conceptual role depends not on truth condition per se but on how the truth condition is expressed or represented. (Much more on all this below.)

Returning now to the salience issue, we note that some philosophers have talked as if it were no issue at all—as if one of our two schemes of role individuation were the *correct* scheme to be chosen in all contexts. The reason is not hard to locate: It stems from the idea that sameness of role is just sameness of "meaning" or (worse) "content" and that one of these two schemes, but not the other, captures meaning and/or really picks out the relevant utterance's content. We have avoided, and shall continue to avoid, fruitless polemics on this topic. So far as we are concerned, both the semantical features and the conceptual roles of sentences reveal important aspects of what this theorist or that might be pleased to call their "meanings." [8] The question, in connection with (4), of whether John's alleged utterance "has the same meaning" as the speaker's display sentence evinces precisely such teleological relativity. If our interest is in the truth-relevant properties of these sentences, we are in effect concerned with whether they play the same semantical role. But if our interest is in the behavior-modifying characteristics of what John supposedly uttered, we are in effect wondering whether the sentence produced by John and the sentence displayed by the speaker play the same conceptual role for their respective utterers. What renders salient the application to (4) of one scheme of role individuation rather than another in a particular context is the interests and background information that as potential interpreters we bring to bear on the utterer and subject of (4) in that context. We see later that this interpretive latitude has important consequences for our treatment of the opacity issue.

3   Logical Form and Semantic Interpretation

We have arrived at an impressionistic picture of how a paratactic account of (3) might work. But a picture is not yet a theory, and even as an intuitive sketch, our picture's potential shortcomings are fairly clear. The moment we try to extend the account to *oratio obliqua* in general, we are blocked by English grammar, which incorporates recognition of differences in perspective between the utterer and the subject of a "says that" construction and dictates corresponding shifts in verbal and pronominal forms. For example, in "John said that Tom was a fool," the display sample "Tom was a fool" is in the past tense, yet the utterer is intuitively attributing to John the utterance at some past time of a *present*-tense sentence, such as "Tom is a fool." If what

John uttered at that past time was not in the present tense but, say, in the past tense, then the reporter should move to the pluperfect "John said that Tom had been a fool," and so on. The problem posed by these shifts of perspective is glaring: that the relevant class of sentences cannot in general be specified in terms of the role played by the *actual* display sample. Of course, the relevant grammatical rules can be run backward to obtain the intuitively appropriate sentence type, which we may call the *progenitor* of the displayed sentence. Thus, e.g., "Tom is a fool" is the progenitor of the complement in "John said that Tom was a fool"; "Tom will be a fool" is the progenitor of the complement in "John said that Tom would be a fool," and so on. (Similar remarks apply, mutatis mutandis, to certain reflexive pronouns, which concerns us later.) But what the speaker tokens as a display sample is not in general a token of its progenitor; the latter occurs in *our* mouths in the course of explaining what is going on but might never be tokened by anyone else. There is no guarantee that the role that the actually displayed sentence plays for the utterer coincides with the role that its progenitor plays in our mouths. At this point one begins to see the need to embody the intuitive picture in a formal mechanism powerful enough to untangle these threads. We turn now to a sketch of the necessary components.

We have casually envisioned positing "logical forms" for sentences of English (and, by implication, for sentences of other natural languages). These logical forms can presumably be represented by formulas (or, in the paratactic case, sets of formulas) of some canonical idiom, a privileged artificial language that is somehow related to various natural languages—this relation being what makes a given logical form the or a logical form *of* such-and-such a natural-language sentence. Various accounts of this relation have been proposed by linguists and philosophers. Just for a modest definiteness, we adopt the pretense that there is a single canonical idiom (whose syntax may for our limited purposes be regarded as that of a standard first-order calculus) from which the sentences of any particular natural language are derived by means of a complicated set of "transformations" peculiar to and definitive of that language. (With some trepidation we use "transformation" here in the widest possible sense appropriate to Montague's universal grammar, asking the reader to bracket the term's various traditional associations with one or another internecine dispute between syntactic theorists.[9]) A natural language itself is taken to be a set of purely formal rules for projecting logical forms singly or in groups onto the types of marks and noises that are the coin of actual writing and speech.[10] We assume that the semantical properties of a natural-language sentence derive from and are just those of its underlying logical form. Thus we view our chosen canonical idiom as a system of "universal semantic representation": Whatever the correct semantical theory for the canonical idiom is, that theory automatically interprets the sentences of any natural language whose transformational apparatus is available.[11]

3.1 Fragments of the Canonical Idiom

Since the ideas adumbrated above do some fairly heavy duty for us later, we must clarify certain background assumptions that we make about the syntax and semantics of the canonical idiom. (What follows is technical and fairly dense; some readers may want to spare themselves and leap ahead to the informal summaries (sections 3.5 and 4.5).) To begin with, we are concerned only with a certain fragment F^{++} of the canonical idiom, a fragment that underlies the sorts of nonembedded "attitudinal" constructions of English which comprise our topic, viz., the instances of "X says that p," "X believes that p," "X knows who N is," etc. The fragment F^{++} can be specified in the following manner.

First, let T be the set of all primitive (i.e., syntactically simple) singular terms of the canonical idiom *excluding* (i) **THAT** and the related quasidemonstratives **FACTTHAT** and **THE-WHO-OF-IT** (to be introduced and discussed later), (ii) deictic terms, and (iii) token reflexives other than **I**. (Ignoring (ii) and (iii) is merely a convenience that simplifies our later remarks about the semantics of F^{++}.) Let P be the set of all primitive predicates of the canonical idiom *excluding* "attitudinal" predicates like **SAY**. If we suppose that the canonical idiom contains a semantically inert, noniterable termforming operator $*$ on variables, F can be specified as the set of primitive formulas constructed from T and P by means of the usual provisions for connectives, quantifiers, identity, tense operators, and iota-terms. Now let T^{+} be the set of all primitive and derived (i.e., iota-) terms figuring in F, and let P^{+} be the result of adding to P as derived k-ary predicates every abstract $\hat{v}_1 \ldots \hat{v}_k$ (A) in which A is a formula of F containing at least the distinct variables $v_1 \ldots v_k$ free and having no variable with both free and bound occurrences. Let F^{+} be the set of formulas generated from T^{+} and P^{+} by means of connectives, quantifiers, identity, and tense operators alone (i.e., no derived terms not already in T^{+} figure in F^{+}). Finally, let T^{++} be the result of adding to T^{+} **THAT**$_i$, **FACTTHAT**$_i$, and **THE-WHO-OF-IT**$_i$ for $i = 1, 2, \ldots$, and let P^{++} be the result of adding P^{+} the three attitudinal predicates **SAY**, **BELIEVE**, and **KNOW**. Then the desired fragment F^{++} can be identified with the set of formulas generated from T^{++} and P^{++} by the same apparatus employed in connection with F^{+}. (Notice that, by this specification, no formula of F^{++} contains an abstract embedding another abstract nor any iota-term embedding an abstract. No expressive power is thereby sacrificed, as we shall see when we turn to semantical considerations, where the reasons for this somewhat baroque specification of F^{++} emerge.)

We next introduce, for arbitrary natural language L, the general notion of a *categorematic expression under analysis* (CEUA) in L, in terms of which we define a *sentence under analysis* (SUA) of L and a *predicate abstract under analysis* (PAUA) of L. A CEUA in L is an ordered pair $\langle G, J \rangle$ such that (i) $J \in \mathbf{T}^{++} \bigcup \mathbf{P}^{++} \bigcup \mathbf{F}^{++}$; (ii) if $J \in \mathbf{F}^{++}$, then G is a surface sentence derivable from J under L; and (iii) if $J \in \mathbf{T}^{++} \bigcup \mathbf{P}^{++}$, then G is the output of some lexicalization transformation in L which takes J as an admissible input.

To define SUAs and PAUAs of L, we need the notion of a *regimented* formula or abstract (derived predicate). Let us say that a formula $A \in \mathbf{F}^{++}$ is regimented iff (i) A's k distinct free variables (if any) comprise exactly the alphabetically first k variables of the canonical idiom (the variables of the canonical idiom being, say, $\mathbf{x}_1, \mathbf{x}_2, \ldots$); (ii) no variable has both bound and free occurrences in A; and (iii) no variable v occurs in A in a term v^* unless it so occurs everywhere in A and is alphabetically the last free variable in A. And let us say that a derived predicate $\hat{v}_1 \ldots \hat{v}_k(A)$ in $\mathbf{P}^+$ is regimented iff either (i) it is closed (contains no free variables) and $v_1, \ldots, v_k$ are, respectively, $\mathbf{x}_1, \ldots, \mathbf{x}_k$, or (ii) it is open in $\mathbf{x}_1, \ldots, \mathbf{x}_n$, and $v_1, \ldots, v_k$ are, respectively, $\mathbf{x}_{n+1}, \ldots, \mathbf{x}_{n+k}$, and no variable v occurs in A in a term v^* unless $v = \mathbf{x}_n$ and v so occurs everywhere in A. A SUA of L is, then, a CEUA $\langle G, J \rangle$ in L in which J is a *regimented* formula and G is a surface sentence; and a PAUA of L is a CEUA $\langle G, J \rangle$ in L in which J is a *regimented* abstract in $\mathbf{P}^+$ and G is an appropriate surface form. When the fact the logical form component of a SUA of L belongs to $\mathbf{F}$ or $\mathbf{F}^+$ is relevant, we accordingly speak of $\mathbf{F}$-SUAs of L or $\mathbf{F}^+$-SUAs of L. (And when the identity of L is not important, we speak simply of SUAs and PAUAs.)

Finally, we say that an expression token e, produced by utterer u at time t, is a *token of the CEUA* $\langle G, J \rangle$ *in* L—or that u *tokens the CEUA* $\langle G, J \rangle$ *in* L by producing e at t—iff (i) e is a token (in the ordinary sense) of type G; (ii) u's production of e at t is the result of psychological processes in u that realize the rules under which G is derived from J in L. (Given our assumption about the purely formal character of such rules, "tokening a CEUA in L" is not a semantic notion; hence it can be employed in formulating semantical rules without threat of hidden circularity.) We turn now to the semantics of our fragment of the canonical idiom.

3.2 Indexical Semantics and Order of Priorities

The framework we envisage for interpretation of the canonical idiom is a modified version of the familiar Tarskian truth-theoretic format. The modifications in question are of two sorts. First, denotation and satisfaction (hence truth conditions) are relativized to utterance contexts (represented by the *indices* defined below).[12] And second, *primitive* predicates are assigned *properties* and *relations* as denotata at indices, their corresponding *extensions* at indices being defined in terms of the metaphysical notion of *instantiation*, taken as primitive in the metalanguage. (If possible worlds were added as coordinates of indices, instantiation would be a matter of functions from worlds to extensions; but we forego the extra baggage here.)

Accordingly, we define an *index* as a sextuple $I = \langle u, t, C, D, E, P \rangle$ in which (i) u, t, P are, respectively, an utterer, time, and classificatory purpose (about which more later); (ii) C is a function from persons to language games (conceptual schemes); (iii) D is an infinite sequence of pairs $\langle M, A \rangle$ in which A is a (regimented) F^+-formula and $M \in \{SEM, CON\}$, where SEM and CON are two arbitrarily chosen objects that serve as role markers; and (iv) E is an infinite sequence of pairs $\langle M, J \rangle$ in which $M \in \{SEM, CON\}$ and J is a regimented abstract.[13] This account of indices is deliberately oversimplified: In the interest of brevity we have omitted "audience," "place," and "demonstrated objects" coordinates; and the coordinates D and E are tailored to our pretense that the semantics of the fragment F^{++} is called on only to provide interpretations of the structures underlying nonembedded attitudinal constructions of English—a vastly more complicated account would otherwise be called for.[14] If we were undertaking a full account of proper names and natural-kind terms, we would need yet another coordinate representing their connection with historical "dubbings," "paradigms," and the like to handle the familiar problems engendered by such phenomena as Twin Earth cases and the multiple ambiguity of names. Since this further etiological relativization would complicate our account of *oratio obliqua* and our later theory of propositional-attitude ascriptions without further benefit, we choose to forego it in favor of artificially treating the primitive terms and predicates of F as *indexically rigid*, i.e., as denoting the same object or property at every index $\langle u, t, C, D, E, P \rangle$. This artifice is only a temporary expedient for avoiding entanglement in related problems of philosophical semantics: Once we have articulated our theory (in admittedly oversimplified form) with its aid, there are clear enough ways of dispensing with the pretense and blending in a more realistic treatment of names and natural-kind terms.

The account of (index-relativized) satisfaction and truth conditions for formulas of F^{++}, and their connection with the interpretation of paratactic constructions of English such as (3), must be approached with caution, lest we fall into vicious circularity. The threat of circularity stems from the fact that the natural order of introducing and motivating our semantical remarks about English paratactic constructions tends to invert the strict logical order of these remarks. So it is crucial that we understand what place in the logical order each of our subsequent proposals occupies. This is pedagogically ugly (since it forces us to discourse about matters that have not yet been articulated or motivated) but worth the price. Accordingly, we stipulate the following five-stage ordering of priorities:

Stage 1: a truth theory for $\mathbf{F}^+$ couched in meta-English and incorporating all the definitions introduced thus far.

Stage 2: a truth theory for $\mathbf{F}^+$-SUAs using only semantical notions definable from stage 1.

Stage 3: a truth theory for $\mathbf{F}^{++}$ whose only semantical notions are definable from earlier stages.

Stage 4: a truth theory for $\mathbf{F}^{++}$-SUAs using only semantical notions definable from earlier stages.

Stage 5: a truth theory for readings of English paratactic constructions and their components, invoking only semantical notions definable from the earlier stages.

Now $\mathbf{F}^+$ is merely a foil for later constructions; so, betraying our taste for theft over honest toil, we simply assume that stage 1 has been accomplished, hence that suitably relativized term- and predicate-denotation functions ($\mathbf{T}^+\mathbf{DEN}_I$ and $\mathbf{PDEN}_I$) and a relation of formula satisfaction ($\mathbf{F}^+\mathbf{SAT}_I$) have been defined for all indices I in such fashion as to meet three minimal requirements: (i) Derived predicates in $\mathbf{P}^+$ are accommodated by requiring that a denumerable sequence satisfy $\hat{v}_1 \ldots \hat{v}_k (A) (e_1, \ldots, e_k)$ at I iff (where A' is an alphabetical variant of A in which each v_i is free for e_i) it satisfies the formula $A'(e_1 \ldots e_k/v_1 \ldots v_k)$ at I (since, by our earlier stipulation, no abstract can contain another, this is easy to accomplish without circularity[15]); (ii) some provision is made for *non*denoting terms in $\mathbf{T}^+$ that does *not* deprive formulas containing such terms from having determinate truth conditions[16]; and (iii) the semantical metalanguage uses the notation of lambda-abstraction to designate the properties and relations assigned to primitive predicates, defines the *extension* (relative to a denumerable sequence z) of an n-ary primitive predicate H at an index I (i.e., $\mathbf{PExt}_I(z, H)$) as the set of n-tuples that instantiate $\mathbf{PDEN}_I(z, H)$ at I, and contains an abbreviative convention of the sort represented by the following schema:

$$\langle a_1, \ldots, a_n \rangle \text{ instantiates } \lambda u_1 \ldots u_n(\text{—}u_1\text{—} \ldots \text{—}u_n\text{—}) \text{ at } I \text{ iff —}a_1\text{—} \ldots \text{—}a_n\text{— at } I.$$

(In other words, if the denotation of H at I relative to z is specified as, say, $\lambda u_1 u_2(u_1 \text{ hit } u_2)$, then a speaker of the metalanguage is allowed to use, e.g., "John hit Mary" as shorthand for "$\langle \text{John}, \text{Mary} \rangle$ instantiates $\lambda u_1 u_2(u_1 \text{ hit } u_2)$," and so on. This, of course, is not a definition of instantiates, which is a primitive of the metalanguage; it is merely a verbal convenience regarding talk about those properties and relations that we are lucky enough to have the resources to describe with lambda-abstracts). Given $\mathbf{F}^+\mathbf{SAT}_I$, we have $\mathbf{F}^+\mathbf{TRUE}_I$ by the usual definition.

Stage 2 is trivial extension of stage 1 effected by the two obvious definitions for $\mathbf{F}^+$-SUAs:

DEFINITION. For any $\mathbf{F}^+$-SUA $s = \langle S, A \rangle$, index I, and denumerable sequence z, z satisfies$_I$ s iff $\mathbf{F}^+\mathrm{SAT}_I(z, A)$.

DEFINITION. For any $\mathbf{F}^+$-SUA s and index I, s is true$_I$ iff every denumerable sequence satisfies$_I$ s.

The semantical properties of $\mathbf{F}^+$-SUAs, as expected, are just those of their logical form components.

The provision, in stage 3, of a truth theory for the fragment $\mathbf{F}^{++}$ is clearly the place where the honest toil begins. In particular, $\mathbf{T}^+\mathrm{DEN}_I$ must somehow be extended to a function $\mathbf{T}^{++}\mathrm{DEN}_I$ through specification of what a denumerable sequence assigns at I to $\mathbf{THAT}_1$, $\mathbf{THAT}_2$, ..., to $\mathbf{FACTTHAT}_1$, $\mathbf{FACTTHAT}_2$, ..., and to $\mathbf{THE\text{-}WHO\text{-}OF\text{-}IT}_1$, $\mathbf{THE\text{-}WHO\text{-}OF\text{-}IT}_2$, ...; and $\mathbf{PDEN}_I$ must be extended to a function $\mathbf{P}^{++}\mathrm{DEN}_I$ through specification of what n-ary relations are assigned at I by a denumerable sequence to an n-ary "attitudinal" predicate in $\mathbf{P}^{++}$. This is the burden of the following sections. Assuming that these requirements can be met, PExt_I extends to $\mathbf{P}^{++}\mathrm{Ext}_I$, by which we get $\mathbf{F}^{++}\mathrm{SAT}_I$ and $\mathbf{F}^{++}\mathrm{TRUE}_I$ in the usual way.

3.3 Semantical and Conceptual Roles

The account of $\mathbf{T}^{++}\mathrm{DEN}_I$ and $\mathbf{P}^{++}\mathrm{DEN}_I$ offered later is facilitated by certain definitions that introduce refined versions of our earlier, informal talk about the semantical and conceptual roles of sentences, recasting it in terms of formulas of the canonical idiom.

Let us use the notation $\ulcorner B(P_1, \ldots, P_k; T_1, \ldots, T_n) \urcorner$ to represent any $\mathbf{F}^+$-formula B whose distinct simple predicates are $P_1, \ldots, P_k$ and whose distinct closed terms are $T_1, \ldots, T_n$, where each P_i and T_i occurs but once in B. And let us write u_I, t_I, etc. as shorthand for "the utterer-coordinate of the index I," "the time-coordinate of the index I," etc. Then a suitable fragment of the general notion of "playing the same semantical role" can be defined as follows for $\mathbf{F}^+$-formulas:

DEFINITION. For any $\mathbf{F}^+$-formulas A and A', A plays for u at t the same *semantical* role as A' iff (for some formula $B(P_1, \ldots, P_k; T_1, \ldots, T_n)$, possibly repetitive sequences $\langle F_1, \ldots, F_k \rangle$ and $\langle G_1, \ldots, G_k \rangle$ of predicates in $\mathbf{P}$, and possibly repetitive sequences $\langle U_1, \ldots, U_n \rangle$ and $\langle V_1, \ldots, V_n \rangle$ of closed terms in $\mathbf{T}^+$):

(i) $A = B(F_1 \ldots F_k / P_1 \ldots P_k)(U_1 \ldots U_n / T_1 \ldots T_n)$;

(ii) $A' = B(G_1 \ldots G_k / P_1 \ldots P_k)(V_1 \ldots V_n / T_1 \ldots T_n)$;

(iii) If T_i lies within [outside] the scope of any tense operator in B, then $\mathbf{T}^+\mathrm{DEN}_I(z, U_i) = \mathbf{T}^+\mathrm{DEN}_I(z, V_i)$ for all denumerable sequences z and indices I such that $u_I = u$ [and $t_I = t$]; and

(iv) $\mathbf{PDEN}_I(z, F_i) = \mathbf{PDEN}_I(z, G_i)$ for all denumerable sequences z and indices I such that $u_I = u$ and $t_I = t$.

The foregoing definition could, at the expense of considerable complication, be generalized to a definition of "A plays for u at t the same semantical role that A' plays for u' at t'," which would cut across *different* utterers and times. However, the "progenitor" strategy, together with our pretense that primitive terms and predicates are indexically rigid, spares us the need for such generality: The progenitor of the complement is already perspectivally adjusted to fit the subject's tokening context, so we need consider only sentences whose logical forms are semantically related to that of the progenitor *as hypothetically put in the subject's mouth*. Later we show that such reference shifts as *are* occasioned by this switch to the subject's perspective are precisely the ones that are intuitively appropriate. (Pure deictic terms in "that" clauses are not adversely affected by this switch, since—given suitable expansion of indices to include a "demonstrated objects coordinate"—that coordinate would be fixed by the ascriber's context and held constant throughout subsequent reshuffling of coordinates.)

We do not suppose that the truth theory for $\mathbf{F}^+$ need be capable of proving the salient identities; we suppose only that it can specify the relevant denotations one by one. Whether it is further in a position to "notice," e.g., that Cicero = Tully or that the property of being a Greek = the property of being a Hellene depends on what nonlogical axioms or meaning postulates are allotted to the semantical metalanguage.

The resulting notion of playing the same semantical role, although weaker than "provable semantical equivalence," is nonetheless stronger than mere de facto convergence of truth conditions. In effect, it is a kind of "extensional isomorphism." The need for such extra-semantic constraints—whether in the syntactic form we have given or in the ontologically fancier form of talk about "structured propositions"[17]—is sufficiently well motivated in the literature of the past forty years as to require no further ado here. The reader can judge from our eventual use of the definition whether it fills the bill.

The required definition of "playing the same conceptual role" must, by contrast, be given an intersubjective form. Even though we project an "equivalent" of the progenitor sentence into the subject's mouth, the conceptual role that the progenitor's logical form has for us, the ascribers, is paramount. (A formal reflection of this fact is the holding constant of the conceptual-scheme assignment function.) Accordingly, we offer the following:

DEFINITION. For any $\mathbf{F}^+$-formulas A and A' and any conceptual-scheme assignment function C, A plays for u the same *conceptual* role (modulo C) that A' plays for u' iff

(i) A and A' share the same (starred and unstarred) free variables;
(ii) the pattern of moves [i.e., in Sellarsian terminology, intralinguistic moves, language-entry and language-departure transitions] assigned

by $C(u)$ to A [and hence to the surface reflections of A in u's language(s)]
is functionally equivalent to the pattern of moves assigned by $C(u')$ to
A' [and hence to the surface reflections of A' in u''s language(s)]; and
(iii) either (a) **I** has no occurrence in A or A', or (b) for some variable v
and $B, B' \in \mathbf{F}^+$ containing v free but no occurrence of **I**, $A = B(\mathbf{I}/v)$,
$A' = B'(\mathbf{I}/v)$, and the pattern of moves assigned by $C(u)$ to B is functionally equivalent to the pattern of moves assigned by $C(u')$ to B'.

(Clause (iii) does not come into play until chapter 6; we ignore it until then.)
    As regards this definition, we suppose only that the semantical meta-
language containing it is capable of talking about language games; we do not
suppose that it contains any full-blown *theory* of language games. For present
purposes, "language game," "move," etc. are taken as metalinguistic primitives. (Circularity would threaten if the conceptual roles of $\mathbf{F}^+$-formulas
could be explicated only in terms of semantical notions *richer* than those
provided by the antecedent truth theory for $\mathbf{F}^+$; although there is some
reason for thinking that semantical notions might thus be involved, we see
no reason for thinking that the antecedent truth theory for $\mathbf{F}^+$ is not
adequate to provide them.) The statement of the definition involves the
assumption that language games are defined in the first instance over the
canonical idiom, rather than directly over natural languages. If one thinks of a
theory of language games as simply a different kind of formal semantic
theory (a "conceptual-role semantics"), then the canonical idiom is obviously
the object language of choice. The roles of canonical formulas in a given
game are then projected onto the surface sentences of the players' natural
language(s). The definition thus adverts to *no particular* natural language
employed by u. With the understanding that the conceptual roles of natural-
language sentences are inherited from those of their logical forms, we could,
in principle, omit mention of surface reflections altogether.

3.4 *Truth and Parataxis*
Stage 4 is the trivial extension of stage 3 effected by adding the following
definitions:

> DEFINITION. For any $\mathbf{F}^{++}$-SUA $s = \langle S, A \rangle$, index I, and denumerable
> sequence z, z satisfies$_I$ s iff $\mathbf{F}^{++}\mathrm{SAT}_I(z, A)$.
> DEFINITION. An $\mathbf{F}^{++}$-SUA s is true$_I$ iff every denumerable sequence
> satisfies$_I$ s.

Stage 5, the truth theory for readings of paratactic constructions such as
(3) requires a bit more work. The whole point of introducing SUAs is to
provide constructions that represent "readings" of free-standing sentences of
that fragment of English (or any other natural language) derivable from $\mathbf{F}^{++}$.
"Tokening a SUA" is just a fancy-dress version of Austin's notion of
performing a (phatic) locutionary act. The truth conditions of a sentence on a

reading are obviously just those of the corresponding SUA. Stage 4 thus gives us everything we need to handle free-standing (i.e., *non*paratactic) sentences of our fragment of English. But paratactic constructions do not fit this simple mold.

All our attention so far has been directed to sentences that are derived from *single* formulas of $\mathbf{F}^{++}$, but paratactic constructions are, by hypothesis, derived from *sets* of expressions of $\mathbf{F}^{++}$. In the instances that concern us, the relevant deep structures can be thought of as structures $\langle A, \langle J_1, \ldots, J_n \rangle \rangle$ in which $A \in \mathbf{F}^{++}$ and $J_1, \ldots, J_n \in \mathbf{F}^+ \bigcup (\mathbf{P}^+ - \mathbf{P})$; and a corresponding paratactic surface structure (under some projection L) could be represented as an ordered pair $\langle S, \langle G_1, \ldots, G_n \rangle \rangle$ in which S is an assertive component derived from A and $G_1, \ldots, G_n$ are display clauses derived, respectively, from $J_1, \ldots, J_n$ *in a way that takes account of the original pairing of* $\langle J_1, \ldots, J_n \rangle$ *with A.* The point of the italicized qualification is this: In generating the parataxis, the grammar L may demand surface adjustments in $G_1, \ldots, G_n$ that are *not* reflected in their formal counterparts $J_1, \ldots, J_n$ but are required for the sake of superficial "agreement" with S as derived from A. This is the phenomenon adverted to in our informal notion of a *progenitor*. We propose, in other words, to think of the various "perspectival" adjustments as epiphenomena of L's conventions of parataxis: $J_1, \ldots, J_n$ themselves are devoid of these modifications. A given J_i may be present tense, whereas G_i, owing to the presence in A of the operator **PAST**, is superficially past tense, and so on. What L would derive from J_i in isolation may be, and generally is, different from what it derives from J_i in $\langle A, \langle J_1, \ldots, J_n \rangle \rangle$: The result of the former derivation is the "progenitor" of the result of the latter derivation.

Just as SUAs provide readings for free-standing sentences, so similar constructions—viz., *paratactic sentences under analysis* (PSUAs) of English—provide readings for paratactic sentences such as (3). The relevant constructions are defined as follows:

DEFINITION. A PSUA of L is an ordered pair $\langle X, Y \rangle$ in which X is a surface parataxis $\langle S, \langle G_1, \ldots, G_n \rangle \rangle$; Y is a structure $\langle A, \langle J_1, \ldots, J_n \rangle \rangle$ such that $A \in \mathbf{F}^{++}$ and $J_1, \ldots, J_n \in \mathbf{F}^+ \bigcup (\mathbf{P}^+ - \mathbf{P})$; and X is derivable from Y in L.

The definition of "tokening" a PSUA of L is, mutatis mutandis, the same as for CEUAs in L. Our semantical account of SUAs must now be extended to cover PSUAs. Owing to the peculiarities of the deferred ostension operative in the use of paratactic constructions and to the greater structural complexity of PSUAs, the appropriate definition of satisfaction for the general case is rather complicated.

DEFINITION. For any index I, denumerable sequence z, and PSUA $w = \langle\langle S, \langle G_1, \ldots, G_n \rangle\rangle, \langle A, \langle J_1, \ldots, J_n \rangle \rangle\rangle$ of L, z satisfies$_I$ w iff $\mathbf{F}^{++}\text{SAT}_I$,

(z, A) for every index I' differing from I only in that $D_{I'}$ and $E_{I'}$ are such that if the result of eliminating nonformulas [formulas] from $\langle J_1, \ldots, J_n \rangle$ is a nonempty sequence $\langle A_1, \ldots, A_k \rangle$ of formulas [abstracts], then for all i ($1 < i < k$), $D_{I'}(i) = \langle M, A_i \rangle$ [$E_{I'}(i) = \langle M, A_i \rangle$] for some role marker M such that, for some x, $D_I(i) = \langle M, x \rangle$ [$E_I(i) = \langle M, x \rangle$].

The point of this rather opaque definition is difficult to appreciate in vacuo, since it is designed to mesh with the as yet undiscussed semantics of **THAT** and **THE-WHO-OF-IT** mentioned at stage 3. The underlying idea is that the evaluation of PSUAs as readings of paratactic constructions such as (3) looks only at indices that provide *appropriate* structures to interpret the surface display samples; these structures in turn determine the denotation-in-context of **THAT** and **THE-WHO-OF-IT**. This restriction simply reflects the intuition that "John says that," taken in isolation, puts no constraints on what class of sentences might be at issue, whereas paratactically joining it with another sentence obviously *limits* the range of such classes in a principled way. PSUAs, like SUAs, can be interpreted at *every* index, but the evaluation of a PSUA at a given index is a matter of its evaluation at those indices that are related to the given index in the specified way. We trust that matters will become somewhat clearer when we turn to specific applications.

Given the previous definition, the account of truth is the usual one.

> DEFINITION. For any index I and PSUA w, w is true$_I$ iff every denumerable sequence satisfies$_I$ w.

This completes our technical excursus. In the ensuing discussion, much of which pertains to filling in the gaps in stage 3, we freely avail ourselves of notions from all five stages. Any resulting appearance of circularity can be dispelled by verifying that all subsequently suggested postulates are so formulated as to permit retroactive insertion into the appropriate stage.

3.5 Interim Summary

In our technical excursus, we identified in section 3.1 the relevant fragment F^{++} of the canonical idiom (which would provide the desired logical forms for attitudinal constructions) in terms of a smaller fragment, F^+, which is devoid of attitudinal vocabulary but possesses tense operators, iota-terms, and predicate-abstracts. Formal definitions were given for the key notions "sentence under analysis" (SUA), "predicate abstract under analysis" (PAUA), and "tokening" a SUA or PAUA. The groundwork for an indexical semantics for F^{++} was then laid in section 3.2 by means of the definition of "indices" as ordered sextuples composed of an utterer, time, purpose, assignment of conceptual schemes, and two specialized coordinates bearing on the interpretation of ostended sentences and predicates. This was followed by a stratification of our overall semantic project into five cumulative stages, leading from the semantical vocabulary required by a truth theory for F^+ to that required by a truth theory for English paratactic constructions. We went on in section 3.3 to propose working definitions of sameness of semantical/conceptual role for F^+-formulas. Finally, in section 3.4, we defined the notion of a "paratactic sentence under analysis" (PSUA), which will be used to represent "says that" and related attitudinal constructions of English, and we specified the index-relative satisfaction conditions for PSUAs in terms of those for certain F^{++}-formulas at specially related indices. What remains is to flesh out this schema with actual postulates for the interpretation **SAY** and **THAT**, the posited expressions of the canonical idiom which underlie "say" and the complementizer "that" in English.

4 Oratio Obliqua Constructions

At last we return to (3) ("John says that Tom is a fool"), the problems regarding the paratactic construal of which occasioned our long detour. Let us remind ourselves of where we were. Sentence (3), viewed as a parataxis, is just $\langle$ "John says that", $\langle$ "Tom is a fool" $\rangle\rangle$, whose underlying structure is—in light of (6)—$\langle$**SAY(John, THAT$_1$)**, $\langle$**Fool(Tom)**$\rangle\rangle$. The intuitive idea was that the utterer of (3) asserts "John says that" while forcelessly tokening "Tom is a fool" as a sample of the kind of thing John supposedly uttered, securing reference to that kind by means of deferred ostension. In logical form this means that the quasidemonstrative **THAT$_1$** must somehow link up with the logical form **Fool (Tom)** of the display sample in such a way as to denote a set of appropriately related items. But what is our formal analog of deferred ostension? The answer is provided by indices and their employment in the truth theory. An index $\langle u, t, C, D, E, P \rangle$ portrays (a fragment of) an utterance context, and the coordinates D and E represent the *effects* of deferred ostensions by assigning role-marked formulas and abstracts that provide readings for any paratactically linked sentences or "who" clauses, where the variability of role markers from index to index captures the pragmatic ambiguity of deferred ostension discussed earlier. So what we need is an account of the quasidemonstratives **THAT$_1$**, **THAT$_2$**, ... which makes their denotations *index dependent* and enables us to specify their denotations at an index by looking at the D-coordinate of that index.

4.1 Postulates for **SAY** and **THAT**

In light of all this, the required (stage 3) postulate is straightforward. We offer the following as a provisional formulation:

For any denumerable sequence z and index $I = \langle u, t, C, D, E, P \rangle$ in which $D = \langle \langle M_1, A_1 \rangle, \ldots, \langle M_i, A_i \rangle, \ldots \rangle$, if $M_i = \text{CON}$, then

$T^{++}DEN_I(z, THAT_i)$ = that function d^i_{CON} from utterer–time pairs $\langle u', t' \rangle$ to sets of closed F^+-formulas such that $d^i_{CON}(\langle u', t' \rangle) = \{A: A$ is a closed F^+-formula & A plays for u' the same conceptual role modulo C that A_i plays for $u\}$; and if M_i = SEM, then $T^{++}DEN_I(z, THAT_i) =$ that function d^i_{SEM} from utterer–time pairs $\langle u', t' \rangle$ in which $t' = t$ to sets of closed F^+-formulas such that $d^i_{SEM}(\langle u', t' \rangle) = \{A: A$ is a closed F^+-formula & A plays for u' at t' the same semantical role as $A_i\}$.[18]

Having $THAT_i$ denote a function taking us *to* the desired set rather than denoting that set directly is merely a technical artifice that simplifies certain later constructions: The upshot for (3)'s truth condition is the same in either approach. Given the notion of "tokening a SUA," the predicate-denotation postulate for $SAY \in P^{++}$ is equally simple. Again provisionally:

For any denumerable sequence z and index $I = \langle u, t, C, D, E, P \rangle$, $P^{++}DEN_I(z, SAY) = \lambda xy[x$ is a person & y is a function from utterer–time pairs to sets of closed F^+-formulas & for some L and F^+-SUA $\langle S, A \rangle$ of L, x assertively tokens $\langle S, A \rangle$ at t & $A \in y(\langle x, t \rangle)]$.[19]

The provisional character of the denotation postulate for $THAT_i$ owes to the need for a slight adjustment—to be introduced in chapter 5. Since the effect on (3) is null, we postpone introducing the modification until it becomes germane and can be appropriately motivated. We regard the predicate-denotation postulate for SAY as provisional in that it has been tailored to fit *oratio obliqua* without regard for the logical form of *oratio recta* constructions. If "says" really has different "senses" as it occurs in these two sorts of constructions, then there is no problem: The postulate pertains to the *oratio obliqua* sense, and separate provisions could be made for the other sense of "say." If, on the other hand, it is insisted that "says" is univocal, then the suggested postulate would require revision (e.g., quotation names could be construed as themselves denoting functions of the indicated sort, only having sets of noise- and mark-types as their ranges, etc.) Since our main concern is *oratio obliqua* and its ultimate connection with ascriptions of propositional attitudes, we do not pause here to debate the univocality issue.

4.2 Truth Conditions

Let us now see how (from the viewpoint of stage 5) this apparatus bears on the interpretation of (3). Since we are treating (3) as the parataxis $\langle$"John says that", $\langle$"Tom is a fool"$\rangle\rangle$, the first step is to pick an English PSUA w as (3)'s reading—say, $\langle\langle$"John says that", $\langle$"Tom is a fool"$\rangle\rangle$, $\langle SAY(John, THAT_1), \langle Fool(Tom) \rangle \rangle\rangle$. Then (3)/$w$ is true at an index $I = \langle u, t, C, D, E, P \rangle$ iff w is true$_I$, i.e., iff every denumerable sequence satisfies$_I$ w. By our definitions and postulates we have:

[For all z, z satisfies$_I$ w] iff

[For all z, $\mathbf{F}^{++}\mathrm{SAT}_{I'}(z, \mathbf{SAY}(\mathbf{John}, \mathbf{THAT}_1))$ for each I' different from I only in that $D_{I'}(1) = \langle M_1, \langle \text{"Tom is a fool"}, \mathbf{Fool}(\mathbf{Tom}) \rangle \rangle$, where M_1 is fixed as in $D(1)$] iff

[For every such I' and z, $\langle \mathbf{T}^{++}\mathrm{DEN}_{I'}(z, \mathbf{John}), \mathbf{T}^{++}\mathrm{DEN}_{I'}(z, \mathbf{THAT}_1) \rangle \in \mathbf{P}^{++}\mathrm{Ext}_{I'}(z, \mathbf{SAY})$] iff

[$\langle \mathbf{John}, d_{M_1}^1 \rangle \in \{ \langle x, y \rangle : x$ is a person & y is a function ... & for some L and $\mathbf{F}^+$-SUA $\langle S, A \rangle$ of L, x assertively tokens $\langle S, A \rangle$ at $t_{I'}$ ($= t$) & $A \in y(\langle x, t_{I'} \rangle)$}] iff

[For some L and $\mathbf{F}^+$-SUA $\langle S, A \rangle$ of L, John assertively tokens $\langle S, A \rangle$ at t & $A \in d_{M_1}^1(\langle \mathbf{John}, t \rangle)$].

So, in the end, we have the desired result. If $M_1 = \mathrm{CON}$, then $d_{M_1}^1(\langle \mathbf{John}, t \rangle) = d_{\mathrm{CON}}^1(\langle \mathbf{John}, t \rangle) = \{A: A$ plays for John the same conceptual role modulo C that $\mathbf{Fool}(\mathbf{Tom})$ plays for $u\}$. And so, relative to an index I marking conceptual role:

(3)/w is true at I iff, for some language L, sentence S, and $A \in \mathbf{F}^+$, John assertively utters S at t_I *qua* sentence of L with deep structure A, and A is a functional equivalent in $C_I(\mathbf{John})$ of the formula $\mathbf{Fool}(\mathbf{Tom})$ in $C_I(u)$.

And if $M_1 = \mathrm{SEM}$, then $d_{M_1}^1(\langle \mathbf{John}, t \rangle) = d_{\mathrm{SEM}}^1(\langle \mathbf{John}, t \rangle) = \{A: A$ plays for John at t the same semantical role as $\mathbf{Fool}(\mathbf{Tom})\}$. And so, relative to an index I marking semantical role:

(3)/w is true at I iff, for some sentence S, language L, and $A \in \mathbf{F}^+$, John assertively tokens S at t_I *qua* sentence of L with deep structure A, and $A = Q(T)$ for some $Q \in \mathbf{P}$ and $T \in \mathbf{T}^+$ such that $\mathbf{T}^+\mathrm{DEN}_{I'}(z, T) = \mathrm{Tom}$ and $\mathrm{PDEN}_{I'}(z, Q) = \lambda y(y$ is a fool) for every denumerable sequence z and index I' in which $u_{I'} = \mathrm{John}$ and $t_{I'} = t_I$.

(If, for each formula $A \in \mathbf{F}^+$ and each admissible C and u, the "moves" assigned by $C(u)$ to A could be characterized directly without essential reference to particular formulas of the canonical idiom (but perhaps allowing quantification over such), then the mention of $\mathbf{Fool}(\mathbf{Tom})$ would disappear when $M_1 = \mathrm{CON}$ just as it does when $M_1 = \mathrm{SEM}$. At present, the direct method is beyond our reach, and we must be content with the comparative method, trusting that the residual mention of particular formulas will someday be otiose.)

We have arrived at the fancy-dress version of our initial rough idea of (3)'s truth condition, viz., that John utter something which plays the same salient role for John that the complement of (3) plays in the mouth of (3)'s utterer. One advantage to the fancy-dress version is that it mentions no particular natural language or natural-language sentence, thus respecting the intuition that John's saying that Tom is a fool does not require the existence of the

English sentence "Tom is a fool" or the like. This may seem a small triumph in light of the residual *quantification* over grammars, formulas of the canonical idiom, and surface forms, but we are unrepentant, for "say" is, after all, a *speech act* verb (at least in *oratio obliqua*). How could there be full-blown illocutionary acts of contentful saying-that unless there exists something like sentences constructed according to grammars internalized by speakers? One may or may not like the particular theoretical format we have adopted for representing these factors, but it is a mystery how one could construct a rival theory that has nothing analogous to these factors in its ontology. Pending oracular revelation, we press onward.

We remarked earlier that the notion of a progenitor is built into our treatment of sentences such as

(7) John said that Tom was a fool.

This building-in occurs at the level of assigning a PSUA as reading of the parataxis ⟨"John said that", ⟨"Tom was a fool"⟩⟩, and it takes the shape of an assumption that, at least where English is concerned, the relevant paratactic deep structure is the pair

⟨**PAST(SAY(John, THAT₁))**, ⟨**Fool(Tom)**⟩⟩.

Though it is possible to construct a paratactic account that does not require this assumption, making it has the virtue of enabling us to get the truth conditions right while avoiding the further formal machinery that would otherwise be needed to readjust the relevant formulas and/or postulates.

4.3 Modified Dot Quotes and Informal Glosses

Still, matters could be a lot simpler. The relativized truth conditions for paratactic constructions, even when only partially spelled out as above for (3)/*w*, are cumbersome. Since talk about such truth conditions figures prominently in this chapter, it would be nice to have some casual but reasonably perspicuous way of condensing all this talk about SUAs and role playing into a drop (well, a puddle) of metalinguistic notation. As it happens, a modified version of Sellarsian "dot quotes" can be pressed into service for this purpose.

Let us say that a *partial utterance context* for a sentence "S" of a natural language *L* is a structure ⟨*u, C, A*⟩ in which *C* is a conceptual-role assignment function, *A* is a logical form such that ⟨"S", *A*⟩ is a SUA of *L*, and *u* is a hypothetical tokener of ⟨"S", *A*⟩. Then, given some partial utterance context ⟨*u, C, A*⟩ for "S," we stipulate that something is a conceptually [semantically] individuated ·S· for *u'* at *t'*—for short, a conceptually [semantically] individuated ·S·⟨*u', t'*⟩—iff it is a SUA whose logical form component plays for *u'* the same conceptual role modulo *C* that *A* plays for *u* [plays for *u'* at *t'* the same semantical role as A]. In practice, when surrounding discourse not only specifies a partial utterance context for "S" but also makes plain the identity of u' and t', we drop the "for so-and-so ..." and speak simply of conceptually [semantically] individuated ·S·'s. And when, in addition, we wish either to leave the salient role-kind open or to trust the surrounding discourse to identify it, we speak simply of ·S·'s.

Using this version of dot quotes, we can give fairly brief glosses of the truth conditions for paratactic constructions. In the case of (3)/w, we could say that it is true at an index $I = \langle u, t, C, D, E, P \rangle$ iff John (at t) assertively tokens a ·Tom is a fool·$_{\langle John, t \rangle}$—since the reading of "Tom is a fool," its hypothetical utterer, etc., are provided by I itself. And since the ingredients of $\langle John, t \rangle$ are also fixed by the context of evaluation, we could further abbreviate matters by saying simply that (3)/w is true at I iff John assertively tokens a ·Tom is a fool·. (It must be stressed, however, that these dot glosses are *merely* paraphrastic conveniences for talking about the deliverances of the truth theory: Dot quotes themselves are *not* part of that theory and do no theoretical work whatever.) Similarly, given an English reading for (7) that incorporates the underlying structure proposed two paragraphs ago, we could say that (7), so read, is true at I iff, at some t' earlier than t_I, John assertively tokens a ·Tom is a fool·. Whether John's ·Tom is a fool·'s (relative to I) are to be conceptually or semantically individuated depends, of course, on what roles are marked by I. Though tailored for use in the context of glossing theorems of the truth theory, dot quotes can in principle be used outside such contexts, provided that we keep a firm grip on the reading and hypothetical utterer of the dot-quoted sentence and are clear about *whose* analogs (at what common time) are in question. When using dot quotes in this independent way, we always think of the dot-quoted sentence as in *our* mouths (at the salient time), and we dot quote only structurally unambiguous English sentences, indicating whose analogs are in question by means of phrases such as *"John's* ·Tom is a fool·," "a ·Snow is white· *for Mary*," etc. Since the identity of the common time, when important, is clear from the context, we do not mention it explicitly.

(Objectual) quantification and substitution into dot quotations are obviously *verboten*. Substitutional quantification and the use of schematic letters with respect to dot quotations are harmless. Thus, where "N" is a schematic letter whose replacements are, say, English proper names, we can sensibly talk of, e.g., John's ·N is a fool·'s. Even the use of contextual *abbreviations* within dot quotations can be managed, so long as it is clear how to eliminate the abbreviations, in whose mouth the *un*abbreviated version is supposed to occur, etc. Thus, in later sections, we treat "·Tom alone ran·" as contextual shorthand for "·One and only one thing ran and that thing was Tom·," trusting that no confusion results.

4.4 Opacity and Indices

In the informal discussion that preceded our technical excursus, we noted that the deferred ostension involved in (3) creates a pragmatic ambiguity regarding the saliency of conceptual versus semantical roles, and we claimed that this fact has important fallout for the opacity issue. We are now in a position to unpack this claim more fully. Nothing in our apparatus commits us to the idea that a sentence such as (3) must be assigned different "readings" in order to account for opaque versus transparent construals of the embedded occurrence of "Tom." The single PSUA w assigned to (3) as its English reading suffices, since we now regard opacity and transparency as *indexical* phenomena, dependent on the role saliencies marked by indices. The question of whether "Tom" in (3) occurs transparently or opaquely is not a syntactic but a semantic question, pertaining to the contribution made by "Tom" to the truth condition of (3)/w *at a particular index*. Since the truth condition of (3) is just that of its reading w, the question reduces to one about PSUAs, viz., under what conditions does a term occurrence in the surface-structure component of a PSUA (and the corresponding term occurrence in the logical-form component) count as transparent relative to an index I? Shorn of technicalities, the answer is fairly simple.

An occurrence $/N/$ of a closed term N in the surface component X of a PSUA $\langle X, Y \rangle$ of L—where $/N/$ in X reflects under L an occurrence $/T/$ of a closed term T in Y—is *transparent at I* iff, for any well-formed PSUA $\langle X', Y' \rangle$ of L resulting from replacement of $/N/$ in X by an occurrence of a closed term N' and replacement of $/T/$ in Y by an occurrence of a closed term T', the co-denotation of T with T' at I is *provably sufficient* for $\langle X, Y \rangle$ and $\langle X', Y' \rangle$'s being satisfied at I by exactly the same sequences.

An important consequence of this criterion for transparency of a term occurrence at an index is that the single occurrence of "Tom" in (3) is transparent at just those indices that mark *semantical* role as salient. That this is so at all such indices follows from the definition of "playing the same semantical role," the definiens of which is automatically satisfied by **Fool(Tom)** and by any formula **Fool(T)** such that T co-denotes with **Tom** at I. If, say, "Tom" and "Bozo" co-denote at I, then (at I) John's tokening a ·Tom is a fool· is, *semantically* speaking, the same thing as John's tokening a ·Bozo is a fool·—i.e., to be a ·Tom is a fool· for John is to be a ·Bozo is a fool· for John (relative to I). That "Tom" occurs transparently in (3) *only* at such indices may be less obvious.

Suppose that the index I marks conceptual role as salient. By the above criterion, "Tom" would occur transparently in (3) relative to I just in case (schematically speaking) John's tokening a conceptually individuated ·Tom is a fool· could be shown to come to the same thing as his tokening a conceptually individuated ·N is a fool· whenever it is given that "Tom" and "N" co-denote at I. As we have set things up, the truth theory for PSUAs clearly cannot show this. Now it might be thought that this failure shows an inadequacy in the truth theory. But it would not matter if we had built in a comprehensive "conceptual-role semantics." Although such a complication would enable the truth theory to *identify* the conceptual roles played by sentences in the scheme assigned to the utterer, it would still not permit the infinitely many required derivations relative to any conceptual scheme that could plausibly be assigned to a finite creature. The only conceptual scheme relative to which ·Tom is a fool·'s and ·N is a fool·'s count as the same whenever "Tom" and "N" happen to co-denote would be one in which *every* true equation "Tom = N" had somehow managed to acquire *axiomatic* status already! (The mere extra-mental fact of co-denotation, being outside the utterer's head, cannot dictate conceptual roles; so the only way the derivations could all go through is if the specified conceptual scheme already treats the equations in question as "axiomatic.") Such a conceptual scheme is a Rationalist's dream, in which all true identities are analytic and a priori. Only God (if even He) could qualify for this kind of internal organization! In short, there is no reason to think that any plausible account of human conceptual organization would, when grafted onto the truth theory for PSUAs, permit the wholesale conflation of conceptually individuated ·Tom is a fool·'s with ·N is a fool·'s because of, much less independently of, the premise that "Tom" and "N" co-denote.

In general, a term occurrence in the complement of an *oratio obliqua* construction is opaque at an index specifying individuation by conceptual role and transparent at an index specifying individuation by semantical role—provided in the latter case that the term in question is *temporally rigid* at that index (i.e., has the same denotation at any index that differs from the given one at most in its time-coordinate). Whether a temporally flaccid term, such as "the mayor of New York City," whose denotation at an index varies with shifts of the time-coordinate, occurs transparently with respect to indices marking semiatical role depends, of course, on the tense structure of its linguistic environment. Thus, e.g., in "John says that the mayor of New York City is a fool," the indicated term occurrence is transparent relative to such an index I, but *not* in "Abraham Lincoln said that the mayor of New York City was a fool." In the former, the index-time t_I and John's alleged saying-time are taken to coincide, so that the term occurrence in question is replaceable salva veritate by an occurrence of any term co-denoting with it at I. But in the latter sentence, Lincoln's alleged saying-time is taken to precede the index-time t_I; hence mere co-denotation at I does not guarantee replaceability. What matters at I is not what the indicated expression denotes in the ascriber's mouth at the ascription-time t_I, but, so to speak, what it *would* denote in the subject's mouth at the subject's saying-time. (The same phenomenon arises with respect to "John *says* that the mayor of New York City *was* a fool," which is ambiguous as regards the scope of the description with respect to the past-tense operator in the complement. On the wide-scope reading—paraphrasable by "John says that the mayor of New York City [is someone who] was a fool"—the description occurs transparently at indices marking semantical role; but on the narrow-scope reading—paraphrasable by "John says that [at some earlier time t] the mayor of New York City [at t] is a fool [at t]"—the description would occur opaquely.) By contrast, names, eternal descriptions, "I," and—with suitable expansion of indices to accomodate deixis—deictic terms, such as "this" or "that person" all count by our lights as temporally rigid at a given index, hence as occurring transparently at indices marking semantical role as salient. (It must of course be remembered that a term that is temporally rigid at an index may not be rigid in other respects at that index; "I" is an obvious case in point.)

In earlier chapters, we tried to account for the transparent versus opaque term occurrences by using a strong syntactic–semantic version of the referential/attributive distinction. We see now that, at least where *oratio obliqua* is concerned, there is no need for such a strong hypothesis. There is nothing amphibolous about (3): It has a single paratactic logical form *qua* sentence of English, and our ability to hear the embedded occurrence of "Tom" either transparently or opaquely betokens no hidden structural shift but is merely an epiphenomenon of the pragmatic ambiguity of deferred ostension—as formally reflected in the different truth conditions associated with (3) at indices with different role markers.

4.5 Interim Summary

In section 4.1 we provided index-sensitive denotation postulates for **SAY** and **THAT** which formally captured the pragmatic ambiguity of deferred ostension with respect to choice of computational or semantical individuation of contents. Then in section 4.2 we applied this apparatus to our paratactic construal of "John says that Tom is a fool"—represented as the PSUA ⟨⟨"John says that", ⟨"Tom is a fool"⟩⟩, ⟨**SAY**(**John**, **THAT**$_1$), ⟨**Fool**(**Tom**)⟩⟩⟩—computing its truth condition at an arbitrary index and arguing that it is at least approximately what one should expect. We went on in section 4.3 to show how, with slight modifications, the familiar Sellarsian device of "dot quotation" could be defined in our semantical metalanguage and used to give conveniently short informal glosses of the truth conditions assigned to PSUAs by our theory—allowing us to say, e.g., that "John says that Tom is a fool" is true at an index I iff John assertively tokens a ·Tom is a fool· at the time in I. Finally, we saw in section 4.4 how opacity [transparency] of "says that" complements can be explained in terms of our indexical semantics as arising at indices marking the salience of sameness of conceptual [semantical] role in assessing the contribution of the ostended complement to the truth condition of the whole. The proliferation of representations in chapter 2 to account for opaque versus transparent readings is thus potentially undermined. Of course, such a result regarding *oratio obliqua* bears on knows-who locutions only to the extent that the paratactic apparatus applied to the former can somehow be extended to the latter as well. Our next task is to implement this extension, encompassing first belief and knowledge ascriptions in the familiar "that"-clause format and later knowledge ascriptions in the "who"-clause format.

Chapter 4
De Dicto Attitude Ascriptions

We have labored so long over "says that" because we are moved by the obvious parallels between says-that constructions and propositional-attitude constructions, such as "believes that" and "knows that," to follow Ockham and Sellars in regarding thought as a kind of inner speech. Just as we construed John's saying that Tom is a fool in terms of John's assertively tokening a ·Tom is a fool,· so too we wish to construe John's believing or knowing that Tom is a fool in terms of John's standing in certain relations to ·Tom is a fool·'s in his language of thought. We believe the nature of these relations is best understood by means of a version of Functionalist psychology, though we cannot pursue the psychological dimension here.[1] For our limited purposes, we simply assume that "believe-true" and "know-true" are antecedently understood verbs of the semantical metalanguage of the stage 3 truth theory for $\mathbf{F}^{++}$ and that the predicates **BELIEVE** and **KNOW** in $\mathbf{P}^{++}$ are given predicate-denotation conditions couched in terms of these verbs. A complete unpacking of "knows-true" would, of course, relate it appropriately to "believes-true," bring out the connection with evidential considerations, and so on. At present, we venture no further than to remark that we understand believing-true and knowing-true to be relations to *tokens* of SUAs, i.e., to involve the subject's tokening, or being appropriately disposed to token, such-and-such a SUA in foro interno.[2] We switch from calling our view "sententialist" to the more general term "representationalist," for the metaphor of "*sentences* in the head" has garnered much misguided derision and, in train, a host of even more misguided objections that we have turned aside in earlier works.[3]

1 From "Says That" to "Believes/Knows That"

Given the amount of attention we have lavished on *oratio obliqua*, we can be brief about the likes of (1a–b):

(1) a. John believes that Tom is a fool.

  b. John knows that Tom is a fool.

Provisionally, we can think of the logical form of (1a) as the parataxis $\langle\textbf{BELIEVE(John, THAT}_1), \langle\textbf{Fool(Tom)}\rangle\rangle$, and hence of (1a)'s standard English reading as the PSUA

$\langle\langle$"John believes that", $\langle$"Tom is a fool"$\rangle\rangle$,
$\langle\textbf{BELIEVE(John, THAT}_1), \langle\textbf{Fool(Tom)}\rangle\rangle\rangle$.

(We say "provisionally" because our account of *de re* ascriptions in chapter 5 requires us to think of **BELIEVE** and **KNOW** as triadic rather than dyadic; but since the impact on (1a–b)'s truth conditions is null, we stick with the dyadic version here.) Since the predicate-denotation postulates (at stage 5) for **BELIEVE** and **KNOW** are just like the one given for **SAY**, except for having "believes-true" and "knows-true," respectively, in place of "assertively tokens," we can spare the reader a return trip through the formal apparatus and simply note, by way of a gloss, that (1a) on the given reading is true at an index I iff John believes-true at t_I a · Tom is a fool ·. The treatment of (1b) involves one extra wrinkle, owing to the factive character of knows-that constructions. The truth of (1b) at an index must, of course, ensure the truth at that index of "Tom is a fool." But our postulate for **THAT**, even if coupled with a truth proviso in the postulate for **KNOW**, would not vouchsafe this, for the latter concerns only the inner token that the subject knows-true, not the ascriber's display sentence. The simplest way of handling this difficulty is to concede something that has been maintained by many linguists and philosophers,[4] viz., that there is a "factive complementizer" which also surfaces in English as "that." In our framework, the job of this factive complementizer would be performed by the quasidemonstrative **FACTTHAT** in $\textbf{T}^{++}$, alluded to in the technical excursus of the preceding chapter, and (1b) would accordingly have as its logical form the parataxis $\langle\textbf{KNOW(John, FACTTHAT}_1), \quad \langle\textbf{Fool(Tom)}\rangle\rangle$. The postulate for **FACTTHAT** is straightforward:

For any denumerable sequence z and index $I = \langle u, t, C, D, E, P\rangle$ in which $D = \langle\langle M_1, A_1\rangle, \ldots, \langle M_i, A_i\rangle, \ldots\rangle$, if $M_i = \text{CON}$, then $\textbf{T}^{++}\text{DEN}_I(z, \textbf{FACTTHAT}_i) = $ that function f_{CON}^i from utterer–time pairs $\langle u', t'\rangle$ to sets of closed $\textbf{F}^+$-formulas such that $f_{\text{CON}}^i(\langle u', t'\rangle) = \{A:$ A is a closed $\textbf{F}^+$-formula and A plays for u' the same conceptual role modulo C that A_i plays for u & $\textbf{F}^+\text{TRUE}_{\langle u',t',C,D,E,P\rangle}(A)\}$, *provided that* $\textbf{F}^+\text{TRUE}_{\langle u',t',C,D',E,P\rangle}(A_i)$, and $f_{\text{CON}}^i(\langle u',t'\rangle) = $ the empty set, otherwise; and if $M_i = \text{SEM}$, then $\textbf{T}^{++}\text{DEN}_I(z, \textbf{FACTTHAT}_i) = $ that function f_{SEM}^i from utterer–time pairs $\langle u', t'\rangle$ in which $t' = t$ to sets of closed $\textbf{F}^+$-formulas such that $f_{\text{SEM}}^i(\langle u', t'\rangle) = \{A: A$ is closed $\textbf{F}^+$-formula & A plays for u' at t' the same semantic role as $A_i\}$, *provided that* $\textbf{F}^+\text{TRUE}_{\langle u',t',C,D,E,P\rangle}(A_i)$, and $f_{\text{SEM}}^i(\langle u',t'\rangle) = $ the empty set, otherwise.

(Some authors[5] have suggested that there is a reading of negative ascriptions such as "John does not know that Tom is a fool" on which they too imply their complements. For reasons we have discussed at length elsewhere,[6] we think this view is mistaken; we have formulated the postulate for **FACTTHAT** accordingly, though nothing important to our enterprise hinges on this decision. We note in passing that this postulate obviates the need for any truth proviso in the postulate for **KNOW**.)

To avoid the need for circumlocution in glossing (1b)'s truth condition, it is handy to introduce *colon quotes*—a factive version of dot quotes. Assuming as always some $\mathbf{F}^+$-SUA $\langle "S", A \rangle$, let us say that something is an $:S:$ for u' at t' iff it is an $\cdot S \cdot$ for u' at t' such that $\mathbf{F}^+\mathrm{TRUE}_I(A)$ for any I in which $u_I = u'$ and $t_I = t'$. Then, paralleling our gloss on (1a), we can say that (1b) thus interpreted is true at an index I iff John knows-true at t_I a:Tom is a fool:—a state of affairs that can obtain only if Tom is a fool.

Our remarks about the pragmatic ambiguity of deferred ostension, its formal reflection in truth conditions at indices, and the bearing on the opacity/transparency issue carry over in toto.

Our representational account of propositional-attitude ascriptions, illustrated by our treatment of (1a–b), has a number of advantages over rival accounts that appeal, e.g., to Fregean senses or to "possible worlds" as primitives. Briefly: (i) The representational account is the only current candidate that brings semantics and cognitive psychology together in an empirically motivated way. Writing against the background of the "computational paradigm" that dominates current work in cognitive psychology, Jerry Fodor (see note 6, chapter 3) has argued persuasively that the computational processes carried out by any interesting subagency in the brain, being computational, must be couched in some system of representation and that this system needs to share enough of the characteristic features of natural languages as to count as an internal "language" itself.[7] The "formulas" of such a language of thought have physical reality in actual computational processes; unlike Frege's *Gedanken* or "propositions" platonistically construed, they have the causal powers seemingly requisite to any workable account of how the "contents" of beliefs, desires, etc. affect behavior. (ii) As Sellars originally saw, the representational account enables us to understand the intentionality of beliefs and other attitudes to be of a piece with the reference or aboutness of language, especially when the latter is understood in terms of causal chains. Hartry Field[8] makes the related point that the representational account provides what is for now the only attractive answer to the question of how it is possible for a mere aggregate of insensate, purely physical particles to be in an intentional state. (iii) The representational account offers a straightforward explanation of why beliefs have the same standard sorts of semantical properties that sentences have (e.g., truth values, entailments, composition from significant "parts," etc.). (iv) The representational account predicts the many obvious grammatical parallels that appear to hold between verbs of propositional attitude and verbs of saying.[9] Finally, (v) the representational account has strong potential for solving certain puzzles about the attribution of *singular* beliefs. One such puzzle has been posed with great force by Kripke; another, concerning "self-regarding" attitudes, was raised years ago by Geach and by Castaneda and recalled in the 1970s by John Perry. Our representationalist framework has important applications for both. Before embarking on our account of knowing-who ascriptions, it is useful to discuss the first of these puzzles; our treatment of the second requires certain results from chapter 5 and accordingly is postponed until chapter 6.

2 Kripke's Puzzle about Belief

Kripke[10] raises the following problem (which, for brevity, we put in terms of his standard Cicero/Tully case, instead of setting out the more elaborate London/Londres case that Kripke himself emphasizes). Suppose that Jones sincerely says, "Cicero was bald and Tully was not," unaware that Cicero and Tully are one and the same person. It is plausible to think that (i) any competent speaker of English who sincerely says, "Cicero was bald and Tully was not" believes (the proposition) *that* Cicero was bald and Tully was not. But there is considerable reason to believe that proper names are rigid and connotationless designators; and if they are, then (ii) the sentence Jones uttered is false in any possible world, and to believe what it expresses is to believe an explicitly contradictory proposition. Yet (iii) Jones is, we suppose, fully rational and not so confused as to accept any explicit contradictions— Jones is guilty of ignorance but not of crass logical error. The puzzle is just that (i)–(iii) form an inconsistent triad. Also, we are faced by a hard factual question: Does Jones believe that Cicero was bald? Less tractably, *does he believe that Tully was bald?* There seems no obstacle to answering "Yes" to the first of these questions, but intuitions divide sharply over the second.

The approach taken in chapters 1 and 2 (heartily supported by the felt rigidity of names) clearly favors denying (iii), uncharitable toward the luckless Jones as that may seem, and answers Kripke's hard factual question by saying that Jones does indeed believe that Tully (that very person, whom Jones himself happens to be calling Cicero) was bald, even though Jones himself would never express his own belief in that way, *and also* believes that Cicero (= Tully) was not bald.[11] But even if one grants that sometimes a fully rational person might believe a contradiction when mistaken about the references of certain names employed, one still feels that there should be no *unequivocal* answer to Kripke's hard question; the question has a strong "yes and no" feel to it.

Our representationalist account accommodates and explains this air of equivocality, affording an irenic solution to Kripke's entire puzzle—quite straightforwardly in terms of contextual preference for one rather than the other of our two methods of disambiguating deferred ostension in paratactically construed belief ascriptions. Suppose, for the sake of simplicity, that Jones' language of thought is just the canonical idiom itself and that when Jones sincerely says, "Cicero was bald and Tully was not," he does so partly as a result of having tokened in foro interno the formula **Bald(Cicero)** & **∼Bald(Tully)**, which for brevity we call "A". Now consider the following:

(2) a. Jones believes that Cicero was bald and Tully was not bald.

    b. Jones believes that Cicero was bald and Cicero was not bald.

(3) a. Jones believes that Cicero was bald.

    b. Jones believes that Tully was bald.

Does Jones, by internally tokening A, count as believing a contradiction? It depends on whether the semantical or the conceptual role of the formula A is at issue. As we saw earlier, all name occurrences in a sentence such as (2a) are transparent relative to any index marking semantical role as salient: If (2a) is true at such an index, so is (2b). Semantically, Jones' believing-true a · Cicero was bald and Tully was not · comes to the same thing as his believing-true a · Cicero was bald and Cicero was not ·. This is the sense in which Jones does believe a contradiction, but it is *not* the sense in which "believing a contradiction" reflects unfavorably on one's rationality. For Jones has no way of deducing from his mental token of A anything he could recognize as a contradiction; nothing that he carries with him in his head enables him to tell that his mental token of **Cicero** and his mental token of **Tully** represent the same person.

At indices marking conceptual role as salient, the occurrences of "Cicero" and "Tully" in (2a) are resolutely opaque. This is, we have seen, symptomatic of the fact that the computational powers of a formula in a language game are not constrained by the vagaries of extra-mental reference. Jones' internal token of A is not *formally* contradictory at all. If (2b) were true where conceptual role is salient, Jones would internally token the likes of **Bald(Cicero)** & **∼Bald(Cicero)**, as a result of which he would either start madly inferring every formula he could think of (à la C. I. Lewis) or else go into a cognitive spasm of some sort (given a generous helping of "downward causation," his circuitry might turn black and give off smoke). But Jones is unmoved by A in either of these two ways, since, by hypothesis, he internally tokens no · Cicero = Tully ·. Sentence (2a) may be true at the relevant indices even though (2b) is false at those indices. In this sense, Jones does *not* believe that Cicero was bald and Cicero was not bald: He believes-true nothing that plays for him the same conceptual role that the explicit contradiction plays for us.

What about Kripke's hard factual question? Does Jones believe or does he not believe that Cicero was bald? Well, his internal token of A certainly contains the conjunct **Bald(Cicero)**. Sentence (3a) is certainly true at indices marking semantical role and may well be true at indices marking conceptual role. But to the proponent of thesis (ii), this suggests that (3b) must also be true: that Jones must believe that *Tully* was bald. Sentence (3b), of course, is true when (3a) is, provided that only semantical roles are at issue. In this sense, Jones does also believe that Tully was bald. But where conceptual roles are salient, the truth of (3a) does not ensure the truth of (3b), since, as is evident from our account of the alleged contradictory belief, the formulas **Bald(Cicero)** and **Bald(Tully)** have quite different inferential functions for Jones. In this sense, Jones need not also believe that Tully is bald.

To sum up: Relative to semantical roles, (i)–(iii) are all harmlessly true and there is no puzzle; relative to conceptual roles, the triad is inconsistent only if one equivocates on (ii), switching from the harmless sense in which Jones does believe a contradiction to the tendentious sense of "believing a contradiction," which impugns rationality. But nothing in the facts of the case warrants this switch: The semantical properties of A do not determine its conceptual role for Jones. So once again there is no puzzle. Note too that we have succeeded in repudiating the nasty dilemma of Millianism versus Russellianism that has plagued the theory of reference for years: We reject Russell's contention that names abbreviate flaccid descriptions, but we do not thereby commit ourselves to the claim that names serve only to designate their bearers even in belief contexts.

We must deal with a superficially attractive objection, one that goes to the heart of our technical apparatus: Our solution rests on the claim that, where conceptual roles are at issue, (2a) and (3a) could be true, whereas (2b) and (3b) are false. But by the lights of our own semantical theory, this is impossible *unless* the hypothetical utterer of these sentences is also unaware that Cicero = Tully. For if the utterer u is aware of the identity, then u will use "Cicero" and "Tully" interchangeably: In u's game, "Cicero was bald" and "Tully was bald," etc., play the same conceptual role; hence it is impossible for Jones to token something that plays for Jones the same conceptual role that "Cicero was bald" plays for u without ipso facto tokening something that plays for Jones the same conceptual role that "Tully was bald" plays for u. But we, Boër and Lycan, are perfectly aware that Cicero = Tully; so *we* cannot (as we did) truly affirm (3a) while simultaneously denying (3b). Therefore we are hoist with our own petard, and our solution to Kripke's puzzle collapses.

Not quite—though the objection does serve to point out an ambiguity in the notion of "playing the same conceptual role," which we have so far glossed over. As we have loosely defined this notion, it is a matter of what pattern of moves is assigned to a canonical formula by the rules of a particular language game. The ambiguity can be traced back to the phrase "assigned by the rules." In one sense, the rules of the game "assign" patterns of permissible and obligatory moves at the outset, in abstraction from any particular playing of the game; i.e., the rules determine the *intrinsic* combinatory powers of the pieces. In another sense, derived from the first, the rules "assign" moves relative to a particular stage in a particular playing of the game ("Given the point you have just reached, your duties and options are as follows: . . ."). The intrinsic combinatory powers of a piece, together with a particular game-stage environment, determine what we might call its *extrinsic* combinatory powers at that locale. It is the first of these senses that we had in mind in our rough-and-ready characterization of samenesss of conceptual role. The objection, however, trades on the second, derivative sense. The way out is to recognize that pieces with the same extrinsic combinatory powers at some stage in a playing of the game need not have had the same intrinsic powers at the outset. Like many English speakers, we have reached a point in playing our language game where "Cicero = Tully" has been added to our stock of adventitious information, thus allowing us to interderive "Cicero was bald" and "Tully was bald" *using the premise* "Cicero = Tully." But it does not follow that this extrinsic interchangeability of "Cicero" and "Tully" betokens any intrinsic interchangeability: **Cicero = Tully** was never an axiom or meaning postulate of our language game, nor has it become such (any more than "All and only creatures with kidneys are creatures with hearts," to which we also assent). (Perhaps the equation was axiomatic for Cicero himself.) In saying that Jones believes-true a conceptually individuated · Cicero was bald and Tully was not ·, we are saying that Jones believes-true something whose *intrinsic* combinatory powers in Jones' language game are appropriately matched by the *intrinsic* combinatory powers of **Bald(Cicero) & ∼ Bald(Tully)** under the rules of *our* language game. And in our language game there is nothing intrinsically marking this formula as contradictory. So the fact the Boër and Lycan happen to assent to "Cicero = Tully" is irrelevant to what we attribute to Jones in uttering (2a) or (3a), and the same holds for any other utterer. The only utterers who cannot truly affirm the (a) versions while denying the (b) versions are those for whom "Cicero" and "Tully" are *definitionally* related, perhaps after the fashion of "U.N." and "United Nations."

Now, one might think that this extrinsic/intrinsic ploy, though natural, begs the question against Kripke by tacitly assuming that names have Fregean "senses" or the like. After all, the objector may continue, what other than senses or connotations could *antecedently* endow **Bald(Cicero)** and **Bald(Tully)** with different intrinsic combinatory powers in anyone's language game? This is an eminently fair question. For there to be a difference of the sort in question, there must be some rule that intrinsically distinguishes (. . . **Cicero** . . .) from (. . . **Tully** . . .); the question is whether having any such rule is incompatible with treating **Cicero** and **Tully** as connotationless. To see that there is no incompatibility, consider the rule whose English formulation is represented as "N is named 'N.'" Such a rule would antecedently differentiate **Cicero** from **Tully** (though, of course, its effect would be nullified if and when one acquired **Cicero = Tully**), and this intrinsic distinction would remain marked regardless of how one went on to play the game. But having such a built-in connection between a name and a predicate does not amount to embracing senses or connotations, since this connection has nothing to do with determining what, if anything, the name *denotes*. Nothing in our apparatus requires the truth theory to pay the slightest attention to considerations of conceptual role when assigning denotations to names.

3 Ascriptions of "Knowing Who": The Special Case

We turn at last to the case of knowledge ascriptions that involve "who" clauses. In this section we are concerned with "who" complements of the form "who N is" for arbitrary singular term "N"; and we attempt to show that our paratactic framework supplies truth conditions for instances of "X knows who N is" and captures the essential insights of chapters 1 and 2. In the next section, we undertake to show that our new account extends beyond the special case of "X knows who N is" to knows-who locutions in general.

3.1 Logical Form
Let us begin with a simple example, such as

(4) John knows who Mary is.

An apparent obstacle to a paratactic treatment of (4) is that, unlike (1), it does not quite so obviously fall into two parts: Sentence (4) appears to lack an assertive component of the favored sort. If we regard "who Mary is" as the display sample, we are left with just "John knows," which lacks a grammatical object. On the other hand, "who" can sometimes serve as this object: If asked, "Who is Mary?," one might respond "John knows who." To this it is naturally replied that "John knows who" is, in such a case, merely a contextual ellipsis of (4), the missing "Mary is" having been supplied by the question. The basis of this intuition, however, is just the feeling that "John knows who" is somehow incomplete and importantly parasitic on some contextually provided "who" clause. But demonstrative constructions can be incomplete and parasitic in just this way. Indeed, English provides an environment for "who" that brings out this connection with demonstratives rather nicely, viz., the idiomatic though mannered construction "the who of it." (This is not an isolated phenomenon, for we have the systematically related phrases "the how of it," "the why of it," etc.) "John knows the who of it" also feels incomplete and parasitic on context, but this feeling is completely explicable within our paratactic framework.

We propose to think of a free-standing construction such as "John knows who" as tacitly containing "who" in such an stylized environment, i.e., as elliptical for "John knows the who of it." As a first approximation, then, we bifurcate (4) in the way depicted in (5):

(5) John knows the who of it.

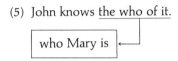

Since the display component is obviously related to the interrogative form "Who is Mary?," it is natural to think of the hypothetical utterer of the parataxis as forcelessly "posing" (as opposed to asking) a question by means of the displayed "who" clause and asserting that John knows the (or an) appropriate answer. The surface form (4) is the result of embedding a trivial transform of the question and deleting "the who of it." Unlike "that," whose deletion is only optional, the deletion of "the who of it" is obligatory when the question is embedded to form a single surface sentence: "The who of it" reaches the surface only in remarks such as "Who is Mary?—John knows the who of it." Where ordinary "pure" demonstratives are concerned, such a deletion might be worrisome, especially if one thinks of the referent of a pure demonstrative as being determined by some causal chain linking an object as distal stimulus to a *token* of the demonstrative as response, for neither (4) nor the likes of "John believes snow is white" contains any overt demonstrative to be tokened. But we have seen that what underlies the complementizer/demonstrative "that" is not a pure demonstrative but rather a quasi-demonstrative whose reference in a canonical parataxis is fixed by an index relative to the structure of the parataxis itself, independently of whether the surface form contains any reflection of **THAT**. As we shall see, something quite similar is true of "the who of it." What matters is not the appearance on the surface but rather the recoverability-in-principle of the underlying logical form that contains the quasidemonstrative in question.

The stylized construction "the who of it" is, to all appearances, a singular term. It would be a bit extravagant to take the occurrence of the definite article too seriously; the phrase is, after all, only an idiom. On the other hand, it does not appear to be a fused name like "The Holy Roman Empire," for what it picks out must obviously be capable of varying from one displayed "who" clause to another. In this respect it is more like a genuine descriptive singular term. To accommodate this mixture of intuitions, we propose an underlying family of indexed quasidemonstratives **THE-WHO-OF-IT$_1$**, **THE-WHO-OF-IT$_2$**, ..., which, though syntactically fused (as all good idioms should be), are semantically sensitive to the coordinates of indices in a way that allows their denotations to vary appropriately from index to index and from one displayed "who" clause to another.[12]

Accordingly, the logical form of "John knows the who of it" would be the simple formula

(6) **KNOW(John, ⟨ ⟩, THE-WHO-OF-IT$_1$).**

Inasmuch as the semantical account of **THE-WHO-OF-IT** is rather complicated and since our current interest is in *de dicto* ascriptions such as (4), it would greatly simplify exposition if we temporarily ignore the sequence parameter in (6) and the role of starred variables in complements and revert to our earlier, dyadic rendering of **KNOW**. Once the basic apparatus has been laid out for the *de dicto* case with dyadic **KNOW**, we can then reintroduce the missing sequence parameter, complicate the denotation postulate for **THE-WHO-OF-IT** to take account of variables and substitution instances, and give a general account of *de re* attributions of "knowing who" that treats (6) as the limiting case. So for the moment, let us regard the logical form of "John knows the who of it" as (7) rather than as (6):

(7) **KNOW(John, THE-WHO-OF-IT$_1$).**

Our next task is to uncover the logical form of "who" clauses. Then we will be in a position to explain the semantical connection between **THE-WHO-OF-IT** and this form and to work out the truth conditions of (4) and its ilk.

The point of our earlier introduction into $\mathbf{P}^+$ of derived predicates (abstracts) $\hat{v}_1 \ldots \hat{v}_n(A)$, and of our subsequent introduction of PAUAs, was to provide the formal apparatus for the representation and interpretation of "who" clauses. The guiding idea is a simple one: The interrogative pronoun "who" in the display sample "who Mary is" is the surface reflection of a capped (abstracted) variable in the prefix of the derived unary predicate $\hat{\mathbf{x}}_1(\mathbf{x}_1 = \mathbf{Mary})$. (Compare "*who* is such that *she* is Mary.") More complex "who" clauses are obviously amenable to the same sort of treatment, but we postpone discussing them until later. Treating "is" as a reflection of " $=$ " is a slight departure from earlier chapters, but one that proves harmless.

So much for the logical form of "who Mary is"; but what is the connection between (7) and $\hat{\mathbf{x}}_1(\mathbf{x}_1 = \mathbf{Mary})$? Given our earlier discussion of attitude ascriptions in the "that"-clause format, one might expect us to claim that display of "who Mary is" involves deferred ostension of a set of items that resemble "who Mary is" in certain ways. Such a ploy would have several disadvantages within our chosen framework. First, "who Mary is" is not a sentence, but what John knows-true *is* a sentence (of Mentalese or whatever). Second, semantical and conceptual roles have been defined only for $\mathbf{F}^+$-formulas; we currently have no apparatus for saying in what the "resemblance" to "who Mary is" would consist. A slightly different though related strategy is therefore required.

In light of our remarks about questions and answers, the required emendation is straightforward. Display of "who Mary is" is an invitation to consider the class of possible grammatically related *answers*, one of which (so the utterer claims) is known-true by John. The resemblance in question is grammatical: The "who" clause determines the *form*, though of course not the specific content, that something must have in order to count as an answer. The content is constrained by the purpose at issue. So the semantics for **THE-WHO-OF-IT** must somehow relate purposes and "who" clauses to an appropriate set of "answers" while providing for the salience of semantical versus conceptual role of answers themselves, so as to capture the transparent versus the opaque "senses" of knowing-who attributions. This is a tall order, but the ingredients for meeting it are already available in the E-coordinates of indices. (Once again, the reader with no taste for the formalities may wish to skip to the last two paragraphs of section 3.3 below, where the upshot of this treatment of (4) is informally glossed.)

3.2 Satisfiers, Answer Formulas, and Purposes: The Initial Postulate for
THE-WHO-OF-IT
If our only task were to account for ascriptions of the form "X knows who N is," the appropriate denotation postulate for indexed occurrences of **THE-WHO-OF-IT** would not be too complicated. But our aim is the broader one of accounting for all (nonembedded) knows-who constructions, so a denotation postulate of extreme generality and considerable complexity is required. The proposal we offer below is only provisional, being tailored to our present exclusive concern with *de dicto* ascriptions (not involving starred variables in the logical forms of their complements) and to our concomitant pretense that **KNOW** is dyadic. Even so, it requires a heavy gloss.

In aid of our project, we define, for each index I and regimented closed abstract $q = \hat{\mathbf{x}}_1 \ldots \mathbf{x}_n(A) \in \mathbf{P}^+$, a correlated set $Z[q, I]$:

$Z[q, I] = \{\langle a_1, \ldots, a_n \rangle : a_1, \ldots, a_n$ are persons & for some denumerable sequence z, $z_i = a_i$ $(1 \leqslant i \leqslant n)$ & $\mathbf{F}^+\mathrm{SAT}_I(z, A)\}$.

Intuitively, this is the set of those sequences of persons that "satisfy" a "who" clause at a given index I. With q as above, we say that a formula $J \in \mathbf{F}^+$ is a $Z[q, I]$-*formula* iff:

(i) for some $k > 0$, $Z[q, I] = \{f^1, \ldots, f^k\}$; and
(ii) there is a sequence $\langle F_1^1, \ldots, F_n^1, \ldots, F_1^k, \ldots, F_n^k \rangle$ of (not necessarily distinct) closed monadic predicates in $\mathbf{P}^+$ such that $F_j^i = F_q^r$ iff $f^i(j) = f^r(s)$ $(1 \leqslant i, r \leqslant k; 1 \leqslant j, s < n)$; and $\mathbf{F}^+\mathrm{SAT}_I(z, \ulcorner F_j^i(x_k)\urcorner)$ for any z such that $z(k) = f^i(j)$; and
(iii) there are distinct variables $v_1^0, \ldots, v_n^0$ and a (possibly repetitive) sequence $V = \langle v_1^1, \ldots, v_n^1, \ldots, v_1^k, \ldots, v_n^k \rangle$ of variables such that

(a) v^0_m differs from v^i_j $(1 \leqslant i \leqslant k; 1 \leqslant j, m \leqslant n)$, and

(b) $v^i_j = v^{i'}_{j'}$ iff $f^i(j) = f^{i'}(j')(1 \leqslant i, i' \leqslant k; 1 \leqslant j, j' \leqslant n)$, and

(c) $v^0_1, \ldots, v^k_n$ are foreign to A and to each F^i_j, and

(iv) J is the existential closure (w.r.t. the distinct variables of V) of the formula

$$\bigwedge \sim (v^i_j = v^{i'}_{j'}) \ \& \ (v^0_1) \ldots (v^0_n)[A' \leftrightarrow \bigvee \bigwedge (v^0_j = v^i_j)] \ \& \ \bigwedge (F^i_j!(v^i_j))$$

in which

(a) $\bigwedge \sim (v^i_j = v^{i'}_{j'})$ is the conjunction of all negated identities whose terms v^i_j and $v^{i'}_{j'}$ are distinct variables in V such that v^i_j alphabetically precedes $v^{i'}_{j'}$;

(b) $\bigvee \bigwedge (v^0_j = v^i_j)$ is the result of deleting from $\bigvee_{1 \leqslant i \leqslant k} \bigwedge_{1 \leqslant j \leqslant n} (v^0_j = v^i_j)$ subsequent repetitions of a conjunct within any disjoined conjunction;

(c) $\bigwedge (F^i_j!(v^i_j))$ is the result of deleting subsequent repetitions of a conjunct within $\bigwedge_{1 \leqslant i \leqslant k} \bigwedge_{1 \leqslant j \leqslant n} (F^i_j!(v^i_j))$; and

(d) A' is the result of simultaneously substituting $v^0_1, \ldots, v^0_n$ for the n free variables $\mathbf{x}_1, \ldots, \mathbf{x}_n$ in A.

Where instances of "X knows who N is" are concerned, we are dealing with unary closed abstracts of the form $\hat{\mathbf{x}}_1(\hat{\mathbf{x}}_1 = N)$, hence $Z[q, I]$ is always either the empty set—in which case there are no $Z[q, I]$-formulas—or else the set $\{\langle a \rangle\}$ for some person a—in which case the $Z[q, I]$-formulas all share the general form

$$(\exists w)((v)(v = N \leftrightarrow v = w) \ \& \ F!w).$$

Now the predicate F in this special case is obviously intended to be something relevantly similar to an important predicate in the sense discussed in chapter 2—as are the various predicates F^i_j in the general case—where importance is relative to contextually specified purposes. As we have defined them, however, $Z[q, I]$-formulas are merely true formulas of a certain *form*: Nothing is said about whether the predicates in question are connected with any purposes. Indeed, since nothing at all has been said so far by way of formally characterizing the P-coordinate of indices, it is as yet unclear how an adequate denotation postulate for **THE-WHO-OF-IT** could make use of $Z[q, I]$-formulas and the coordinate P_I in a way that had anything to do with the lessons of chapter 2! Clearly, we have some explaining to do.

Let us begin by revising slightly the discussion in chapter 2 of Form W. Since we are officially ignoring demonstratives, we can drop line B and instruction box 2. We now stipulate that what occurs on line A or C is always a regimented *n*-ary abstract, with the former line accepting only entries of the sort $\hat{v}(v = T)$ for primitive $T \in \mathbf{T}^+$ and the latter unrestricted except for those of the sort $\hat{v}_1 \ldots \hat{v}_n(\ldots (v_j = T) \ldots)$ for $1 \leqslant j \leqslant n$ and primitive $T \in \mathbf{T}^+$. We further stipulate that a file is labeled with a primitive term T iff it contains $\hat{v}(v = T)$, and contains $\hat{v}(v = \imath x Fx)$ iff it contains $\hat{v}(F!v)$. Now for the instruction boxes. Box 1 requests a predicate $\hat{v}(v = T')$ with primitive $T' \in \mathbf{T}^+$ distinct from T from the file (if any) containing $\hat{v}(v = T)$ when $\hat{v}(v = T)$ occurs on line A and *one* predicate $\hat{v}(v = T')$ with primitive $T' \in \mathbf{T}^+$ from *each distinct* file containing $\hat{v}_j((\exists v_1) \ldots$ $(\exists v_{j-1})(\exists v_{j+1}) \ldots (\exists v_n)B)$ for $1 \leqslant j \leqslant n$ if $\hat{v}_1 \ldots \hat{v}_n B$ occurs on line C. Box 3 requests a predicate $\hat{v}(F!v)$ in which F is an appropriately formatted noncircular catalog entry from the file (if any) containing $\hat{v}(v = T)$ when $\hat{v}(v = T)$ appears on line A and *one* such predicate $\hat{v}(F!v)$ from *each distinct* file containing $\hat{v}_j((\exists v_1) \ldots (\exists v_n)B)$ for $1 \leqslant j \leqslant n$ when $\hat{v}_1 \ldots \hat{v}_n B$ occurs on line C. (Thus, in the former case, the output $\hat{v}(F!v)$ could not contain T, and in the latter case each of the required outputs would have to be novel with respect to the input $\hat{v}_1 \ldots \hat{v}_n B$. For future reference, let us call the result of these revisions "Form W(Rev.)" and say that its deliverances are "important predications" with respect to the input on line A or C.

We now need a characterization of the *P*-coordinate of an index that provides an extensional representation of the bearing of purposes on important predications. The following definition—subject to a small qualification to be made in the final section of this chapter—suffices.

> DEFINITION. P (the final coordinate of an index) is any function from the set of *n*-ary abstracts $q \in \mathbf{P}^+$ such that $P(q)$ is the set of monadic predicates in $\mathbf{P}^+$ that are admissible for complying with a fully filled-out copy of Form W(Rev.) that has q on line A or C.

(One final terminological matter: Let us say that two regimented *n*-ary abstracts play the same semantical role for *u* just in case their respective matrices do.)

We are at last in a position to give a denotation postulate for **THE-WHO-OF-IT**$_h$ that appropriately connects $Z[q, I]$-formulas with our account of the *P*-coordinate in a way that begins to do justice to our original notion of an important predicate *without invoking the latter explicitly*.

Where z is any denumerable sequence, $I = \langle u, t, C, D, E, P \rangle$ and $E(h) = \langle M_h, q_h \rangle$ for some regimented abstract $q_h \in \mathbf{P}^+$:

> If $M_h = \text{CON}$, then $\mathbf{T}^{++} \text{DEN}_I(z, \textbf{THE-WHO-OF-IT}_h) =$ that function W_{CON}^h from utterer–time pairs $\langle u', t' \rangle$ to sets of closed $\mathbf{F}^+$-formulas such that $W_{\text{CON}}^h(\langle u', t' \rangle) = \{A \in \mathbf{F}^+ : \text{for some } J \in \mathbf{F}^+, [J \text{ is a } Z[q_h, I']$-formula for $I' = \langle u', t', C, D, E, P \rangle] \,\&\, [\text{each } F_j^i \text{ in } J \text{ is in } P(q_h)] \,\&\, [A \text{ plays}$

for u' the same conceptual role modulo C that J plays for $u]$}; and if $M_h = $ SEM, then $\mathbf{T}^{++}\mathrm{DEN}_I(z, \mathbf{THE\text{-}WHO\text{-}OF\text{-}IT}_h) = $ that function W^h_{SEM} from utterer–time pairs $\langle u', t' \rangle$ in which $t' = t$ to sets of closed $\mathbf{F}^+$-formulas such that $W^h_{\mathrm{SEM}}(\langle u', t' \rangle) = \{A \in \mathbf{F}^+ :$ for some regimented abstract $q' \in \mathbf{P}^+$, $[q'$ plays for u' at t' the same semantical role as $q_h]$ & $[A$ is a $Z[q', I']$-formula for $I' = \langle u', t', C, D, E, P \rangle$ in which each F^i_j is in $P(q')]$}.

This postulate still does not do total justice to our original notion of an important predicate, for it lacks a clause ruling out "importantly false beliefs." Extending our treatment of the matter in chapter 2 and codifying it within the present formalism for insertion into the postulate is a tedious exercise, so we shall just pretend in this and the following chapters that such codification and insertion has taken place.

3.3 Truth Conditions

Let us now see what truth condition is forthcoming for (4) ("John knows who Mary is") in light of our denotation postulate for **THE-WHO-OF-IT**. The appropriate English reading for (4) is presumably the following PSUA w:

$\langle\langle$"John knows the who of it", $\langle$"who Mary is"$\rangle\rangle$, $\langle\mathbf{KNOW}(\mathbf{John},$ $\mathbf{THE\text{-}WHO\text{-}OF\text{-}IT}_1), \langle$"$\hat{\mathbf{x}}_1(\mathbf{x}_1 = \mathbf{Mary})\rangle\rangle\rangle$.

Now (4)/w is true at an index $I = \langle u, t, C, D, E, P \rangle$ iff w is true$_I$, i.e., iff every denumerable sequence z satisfies$_I$ w. So we have:

[For all z, z satisfies$_I$ w] iff
[For all z, $\mathbf{F}^{++}\mathrm{SAT}_{I'}(z, \mathbf{KNOW}(\mathbf{John}, \mathbf{THE\text{-}WHO\text{-}OF\text{-}IT}_1))$ for each I' differing from I only in that $E_{I'}(1) = \langle M_1, \hat{\mathbf{x}}_1(\mathbf{x}_1 = \mathbf{Mary}) \rangle$, where M_1 is fixed as in $E_{I'}(1)$] iff
[For each such I and z, $\langle \mathbf{T}^{++}\mathrm{DEN}_{I'}(z, \mathbf{John}), \mathbf{T}^{++}\mathrm{DEN}_{I'}(z, \mathbf{THE\text{-}}$ $\mathbf{WHO\text{-}OF\text{-}IT}_1) \rangle \in \mathbf{P}^{++}\mathrm{Ext}_{I'}(z, \mathbf{KNOW})$] iff
[$\langle$John, $W^1_{M_1} \rangle \in \{\langle x, y \rangle : x$ is a person & y is a function … & for some L and $\mathbf{F}^+$-SUA $\langle S, A \rangle$ of L, x tokens $\langle S, A \rangle$ at $t_{I'} (= t)$ in foro interno & $A \in y(\langle x, t \rangle), … \}$] iff
[For some L and $\mathbf{F}^+$-SUA $\langle S, A \rangle$ of L, John tokens $\langle S, A \rangle$ in foro interno at t & $A \in W^1_{M_1}(\langle \mathrm{John}, t \rangle)$ etc.].

If $M_1 = $ CON, then $W^1_{M_1}(\langle \mathrm{John}, t \rangle) = W^1_{\mathrm{CON}}(\langle \mathrm{John}, t \rangle) = \{A \in \mathbf{F}^+ :$ for some $J \in \mathbf{F}^+$, J is a $Z[\hat{\mathbf{x}}_1(\mathbf{x}_1 = \mathbf{Mary}), I']$-formula for $I' = \langle \mathrm{John}, t, C, D, E, P \rangle$ each of whose predicates F^i_j is in $P(\hat{\mathbf{x}}_1(\mathbf{x}_1 = \mathbf{Mary}))$, and A plays for John the same conceptual role modulo C that J plays for u}—in which case:

(4)/w is true at I iff for some object o, monadic predicate $F \in \mathbf{P}^+$, language L, and $\mathbf{F}^+$-SUA $\langle S, A \rangle$ of L, $o = $ Mary & $F \in P(\hat{\mathbf{x}}_1(\mathbf{x}_1 = $

Mary)) & John knows-true $\langle S, A \rangle$ at t & A plays for John the same conceptual role modulo C that is played for u by

$$(\exists \mathbf{x}_1)[(\mathbf{x}_2)(\mathbf{x}_2 = \mathbf{Mary} \leftrightarrow \mathbf{x}_2 = \mathbf{x}_1) \ \& \ F!(\mathbf{x}_1)].$$

And if $M_1 = \text{SEM}$, then $W^1_{M_1}(\langle \text{John}, t \rangle) = W^1_{\text{SEM}}(\langle \text{John}, t \rangle) = \{A \in \mathbf{F}^+$ for some $q \in \mathbf{P}^+$, which plays for John at t the same semantical role as $\hat{\mathbf{x}}_1(\mathbf{x}_1 = \mathbf{Mary})$, A is a $Z[q, I']$-formula for $I' = \langle \text{John}, t, C, D, E, P \rangle$ in which each F^i_j is in $P(q)\}$ — in which case:

> (4)/w is true at I iff for some object o, monadic predicates F, $G \in \mathbf{P}^+$, language L, and $\mathbf{F}^+$-SUA $\langle S, A \rangle$ of L, $o = \text{Mary} \ \& \ G$ plays for John at t the same semantical role as $\hat{\mathbf{x}}_1(\mathbf{x}_1 = \mathbf{Mary})$ & $F \in P(G)$ & $A = (\exists \mathbf{x}_1)[(\mathbf{x}_2)(\mathbf{x}_2 = \mathbf{Mary} \leftrightarrow \mathbf{x}_2 = \mathbf{x}_1)$ & $F!(\mathbf{x}_1)]$ & John knows-true $\langle S, A \rangle$ at t.

Where "S" is an English sentence whose logical form is a $Z[q, I]$-formula A, we can continue to speak as before of conceptually individuated $\cdot S \cdot$'s and $:S:$'s, since preservation of A's computational role involves preservation of A's "informativeness" and hence of A's internal noncircularity. But a small caveat must be entered as regards speaking in this case of *semantically* individuated $\cdot S \cdot$'s and $:S:$'s, for a mere extensional isomorph A' of a $Z[q, I]$-formula A is *not* guaranteed to preserve any semantical analog of A's informativeness: The counterpart q' in A' of q in A may not (as the postulate requires when $M_h = \text{SEM}$) have counterparts of the predicates F^i_j which themselves are in $P(q')$. So it would not be strictly correct in glossing a transparent knows-who ascription to speak of knowing-true a semantically individuated $:S:$ for "S" containing such-and-such interesting predicates. Since dot quotes and colon quotes are such handy paraphrastic devices, we propose a modest convention that will enable us to exploit them with a clear conscience in connection with transparent knows-who constructions: viz., *solely* in the context of discussing what is ascribed by some transparent knows-who ascription, talk about the subject's knowing-true a semantically individuated $:S:$ (or believing-true a semantically individuated $\cdot S \cdot$) for "S" containing such-and-such a predicate "F" is to be understood as talk about a *restricted* class of semantically related sentences, viz., those having logical forms whose counterparts q' and $F^{\prime i}_j$ of q and F^i_j in A (= the $Z[q, I]$-formula which is the logical form of "S") are such that $F^{\prime i}_j \in P(q')$.

Using the original notion of an important predicate in a purely informal way (which we trust is readily understood in light of the foregoing), we can mobilize (restricted) colon quotes to gloss the truth condition of (4) as follows:

> (4) is true at I iff John knows-true at t_I a $:$ One and only one thing is Mary and that thing is uniquely $G:$, where "G" reflects an important predicate for purpose P_I (i.e., something in $P_I(\hat{\mathbf{x}}_1(\mathbf{x}_1 = \mathbf{Mary}))$.

Exploiting our convention for the use of abbreviations within dot quotes, we could say even more succinctly that

> (4) is true at I iff John knows-true a : G!(Mary): for "G" reflecting an important predicate relative to P_I.

Several features of this result call for comment. First, we regard " = " in the usual way as tenseless and so do not insist on a distinction between knowing who a currently living person is and knowing who a previously but not currently living person was. Nothing important to our project hinges on this liberality, and appropriate complications for tensed identities could harmlessly be added if desired. Second, for genuinely empty names we have the result urged in previous chapters: if "N" is empty, then every instance of "X knows who N is" is false at every index (assuming, of course, that $x_1 = N$ is assigned determinate satisfaction conditions that no sequence meets—a matter that we assume was taken care of in one of the ways mentioned earlier). "Knowing who" is a species of "knowing that," and one can no more literally know who, e.g., Santa Claus is than one can literally know that Santa Claus brings toys at Christmas. (One can wonder/venture an opinion as to/speculate about/ … who Santa Claus is; but we would argue that such nonfactive attributions involving "who" clauses have logical forms importantly different from those of the corresponding factive attributions.)

3.4 Plausible Inferences and Residual Ambiguities: Some Test Cases
Our theory makes the connection between the opaque construals of (4) and (8) as tight as could be wished:

> (8) John knows that one and only one thing is Mary and that thing is uniquely G.

Relative to a common index specifying individuation of their respective complements by conceptual role, any instance of (8) in which "G" is replaced by an English reflection of an important predicate (relative to that index) is such that its truth guarantees the truth of (4). Indeed, under these assumptions the truth of an instance of "X knows that one and only one thing is N and G!(it)" ensures the truth of the corresponding instance of "X knows who N is." The inference *fails*, however, where transparent construals are concerned. Formally, the reason is just that extensional isomorphism of $\hat{x}_1(x_1 = T)$ and $\hat{x}_1(x_1 = T')$ does not imply that that $P(\hat{x}_1(x_1 = T)) = P(\hat{x}_1(x_1 = T'))$. Informally, the failure can be illustrated as follows: For certain purposes, "John knows that Mary = the murderer of Smith" implies that "John knows who Mary is"; but *transparently* construed, the former is truth-conditionally equivalent to "John knows that Mary = Mary," which clearly does *not* imply "John knows who Mary is" even when the latter is also transparently construed!

An adequate account of ascriptions of "knowing who" must also explain the attractiveness of inferring instances of "*X* knows who N is" from corresponding instances of "*X* knows that N = M." Why, e.g., does it seem that the truth of "John knows that Tully = the author of *De Fato*" or even of "John knows that Tully = Cicero" might suffice for the truth of "John knows who Tully is"? The first thing to see is that these inferences are plausible only when the ascriptions are taken *opaquely*; taken transparently, "John knows that Tully = Cicero/the author of *De Fato*" merely attributes to John the knowing-true of some equation whose terms have the relevant denotations; but, in principle, nothing prevents this equation from being a trivial self-identity (since Cicero = Tully = the author of *De Fato*)—in which case it would be ludicrous to infer the truth of "John knows who Tully is."

When the ascriptions are taken opaquely, our theory can easily predict the intuitively correct results. If John knows-true a *conceptually* individuated : Tully = the author of *De Fato* : [or : Tully = Cicero :], then, assuming that he is logically competent, he knows-true a conceptually individuated : Tully alone authored *De Fato* : [: Tully alone is Cicero :], hence counts as knowing who Tully is (opaque sense) for any purpose for which "authored *De Fato*" [" = Cicero"] counts as an important predicate.

It is worth pointing out here (and it is important in chapter 6) that the opaque sense in which (relative to certain purposes) we can get "*X* knows who N is" from "*X* knows that N = M" does *not* guarantee that we can also get "*X* knows who M is." This may sound paradoxical, for if "*X* knows who N is" and "*X* knows that N = M" are both true, must not "*X* knows who M is" also be true (provided, of course, opaque readings throughout)? Surprisingly, as our theory now stands the answer is "No!" Under the given proviso, the inference works only in relation to indices *I* whose *P*-coordinates are such that "*X* knows who N is" is true at *I independently* of the truth at *I* of "*X* knows that N = M." But the case at hand is precisely of the degenerate sort which is thus excluded, viz., one in which P_I is such that "*X* knows who N is" is true at *I because* "*X* knows that N = M" is. To see why independence is required, consider the following example involving Form W(Rev.). Suppose that P requires some sort of descriptive catalog entry to match $\hat{x}_1(x_1 = $ **Sir Alexander Fleming**$)$ and that $\hat{x}_1(x_1$ **discovered penicillin**$)$ is a predicate of the required sort (i.e., $\hat{x}_1(x_1$ **discovered penicillin**$) \in P(\hat{x}_1(x_1 = $ **Sir Alexander Fleming**$)))$. Suppose further that John knows that Sir Alexander Fleming = the discoverer of penicillin, hence that Fleming (alone) discovered penicillin. Then John knows (for P) who Sir Alexander Fleming is. But John does *not* necessarily know (opaque sense) who the discoverer of penicillin is *for that same cataloging purpose P*—though he certainly does for certain *other* purposes, such as label finding—since by hypothesis P rejects the predicate $\hat{x}_1(x_1 = $ **Sir Alexander Fleming**$)$ as not being a descriptive catalog entry *and* rejects $\hat{x}_1(x_1$ **discovered penicillin**$)$

as an inappropriately circular match for $\hat{x}_1(x_1 = \imath x_2(x_2$ **is a discoverer of penicillin**)—i.e., $\hat{x}_1(x_1$ **discovered penicillin**) is in $P(\hat{x}_1(x_1 =$ **Sir Alexander Fleming**)) but *not* in $P(\hat{x}_1(x_1 = \imath x_2(x_2$ **is a discoverer of penicillin**))). In defense of this consequence of our theory, we point to the counterintuitiveness of allowing that someone's knowing-true a conceptually individuated :F!(the F): should ever suffice for that person's knowing *who* the F is!

As a final sort of test-case, consider

(9) Castro knows who the CIA's Havana agent is.

In laying out our original account, we noted that sentences such as (9) have an "intermediate" interpretation that falls between their "referential" and "attributive" construals. Sentence (9) can be heard as ascribing to Castro any of the following: (i) the ability appropriately to identify so-and-so as *the* CIA agent in Havana; (ii) the ability appropriately to identify *that very person*, but not necessarily to identify that person as *the* (or even as *a*) CIA agent; (iii) the ability appropriately to identify that person as *a* (but perhaps not as *the*) CIA agent in Havana. Our "two-schemes" approach obviously provides—by means of conceptual versus semantical individuation of :G!(the CIA's Havana agent):'s—for the sense in which (9) attributes to Castro (i) or (ii) but does not by itself seem to provide for attribution of (iii). Is this a defect in our theory? We think not.

The intermediate interpretation in question is, we suggest, merely an artifact of interpreting (9) at indices that mark semantical role as salient *and* that specify certain special sorts of purposes. For the utterer's choice of words for talking about the victim can often conversationally suggest what purpose or range of purposes the utterer has in mind, and when we register such suggestions, it is only natural that these purposes would come first to mind in evaluating the utterance. In the case of (9), describing the victim as a *foreign agent* taps our background lore about espionage and brings to mind the familiar purposes and projects relating to internal security, counterintelligence, etc., relative to which predicates such as "is a CIA agent" would, if applicable, surely rank as prominent items in the victim's dossier. Small wonder, then, that we might be prepared to deny (9) if Castro's identification of the person in question included nothing about being a CIA agent. But such a denial is defeasible in principle: It is just difficult to focus on more mundane purposes when a particularly exciting one is on stage. As additional support for this treatment of the "intermediate" interpretation, we note that (at least to our ears) such an interpretation becomes increasingly difficult to hear the more "neutrally" the victim is described. Consider, e.g.,

(10) Castro knows who John's uncle is.

Precisely because there is no standard stock of "uncle-related" purposes, what comes to mind is just that Castro knows-true some semantically or conceptually individuated : G!(John's uncle) : for "G" reflecting an important predicate relative to *some purpose or other*.

3.5 Departures from the Prototheory Explained and Defended

It should be apparent by now that our proposal for the paratactic analysis of sentences of the form "X knows who N is" has many affinities with the account offered in chapter 2; nevertheless, it differs from the latter in two obvious and significant respects. One the one hand, the present account says nothing about X having any "Mentalese referential designator" of N to which X attaches the important predicate in the inwardly tokened Mentalese sentence. Where conceptual role is concerned, there is no a priori guarantee that the subject's : G!(N) : contains any singular term answering to "N", the term *we* use in specifying the conceptual role of what the subject knows-true. Isomorphism is not a condition of two $\mathbf{F}^+$-formulas' playing the same conceptual role. On the other hand, the present analysis is unitary: It assigns the same logical form to an instance of "X knows who N is" regardless of the status of the term replacing "N"—i.e., it pays no attention at the level of logical form to the referential/attributive distinction that exercised us in earlier chapters. If defensible, both of these departures would be welcome contributions to the simplicity and philosophical neutrality of our theory. But what entitles us to these modifications?

Both points of divergence are intimately connected with worries about the referential/attributive distinction, and both are motivated by our new-found ability to handle the relevant data about opacity and transparency while remaining neutral on the existence and status of such a distinction. We do not need two potential logical forms for each instance of "X knows who N is"—one for "referential" readings of what replaces "N" and another for "attributive" readings thereof—since the term replacing "N" is now re-garded as part of the displayed "who" clause, tokened in the course of making deferred reference to the class of "answers" structurally related to the question it "poses." And the concomitant pragmatic ambiguity regard-ing the individuation of : G!(N) :'s explains, by means of the appeal to semantical versus conceptual schemes of individuation, the very data re-garding duality of interpretations for which the referential/attributive distinction and the attendant proliferation of paraphrases were earlier invoked.

Thus, e.g., we can readily account for the transparent versus the opaque "senses" of (4). (We assume in what follows that "Mary" is a nonempty name.) Relative to any index that marks semantical role as salient and at which "N" has the same denotation (with respect to every denumerable sequence) as "Mary," John's knowing-true a : G!(Mary) : and his knowing-true a : G!(N) : come to exactly the same thing, regardless of whether "N" is a proper name or definite description. (With suitable expansion of indices, the same would hold for deictic pronouns, which we are ignoring at present.) The occurrence of "Mary" in (4) is fully transparent in such a case. Relative to indices marking conceptual role as salient, the opaque construal is immediately forthcoming, since—for the same sort of reasons invoked in connection with our discussion of the Cicero/Tully case—the coreferentiality of "Mary" and "N" in the attitude-ascriber's mouth does not ensure that John's :G!(Mary):'s and :G!(N):'s coincide. This is the sense in which John can know who Mary is without knowing who, e.g., Fred's wife is, even though Mary = Fred's wife.

Turning now to the remaining point of difference (viz., the lack of any "referential designator requirement"), we must return to our original motives in chapter 2 for switching from important names to important predicates. Having there proliferated logical forms for "X knows who N is" to account for referential versus attributive construals of what replaces "N", we were suddenly seized by the belated realization that the posited important names, taken as Mentalese definite descriptions, might *also* evince a referential/attributive ambiguity and that, when taken referentially, they would fail to make the needed predicative contribution to the content of what X must know-true. To avoid this difficulty, we separated the referential function of an important name from its attributive or predicative contribution and posited a referential designator in the language of thought to serve the former and a concatenated important predicate to make the latter. In defense of the posited referential designator, we cited (i) a need for the subject to be en rapport with the victim and (ii) a desire to have the content of the subject's knowledge conform to a terminal (purpose-satisfying) answer in the question-and-answer game. Our new theory avoids the proliferation of logical forms while capturing the role of important predicates *qua* predicates; so if there is any residual need for the posited Mentalese referential designator, it must presumably lie in (i) or (ii).

Let us begin with (i). In the present context, the only apparent reason for insisting on (i) would be a desire to ensure that all knowledge of who someone is should be *de re* knowledge regarding that person, knowledge *of* so-and-so that he or she possesses such-and-such important characteristics. There are, however, reasons for thinking that such a desire is misguided. Consider a person (call her "Bertie") whose only language is a Russellian "ideal" language, in which simple demonstratives—including "I" and "now" as well as "this," "that," and the like—are the sole singular terms (logically proper names). Bertie can accumulate and express a vast amount of highly detailed information but can *designate* (rigidly or otherwise) only items immediately present to her (and only while they are thus present). In particular, it seems that Bertie can have no *de re* knowledge of things with which she is not directly acquainted. But this seems rather feeble ground for denying that Bertie can know the identities of various temporally and/or spatially remote persons, for she might well be able to describe them (in her Russellian fashion) in arbitrarily great detail! For a wide range of ordinary classificatory purposes, Bertie can provide satisfactory (albeit clumsy) answers to her Russellian version of attributive "who" questions of the form "Who is/was the F?"—answers of the sort

$$(\exists x)(\exists y)((w)(Fw \leftrightarrow w = x) \ \& \ (z)(Gz \leftrightarrow z = y) \ \& \ x = y),$$

for some important predicate "G".

But what about referential "who" questions? This is where (ii) comes in. If we ask, "Who is Quine?," we expect an answer of the form "Quine is the such-and-such" or "He is the such-and-such"—i.e., we expect the respondent to *refer* to the person in question and to predicate appropriate properties of the person thus designated. And it is quite tempting, especially for a representationalist, to suppose that the form of the expected answer must be mirrored in the form of the Mentalese sentence known-true by one who knows who Quine is—hence the notion that, if "Quine" is a referential designator in the mouth of one who makes a true knowing-who attribution to X, it must have a Mentalese counterpart doing the same job for X, the knower. Though not implausible, this line of thought relies too heavily on accidental features of the question-and-answer game, such as the fact that both parties are assumed to speak English and hence to have access to all its referential devices. Consider again our friend Bertie, and suppose that her Russellian idiom is just a truncated and regimented version of English. The question "Who is Quine?" simply does not compute for Bertie: Her language, we may suppose, has an interrogative construction; but, by hypothesis, it has no singular term answering to "Quine." Does this mean that Bertie, learned though she is, cannot know who Quine is? This is one of those questions that invite mixed responses: A blanket "yes" or "no" would be equally dogmatic. The reason is not hard to find.

Granting that "Quine" is, in our mouths, a referential designator of Quine, there is still the residual pragmatic ambiguity anent the individuation of : G!(Quine):'s *qua* answers to the question "posed" by "who Quine is" in our mouths. If we are thinking in terms of *semantical* roles, then there is good reason to doubt that Bertie knows who Quine is, for if Bertie is not in a position to "demonstrate" Quine diaphanously (as few of us are), then *no* sentence of her language has a logical form extensionally isomorphic to that of an appropriate instance of "G!(Quine)." But matters are quite different if we are thinking in terms of *conceptual* roles. From this standpoint, there is no a priori reason why something of the form "One and only one person is F and that person is uniquely G" in Bertie's idiolect could not play for her the same conceptual role that "Quine is uniquely G" plays for us. Indeed, we maintain that this transpires in ordinary English already.[13] In this sense,

Bertie may well know who Quine is. This observation relates directly to our earlier doubts about the necessity of *de re* knowledge for "knowing who" and explains why, given Bertie's reduced linguistic circumstances, (11) seems intuitively less tendentious than (12):

(11) Bertie knows who Quine is.

(12) Bertie knows, of Quine, who he is.

(We make good on this remark in the next chapter, in which we explain how our provisional account of **THE-WHO-OF-IT** can be extended to fit a triadic version of **KNOW** so as to yield an account of *de re* ascriptions of "knowing who" such as (12).) Interpreted in this way, i.e., relative to conceptual role, the occurrence of "Quine" in (11) is resolutely opaque despite the fact that "Quine" is assumed to be a referential designator in the utterer's mouth. Our approach in chapters 1 and 2 was inadequate to allow for this sort of case, and so our new theory is in this respect a substantial improvement.

In the end, then, there seems to be no compelling reason for retaining the referential designator requirement in the analysis of *de dicto* ascriptions of "knowing who" nor any reason for supposing that such ascriptions have more than one basic sort of logical form. The referential designator requirement may, of course, survive as part of a philosophical interpretation of the *"de re* relation," but this is irrelevant to the syntax and semantics of "*X* knows who N is."

4 Ascriptions of "Knowing Who": The General Case

We must now ascertain whether our apparatus, which is admittedly stronger than is required to handle just instances of "*X* knows who N is," is strong enough to accommodate the general case.

In the following discussion we deliberately ignore "mixed" WH—— clauses of the sort that occur in "John knows who ate what at Mary's party" and "Klaus knows who lives where in the village." A full treatment of these cases within our paratactic framework would obviously require generalization of our person-relative **THE-WHO-OF-IT** to an omnibus **THE-WH(?)-OF-IT** and the introduction into abstracts of different styles of restricted variables for persons, places, times, etc., not to mention a swarm of minor adjustments (e.g., in the account of important predicates). Since our chief concern is with knowledge of the identities of persons, we accordingly restrict our attention to "who" clauses containing no other WH—— terms and regard our subsequent remarks about **THE-WHO-OF-IT** as contributing to the partial specification of a more general **THE-WH(?)-OF-IT**, which would ultimately supplant it. The mechanics of such further generalization would conform to the pattern exemplified by the ensuing account of **THE-WHO-OF-IT**.

4.1 Logical Form and Truth Conditions: Restricted Universes and the Null Case
Let us begin with our original examples from chapter 3:

(13) a. John knows who bought tickets.

b. John knows who is conspiring against whom.

c. John knows who insulted who in whose presence.

The three "who" clauses in (13) are unproblematic, having the respective forms $\hat{x}_1(\dots x_1 \dots)$, $\hat{x}_1 \hat{x}_2(\dots x_1 \dots x_2 \dots)$, and $\hat{x}_1 \hat{x}_2 \hat{x}_3(\dots x_1 \dots x_2 \dots x_3 \dots)$. (Notice that our highly restrictive definition of abstracts, together with our regimentation convention for PAUAs, does not constrain the internal ordering of the variables within the matrix of an abstract; so we have no trouble with the kind of overlapping exemplified in the form $\hat{x}_1 \hat{x}_2(\dots x_1 \dots x_2 \dots x_1 \dots)$, which is needed to account for "who" clauses such as *"who* loves whom more than *his* own mother.") English seems to provide no "who" clauses representable by the form $\hat{x}_1 \hat{x}_2(\dots x_2 \dots x_1 \dots)$, thus apparently respecting a convention that, for $i \leqslant j$, the first occurrence of the ith abstracted variable precedes the first occurrence of the jth abstracted variable in the matrix. But other sorts of clauses not involving "who" may require such representation, and there may (for all we know) be some natural language with a colloquial analog of the impermissible "whom who hit," so we refrain from further legislation.

The "who" clauses in (13a–c) do, however, add a semantic wrinkle not encountered in earlier cases, viz., the need for some contextual restriction of the universe of discourse; e.g., an utterer of (13a) is not likely to be attributing to John the ability to identify all the millions of people who ever bought a ticket for anything. There are various ways of accommodating this fact. For one, we could expand indices to include something that determines a salient range of persons and so define the set $Z[q, I]$ that the sequences it contains are formed from persons in this range. For another, we might regard the "who" clauses in question as elliptical for fuller specifications—e.g., treating "who bought tickets" as a contextual ellipsis for the likes of "who bought tickets to *Attack of the Killer Tomatoes* at the Bijou last week." Implementing such strategies would be a purely mechanical affair with no bearing on the essential structure of our theory. So we simply assume that some appropriate adjustment has been made and proceed to ignore the issue in what follows.

The logical form of (13a) is, say, the parataxis

$\langle$**KNOW(John, THE-WHO-OF-IT$_1$),**
$\langle \hat{x}_1($**PAST**$(\exists x_2)($**Ticket**(x_2) & **Buy**$(x_1, x_2))))\rangle \rangle$.

Given the obvious English reading for (13a) incorporating this logical form, our theory dictates that (13a) is true at an index I only if *someone* bought tickets (at a time earlier than t_1); so (13a) is straightforwardly false at I if no one bought tickets. Now, it seems to some people that, to the contrary, (13a) could be true in such a situation, provided that John *knows* that no one bought tickets. Obviously we could amend the denotation postulate for **THE-WHO-OF-IT** to respect this intuition, but we resist the temptation, for the intuition seems to us to be seriously confused.

Knowing who did such-and-such is, roughly, knowing an appropriate answer to the question "Who did such-and-such?" But "who" questions are complex questions: They rest on a prior presumption that one or more persons did such-and-such, and their point is to elicit identification of the culprits. If the presumption is false, the question cannot be answered, since the requested identifications cannot be given. To respond, "*Nobody* did such-and-such!" is not to answer the question but nullify it, by pointing out that it is misguided in light of the facts. The aforementioned intuition conflates answering a question with answering the questioner: If one rejects the presumption of a complex question, one does not try to answer the question itself; rather one answers the questioner by disputing what he or she has taken for granted in posing the question. For this reason is seems to us that (13a) should be false in a situation in which no one bought any tickets.

If these ruminations about complex questions fail to convince,[14] there is a further defense for our treatment. Were we to succumb to the idea that, when nobody F'd, knowing who F'd merely amounts to knowing that nobody F'd, we would get bizarre results for certain values of "F." For example, it is extremely counterintuitive to claim that someone *knows who Nixon's murderer is* merely on the ground that he or she happens to know that Nixon is still alive! By the same token, to announce to a married male friend "I know who your wife is having an affair with!" and then to respond to his startled "Who?" with "Nobody!" seems more like tasteless humor than supporting a serious contention with genuine evidence for its truth. Parallel considerations apply to "knowing which" and "knowing how to": We know that no positive integer lies between one and two and that it is impossible to draw a square circle, but these facts scarcely seem sufficient to warrant the claim that we know *which* positive integer lies between one and two or the claim that we know *how to* draw a square circle.

Having (we hope) dispensed with any residual misgivings about the null case,[15] let us turn to the more interesting situation in which one or more persons (within the contextually specified range of persons) actually did buy some tickets. For the sake of illustration, let us suppose that there are at t just two such persons, Bob and Ted, so that, where $I = \langle u, t, C, D, E, P \rangle$ and $q = \hat{x}_1(\textbf{PAST}(\exists x_2) [\textbf{Ticket}(x_2) \ \& \ \textbf{Buy}(x_1, x_2)])$, the set $Z[q, I']$ is just

$\{\langle \text{Bob}\rangle, \langle \text{Ted}\rangle\}$. Then (13a) is true at an index I marking conceptual [or semantical] role as salient iff somebody bought tickets (prior to t) and, for some L, John knows-true a SUA $\langle S, A\rangle$ of L in which A plays for him the same conceptual role modulo C that J plays for u [or in which A is for John at t a suitably restricted extensional isomorph of J], where J is a $Z[q, I']$-formula of the form

$$(14) \quad (\exists v_1^1)(\exists v_1^2)[\sim (v_1^1 = v_1^2) \,\&\, (v_1^0)[\textbf{PAST}(\exists x_2)(\textbf{Ticket}(x_2) \,\&\,$$
$$\textbf{Buy}(v_1^0, x_2)) \leftrightarrow (v_1^0 = v_1^1 \bigvee v_1^0 = v_1^2)] \,\&\, F_1^1!(v_1^1) \,\&\, F_1^2!(v_1^2)],$$

in which F_1^1 and F_1^2 are in $P(q)$ [or relative to which John's extensionally isomorphic counterparts G, H, q' of F_1^1, F_1^2, q are such that G, $H \in P(q')$].

If we allow, as seems reasonable, that one of the English surface forms of (14) is "The F and the G are the (distinct) people who bought tickets"—"F" and "G" being surface forms of F_1^1 and F_1^2—, then we could gloss (13a)'s truth condition as follows (bearing in mind, of course, that the occurrences of the definite descriptions in the dot glosses are, in light of (14), to be regarded as mere Russellian shorthand, *not* as signaling the presence of iota-terms in logical form):

> (13a) is true at I iff John knows-true at t_I a : The F and the G are the people who bought tickets : for "F" and "G" reflecting P_I important predicates.

For some P_I, "F" and "G" might of course be " $=$ Bob" and " $=$ Ted," in which case we would drop the clumsy "the one who is Bob/Ted" from our gloss in favor of the names themselves. Dropping our assumptions about the facts of the case, we could then say in general:

> (13a) is true at I iff, for some $n > 0$ [n being the number of ticket-buyers], John knows-true at t_I a : The F_1 and ... and the F_n are the people who bought tickets : for $F_1, ..., F_n$ reflecting P_I important predicates.

The treatment of (13b) and (13c) parallels, in obvious fashion, that of (13a). If, e.g., Tom is conspiring against Mary, and Jane is conspiring against Bob, and no other conspiracies are afoot among persons in the salient domain at t_I, then (13b) is true at I iff John knows-true at t_I a : The F_1 is conspiring against the F_2, and the F_3 is conspiring against the F_4, and these (distinct) persons alone are engaged in conspiring :, where "F_1," "F_2," "F_3," and "F_4" are P_I important predicates.

4.2 A Further Test Case

Consider now the question of the proper treatment of an inference such as (15), which undeniably has intuitive appeal:

(15) a. John knows who bought tickets.

   b. Ted bought tickets.

   Therefore

   c. John knows that Ted bought tickets.

The first thing to notice is that the appeal of (15) rests on tacit construal of the (a) and (c) sentences as *transparent*: If these sentences are taken opaquely, then there is no temptation to suppose that Ted's merely falling within the scope of John's "answer" (i.e., happening uniquely to satisfy one of John's important predicates) implies that John must "think of him as Ted," call him "Ted," or anything of the sort. Not surprisingly, our theory does not regard the truth of (15a, b) as guaranteeing the truth of (15c) at indices marking conceptual roles as salient for the simple reason that the truth of (15a) at such indices is obviously compatible with John's lacking any inner computational counterpart of the name "Ted."

The general plausibility of (15) on a transparent construal lies, no doubt, in the conviction that if John has the predicative resources to pick out the culprits, then, since Ted is among them, John has the predicative resources to pick out Ted descriptively, even if he has no *name* designating Ted and nothing that works for him computationally as "Ted" works for us. This line of thought takes for granted a modest logical competence on John's part—e.g., a grasp of the entailment of $G((\imath x)Fx)$ by $(\exists x)(F!x$ & $Gx)$—which leads or at least disposes him to mobilize those predicative resources in term formation.

If we allow ourselves this same assumption about John's minimal intelligence, then it is easy to see that our theory *supports* inference (15) at indices marking *semantical* role as salient throughout! For if, e.g., John knows-true an extensional isomorph of (14) and is logically competent, he presumably knows-true extensional isomorphs of both $\mathbf{BT}[(\imath x)F_1^1(x)]$ and $\mathbf{BT}[(\imath x)F_1^2(x)]$, where $\mathbf{BT}$ is the structure in (14) underlying "bought tickets." But the truth of "Ted bought tickets" guarantees that one of these iota-terms, hence the corresponding term in John's extensional isomorph, denotes Ted. So John knows-true something that is extensionally isomorphic to $\mathbf{BT}(\mathbf{Ted})$, and this suffices to support the inference (15) at the indices in question.

(Sections 4.3 and 4.4 concern predominantly technical details; the impatient reader may wish to skip to section 4.5.)

4.3 Collective versus Distributive Ascriptions of "Knowing Who"

At the beginning of chapter 3, we noted the intuitive inequivalence of the following sentences (we preserve the earlier chapter's numbering):

(1a) John knows who bought tickets.

(2)   John knows who the ticket-buyers are.

Sentences such as (2), containing plural and generic constructions, pose distinctive problems of their own. Until now, we have dealt exclusively with what might be called "distributive" cases of "knowing who," but sentences such as (2) also appear to have a "collective" reading. The question arises as to whether our apparatus can handle this distributive/collective ambiguity, hence provide for the (collective) sense in which (1a) and (2) are not equivalent as well as the (distributive) sense in which they are equivalent. Since the semantics of plural and generic constructions is a matter of some controversy, our remarks on this topic are tentative and somewhat speculative, aimed only at outlining a plausible accommodation.

Where sentences of the form

(16) X knows who the F's are

are concerned, the difference between their collective and distributive readings can plausibly be located in the difference between identity with the *sum* of F persons and membership in the *class* of F persons. For purposes of answering "who" questions, English treats person-sums as, so to speak, "corporate persons" relative to predicates that are satisfied by such sums but not by their person-parts.[16] If John, Bob, and Ted, acting in concert, lifted Mary's Volkswagen, which is too heavy for any one of them to lift, then an appropriate (regress-stopping) answer to the question "Who lifted Mary's Volkswagen?" would saliently identify the person-sum or fusion John-and-Bob-and-Ted as the lifter. From this angle, knowing who the F's are is a matter of knowing who (i.e., which person-sum) = the (sum of) F's and so differs from, e.g., knowing who Mary is only by involving the identity of a "corporate" rather than a natural person. And an appropriate identification of the F's *qua* person-sum need not (though it may) involve individuating information about the incorporated persons severally. On the other hand, knowing who the F's (distributively) are is a matter of knowing which persons are *among* the F's, i.e., who is a member of the class of F's— which reduces ultimately just to knowing who is F. Accordingly, we could represent these differences at the level of logical form by saying that "who the F's are" can derive either from $\hat{x}_1(x_1 = \mathbf{SUM}_z F_z)$ [its collective reading] or from $\hat{x}_1((\exists x_2)(x_2 \in \{x_3 : Fx_3\} \ \& \ x_1 = x_2)$ [its distributive reading]—or similar structures with like import. In this way, the collective and distributive readings of sentences of the form (16) can be accommodated without any alteration of our theory beyond the trivial extension of honorary personhood to certain person-sums.

A potentially more difficult problem is that of capturing the intuitive relations between knowing-who attributions such as (1a) and (2) on the one hand and, on the other hand, (opaque) knowing-that attributions that embed clauses such as (17) and evince a collective/distributive ambiguity:

(17) The bachelors of Podunk (alone) bought tickets.

What, in other words, does our theory have to say about the conditions under which the truth of (18) (on its opaque reading) suffices for that of (1a) or (2):

(18) John knows that the bachelors of Podunk alone bought tickets.

(In our answer below we tacitly avail ourselves of the usual background assumption that our subject is logically competent, hence makes obviously valid inferences, etc. The point of confining our attention to opaque construals was explained in section 3.4.)

To begin with, (17) might have either of the following logical forms (in which "**BT**" and "**P**" denote the structures underlying "bought tickets" and "is a bachelor of Podunk," respectively, and niceties about canonical variables are ignored):

(17coll) $\hat{y}[(\exists x)(x = y \ \& \ \mathbf{BT}!x)](\mathbf{SUM}_z\mathbf{P}_z)$,

(17dist) $\hat{x}[(y)(y \in x \leftrightarrow \mathbf{BT}y)](\{z : \mathbf{P}_z\})$.

Now (17coll) is equivalent to

(17coll.eq) $(\exists x)((y)(\mathbf{BT}y \leftrightarrow y = x) \ \& \ \hat{w}(w = \mathbf{SUM}_z\mathbf{P}_z)!(x))$,

which has the form of a $Z[q, I]$-formula for (1a) in which the abstract $\hat{w}(w = \mathbf{SUM}_z\mathbf{P}_z)$ might be an important predicate of a group (a person-sum). So our theory has no trouble explaining why (18) might imply (1a) when the embedded clause (17) is taken *collectively*, as in (17coll). This is just what we would intuitively expect: If a *group purchase* was the only purchase, then John's ability to identify the purchasing group as such-and-such a person-sum should count as his knowing who bought tickets relative to any purpose for which "being such-and-such a person-sum" is an important predicate. Similarly, (17coll), by the normal definition of "sum of things which are F," entails

(17coll.con) $(\exists x)((y)(y = \mathbf{SUM}_z\mathbf{BT}_z \leftrightarrow y = x) \ \& \ \hat{w}(w = \mathbf{SUM}_z\mathbf{P}_z)!(x))$,

which has the form of a $Z[q, I]$-formula for the collective reading of (2) in which the abstract $\hat{w}(w = \mathbf{SUM}_z\mathbf{P}_z)$ might be an important predicate of a person-sum. So our theory can explain why (18) might imply (2) when *both* are taken collectively. Again, this appears to us to be the intuitively desired result.

But what about the *distributive* reading of (18), i.e., where the embedded clause is taken as in (17dist)? Expression (17dist) is equivalent to $(y)(\mathbf{P}y \leftrightarrow \mathbf{BT}y)$. But even if we generously conjoin $(\exists x)\mathbf{P}x$, the result falls far short of what is needed to obtain a $Z[q, I]$-formula for (1a), since it *neither enumerates nor identifies* the *members* of $\{z : \mathbf{BT}z\}$. So our theory does *not* predict that (18), taken distributively, implies (1a). Knowing that all and only Podunkian bachelors bought tickets is pretty clearly insufficient for knowing *who* bought them, since it is compatible with not knowing who anyone is! Does (18) taken distributively imply (2)? Certainly not if (2) is taken distributively, since on that reading (2) is equivalent to (1a)! But (18) taken distributively might imply the *collective* reading of (2), at least if we assume that there are some Podunkian bachelors. The expression $(\exists x)[\mathbf{P}x \,\&\, (y)(\mathbf{P}y \leftrightarrow \mathbf{BT}y)]$, given the usual definitions, entails $(\exists x)(x = \mathbf{SUM}_z\mathbf{BT}_z \,\&\, x = \mathbf{SUM}_z\mathbf{P}_z)$, which is equivalent to (17 coll.con), a $Z[q, I]$-formula for the collective reading of (2). Thus we allow for the intuitive sense in which knowing that all and only Podunkian bachelors bought tickets, though insufficient for knowing who bought tickets, might (for appropriate group-oriented purposes) be sufficient for knowing who the ticket-buyers (collectively) are. We trust that these examples have convinced the reader that our theory has nothing to fear from such collective/distributive ambiguities.

4.4 The Problem of Promiscuous Predicates: The Revised Postulate for
THE-WHO-OF-IT
Matters are complicated by the existence of predicates that are, so to speak, "promiscuous" with respect to individuals and sums of individuals (cf. Goodman's discussion of "collective" and "cumulative" predicates[17]). Locative predicates like "lives in China" apply not only to individual persons but also to all sums of persons satisfying them. Our strategy of invoking person-sums as honorary persons backfires unless we can somehow allow that an answer to "Who lives in China?" can be adequate without having identify each person living in China *and* each person-sum dwelling therein! The problem here is that of allowing for *interest*-relative fusing and dissecting of the literal satisfiers themselves. It appears, then, that a suitable candidate for the role of purpose coordinate of an index must be capable of determining, in the case of promiscuous predicates, a certain subset of the literal satisfiers as the contextually salient *units* for individual identification.

In the case of a one-place promiscuous predicate such as "lives in China," we want something that takes the totality of persons and person-sums living in China into a subset of such persons and/or person-sums that is "exhaustive" in the sense that any individual person living in China is identical with or is a part of some element of the subset. (Such a subset might, e.g., simply be the set of individual persons living in China, or it might consist entirely of person-sums constructed in terms of ethnic and geographical properties, etc.) In the case of a two-place promiscuous predicate such as "inhabits the same country as," we want something that takes the totality of relevant pairs of persons/person-sums into a subset of such pairs that is exhaustive in the extended sense that, for any pair $\langle a, b \rangle$ of individual persons in the parent set, there is a pair $\langle c, d \rangle$ in the subset such that a is or is part of c and b is or is part of d, and so on in obvious fashion for n-place promiscuous predicates. This is clearly a job for a *"regrouping" function* from sets of finite sequences of persons and/or person-sums (e.g. the "satisfiers" in the $Z[q, I]$ sets) to suitably exhaustive subsets thereof. Since the intuitive idea is clear enough, we forego the tedious formal characterization of such functions and take the general notion of a regrouping function as understood.

The questions now: How should we amend our account of the P-coordinate of indices to accommodate regrouping functions, and what effect does this alteration have on our original formulation of the denotation postulate for **THE-WHO-OF-IT**, which deliberately ignored promiscuous predicates? Earlier, we treated the P-coordinate as a function from n-ary abstracts to admissible monadic predicates in $\mathbf{P}^+$; now we must treat P as a pair $\langle P_1, P_2 \rangle$ consisting of such a function P_1 from n-ary abstracts together with some regrouping function P_2.

The denotation postulate for **THE-WHO-OF-IT** must now be modified to reflect the fact that the indexically specified regrouping function comes into play when and only when promiscuous predicates (abstracts) are involved. However, this in turn forces us to modify our notion of a $Z[q, I]$-formula for the case in which the abstract q is a promiscuous predicate. The reason is simple: Although it is true that the "regrouped" sequences are all "satisfiers" of the promiscuous abstract, it is *false* that *only* they are such (unless, of course, the regrouping function was simply the identity function); but what is known-true must *be* true.

The required changes are relatively simple. Let us retroactively introduce into the canonical idiom a predicate-modifying device Π and stipulate that $\mathbf{P}^+$ contains, in addition to primitive predicates in $\mathbf{P}$ and predicate abstracts q, each modified predicate abstract $\Pi(q)$. The workings of Π are captured in the following postulate.

> For any n-ary regimented abstract q, denumerable sequence z and index I such that $P_I = \langle P_1, P_2 \rangle$:
>
> $\mathbf{F}^+\text{SAT}_I(z, \Pi(q)(v_1, \ldots, v_n))$ iff
> $\mathbf{F}^+\text{SAT}_I(z, q(v_1, \ldots, v_n))$ and
> $\langle \mathbf{T}^+\text{DEN}_I(z, v_1), \ldots, \mathbf{T}^+\text{DEN}_I(z, v_n) \rangle \in P_2(Z[q, I])$.

Intuitively, something of the form $\Pi(\hat{\mathbf{x}}_1 \ldots \hat{\mathbf{x}}_n(A))$ can be read as "is an n-tuple *of the contextually salient sort* such that A," where P_2 determines what these sorts are. We then define the appropriate analog of the set $Z[q, I]$—viz.,

$Z[\Pi(q), I] = \{\langle a_1, \ldots, a_n \rangle : a_1, \ldots, a_n$ are persons or person-sums and for some denumerable sequence z, $z_i = a_i$ $(1 \leqslant i \leqslant n)$ and $\mathbf{F}^+\mathrm{SAT}_I(z, \Pi(q)(\mathbf{x}_1, \ldots, \mathbf{x}_n))\}$.

By simple substitution in the definition of $Z[q, I]$-formulas—together with a change in clause (iv) of that definition to read "$A' = \Pi(q)(v_1^0, \ldots, v_n^0)'$"—we obtain the parallel notion of $Z[\Pi(q), I]$-formulas.

These adjustments having been made, we can amend the denotation postulate for **THE-WHO-OF-IT** along the following lines. Where z is any denumerable sequence, $I = \langle u, t, C, D, E, P \rangle$, $P = \langle P_1, P_2 \rangle$ and $E(h) = \langle M_h, q_h \rangle$ for some regimented closed n-ary abstract q_h:

1. If $M_h = \mathrm{CON}$ and q_h is not promiscuous, then $\mathbf{T}^{++}\mathrm{DEN}_I(z,$ **THE-WHO-OF-IT**$_h) = $ that function W_{CON}^h from utterer–time pairs $\langle u', t' \rangle$ to sets of closed $\mathbf{F}^+$-formulas such that $W_{\mathrm{CON}}^h(\langle u', t' \rangle) = \{A \in \mathbf{F}^+$: For some $J \in \mathbf{F}^+$, $[J$ is a $Z[q_h, I']$-formula for $I' = \langle u', t', C, D, E, P \rangle]$ & [each F_j^i is in $P_1(q_h)]$ & $[A$ plays for u' the same conceptual role modulo C that J plays for $u]\}$; and

2. If $M_h = \mathrm{SEM}$ and q_h is not promiscuous, then $\mathbf{T}^{++}\mathrm{DEN}_I(z,$ **THE-WHO-OF-IT**$_h) = $ that function W_{SEM}^h from utterer–time pairs $\langle u', t' \rangle$ to sets of closed $\mathbf{F}^+$-formulas such that $W_{\mathrm{SEM}}^h(\langle u', t' \rangle) = \{A \in \mathbf{F}^+$: For some regimented abstract $q' \in \mathbf{P}^+$, $[q'$ plays for u' at t' the same semantical role as $q_h]$ & $[A$ is a $Z[q', I']$-formula for $I' = \langle u', t', C, D, E, P \rangle$ in which each F_j^i is in $P_1(q')]\}$; and

3. If $M_h = \mathrm{CON}$ and q_h is promiscuous, then $\mathbf{T}^{++}\mathrm{DEN}_I(z,$ **THE-WHO-OF-IT**$_h) = $ that function W_{CON}^h from utterer–time pairs $\langle u', t' \rangle$ to sets of closed $\mathbf{F}^+$-formulas such that $W_{\mathrm{CON}}^h(\langle u', t' \rangle) = \{A \in \mathbf{F}^+$: For some $J \in \mathbf{F}^+$, $[J$ is a $Z[\Pi(q_h), I']$-formula for $I' = \langle u', t', C, D, E, P \rangle]$ & [each F_j^i is in $P_1(q_h)]$ & $[A$ plays for u' the same conceptual role modulo C that J plays for $u]\}$; and

4. If $M_h = \mathrm{SEM}$ and q_h is promiscuous, then $\mathbf{T}^{++}\mathrm{DEN}_I(z,$ **THE-WHO-OF-IT**$_h) = $ that function W_{SEM}^h from utterer–time pairs $\langle u', t' \rangle$ to sets of closed $\mathbf{F}^+$-formulas such that $W_{\mathrm{SEM}}^h(\langle u', t' \rangle) = \{A \in \mathbf{F}^+$: For some regimented abstract $q' \in \mathbf{P}^+$, $[q'$ plays for u' at t' the same semantical role as $q_h]$ & $[A$ is a $Z[\Pi(q'), I']$-formula for $I' = \langle u', t', C, D, E, P \rangle$ in which each F_j^i is in $P_1(q')]\}$.

Apart from strengthening the theory to deal with promiscuous "who" clauses, these revisions have no effect on our earlier discussions of ascriptions of "knowing who." It is worthwhile pointing out that the crucial purpose-relative implicative relation between certain opaquely construed knows-that attributions and corresponding knows-who attributions is preserved even when the latter involve promiscuous "who" clauses. Consider, e.g., sentences (19) and (20):

(19) John knows that the Abnegonians alone live on Misery Island.

(20) John knows who lives on Misery Island.

Let us suppose that the individual persons living on Misery Island are exactly the Abnegonians. Since "lives on Misery Island" is a promiscuous predicate, it also applies to any sum of individuals living there, such as, e.g., the Abnegonians themselves (i.e., the Abnegonian-sum), families of Abnegonians, Abnegonian political parties, etc. Now it is important to see that our theory—which allowed that (18) on its collective reading might imply (1a) relative to certain purposes—also allows, in its newly expanded form, the parallel result that the collective reading of (19) might similarly imply (20).

The key is provided by the word "alone" in (19). For it is, of course, strictly *false* that the Abnegonians taken collectively (i.e., their sum) is the *sole* inhabitant of the island! Hence John cannot *know* any such thing. Thus, in the intuitive sense in which (19) might relative to certain purposes non-vacuously imply (20), (19) must be taken as elliptical for something like (19^+):

(19^+) John knows that the Abnegonians alone *are a contextually salient group who* live on Misery Island.

Given what has been said so far, it is natural to think of the complement of (19^+) as having a logical form something like

$$(\exists y)[(v)[\Pi(\hat{x}_i(\textbf{Lives on}(x_i, \textbf{Misery Island})))(v) \leftrightarrow v = y]$$
$$\& \ \hat{w}(w = \textbf{SUM}_z\textbf{Abnegonians}_z)!(y)],$$

where the purpose-relative predicate modifier Π does the job of the italicized qualification in (19^+). But then our expanded theory straightforwardly allows that $(19)/(19^+)$ might imply (20)—i.e., relative to indices I specifying the salience of conceptual roles and purposes for which $\hat{w}(w = \textbf{SUM}_z\textbf{Abnegonians}_z)$ is an important predicate vis-à-vis $\hat{x}_i(\textbf{Lives on}(x_i, \textbf{Misery Island}))$.

We have encountered here a way in which knows-that constructions can be taken as purpose relative when their complements contain promiscuous predicates. No doubt other sorts of purpose-relative items might occur in "that" clauses, and there is even the possibility that the verb "knows" itself might evince some such teleological relativity in ways that would allow us to bring our treatments of **THAT** and **THE-WHO-OF-IT** closer together, perhaps even to absorb both into some single, more primitive construction. But this is a project for another occasion.[18]

4.5 Offices and Office-Holders

In chapter 2 we curtly dismissed as irrelevant that species of "knowing who" which concerns knowledge of definitions rather than of the identities of particular persons. The complaint was that a sentence such as

(21) John knows who the Pope is

has a reading in which "the Pope" is neither attributive nor referential in the ordinary way, and that this reading is adequately paraphrased by the likes of "John knows what a Pope is" or "John knows what 'the Pope' means," neither of which ascribes knowledge of anyone's identity. The same feature is found in sentences that lack definite singular terms, such as

(22) John knows who appoints Cardinals,

which could be read as ascribing to John some knowledge concerning the powers of the Papacy—knowledge he could well possess while remaining ignorant of the identity of any person who has ever appointed a Cardinal.

Although we continue to regard these "institutional" readings of sentences such as (21) and (22) as peripheral, it is worth pointing out—if only to quiet possible suspicions of a one-sided diet of cases—that we can accommodate such readings with only slight augmentation of our current theory. We would have to provide alternate underlying structures (say, **THE Pope** as contrasted with $(\imath x)$**Pope**(x)) for the institutional or "office" reading of a description as opposed to the normal "personal" reading. (Since office terms of this sort are essentially *titles*, we suppose that the structures in question are finite in number.)[19] Indices would be expanded to include a Q-coordinate, where Q is a function assigning to each of the titular terms of the canonical idiom a finite (and presumably consistent) set of properties, the latter being the basic powers that constitutively devolve on the title's bearer. (In the case of group titles, $Q(T)$ might be thought of as a set of properties of person-sums.) An office term T would accordingly be said to denote at an expanded index $\langle u, t, Q, C, D, E, P \rangle$ that nonempty set $Cl(Q(T))$ of properties which is the closure under property entailment of $Q(T)$.[20] Q defines the title T, in effect, and $Cl(Q(T))$ stands as the "office" corresponding to T thus defined. To provide for structural disambiguation of "who" clauses corresponding to the dual readings of sentences such as (21) and (22), our canonical idiom would be suitably enriched.[21] Finally, our account of important predicates might be supplemented by some restrictions on the form of such predicates appropriate to the case at hand (e.g., that important office predicates must have such forms as $\hat{x}(\textbf{INC}(\lambda y(\ldots y \ldots), x)$ or $\hat{x}(x = T)$ for some official title T).

With all these emendations in place, our theory readily extends to cover the desired readings of (21) and (22), which require respectively that John should know-true a : G!(**THE Pope**) : and that he should know-true a : The F alone appoints Cardinals: for suitable important office predicates "G" and "F." (Here, either "G" or "F" might correspond, e.g., to $\hat{x}(\mathbf{INC}(\lambda y(y \text{ rules the Roman Catholic Church}), x)$, or "F" to $\hat{x}(x = \mathbf{THE\ Pope})$, etc.) The "definitional" character of what must be known in these cases is reflected in the fact that the truth value of an important "office" predication is determined solely by what properties count in context as conventionally constituting the relevant office. There is still room for teleological relativity, however, since depending on one's purposes, some of an office's associated powers or titles may be more pertinent than others (the Presidency of the United States is a good example here).

One benefit of extending our apparatus in the foregoing way is the concomitant ability to handle sentences such as

(23) John knows who Napoleon became,

which are most naturally heard as attributing knowledge of what important office(s) came to be occupied. (Sentence (23) thus differs from the much weaker "John knows *what* Napoleon became," which might be true for certain purposes simply in virtue of John's knowing that Napoleon was imprisoned on Elba.) If we think of the logical form of "who Napoleon became" as something like $\hat{x}(\mathbf{CAME\ ABOUT}(\mathbf{BE\ IN}(\mathbf{Napoleon}, x)$—where **BE IN** denotes a relation between a person and an office that obtains when the former exemplifies all the properties in the latter—then the intuitively desired truth condition for (23) is readily forthcoming.

We hasten to add that a parallel treatment of "knowing who" as regards *fictional* characters would be inappropriate. Offices, whether construed in the foregoing fashion or as world lines in the manner of Hintikka, are abstract entities that are just as real as their occasional occupants. Transparently occurring office names are clearly open to existential generalization. Moreover, there is an obvious empty/nonempty distinction for office names: Offices, once "created," can also be abolished, and consequently, the corresponding title (such as "Holy Roman Emperor") becomes an empty office name, i.e., one with which no currently sanctioned powers are associated. None of this applies to the likes of "Sherlock Holmes" and "Superman," which are merely semantically empty, make-believe names.

The reader will long ago have noticed our scrupulous avoidance of knows-who locutions involving "I" or "he himself" ("she herself," etc.) in the "who" clause. Moreover, there is another category of "who" clauses about which we have said nothing whatever, viz., *infinitival* "who" clauses of the sort exemplified in

(24) John knows whom to thank for the gift.

In general, attributions of the form "X knows who(m) to VP" (VP = verb phrase) seem paraphrasable without loss of meaning by "X knows whom he himself/she herself is to VP." So an account of reflexive third-person attributions of "knowing who" would seem to be a prerequisite for bringing the likes of (24) within the scope of our theory. But such locutions pose distinctive problems of their own, which in turn are merely special cases of more general difficulties attending the analysis of ascriptions of self-regarding (*"de se"*) propositional attitudes. We bring our theory to bear on these issues in chapter 6, after making some observations about the more general difficulties, but first we must address the more tractable matter of ascriptions *de re*.

Chapter 5

De Re Attitude Ascriptions

Our picture would not be complete without an account of *de re* belief, *de re* attitude ascriptions, and the relation between the two, especially since *de re* belief and "knowing who" are almost universally thought of as closely connected. We offer such an account and argue that the alleged connection is actually quite feeble.

In case any reader is not already aware of the fact, we should mention that philosophers' treatment of belief *de re* over the past decade is a disgusting mess. We doubt that any two contributors to the literature have used the expression *"de re"* in just the same way; between terminological confusion and substantive divergence of theoretical goals and interests, writers on this topic have spent most of their time and ink talking past each other. For this reason one might want to urge a total moratorium on the use of the term *"de re"* and its apparent antonym *"de dicto,"* the moratorium perhaps backed by the death penalty or at least mutilation followed by transportation to Yazoo City, Mississippi. We have considerable sympathy with this proposal, ourselves. Yet we persist, perhaps against our better judgment, in thinking that the phenomena that have occasioned talk of *de re* belief are manifestations of something about believers that is worth tracking down and taking seriously.

1 Initial Data

Our two-scheme theory of content ascription predicts a systematic ambiguity in belief ascriptions, and we have argued that this prediction is confirmed in a way that allowed us to resolve anomalies such as Kripke's Puzzle.[1] For purposes of this chapter, however, we focus our attention on the truth-conditional individuation scheme, for it is appeal to that scheme rather than to the inferential or computational scheme that creates issues about *de re* belief.

What, now, can we say about the *aboutness* of beliefs? A great advantage of the representationalist theory is that in assimilating belief states to linguistic items it allows us to understand their aboutness as being of a piece with that of sentences. Sentences are about objects and states of affairs by containing referring terms that denote those objects and states of affairs; thus if belief states have quasisyntactic and quasisemantic structures of the sort we have suggested, it is natural to suppose that their aboutness too consists in their having referring terms as elements, which denote things in the world (though the referential relations here are admittedly problematic in that they are unmediated by the sorts of convention that do and must figure in public linguistic reference).

As a first pass, then, let us say that a thought or belief is about an object X if and only if it is a case of its subject's hosting (in the appropriate way) a representation containing a "singular term" or individual concept that semantically denotes X, "denote" here being interpreted as broadly as Frege might have intended it. Thus if Ralph says to himself, "The Swan Valley is in Western Australia," his thought is about the Swan Valley, and if Jane says to herself, "The first baby born in the Northern Territory must have had a hard life," her thought is about whichever person was that baby (we do not know if anyone knows who it was) and is true or false according to whether that person did in fact have a hard life.

So far, so good. But readers of Quine's "Quantifiers and propositional attitudes"[2] know that the matter of aboutness only begins here, even if we accept representationalism and all its abundant benefits and advantages, for there seems to be at least one stronger notion of aboutness that is not captured by the fairly liberal criterion we have just formulated. Indeed, that there is such a notion is suggested just by the fact that "believe-that" surface-grammatically functions as a sentence operator, for a sentence operator has scope, and so can give rise to a scope distinction when mixed either with singular terms or with quantifiers:

(1) a. Jane believes that the first baby born in the Northern Territory had a hard life.

   b. The first baby born in the Northern Territory is such that Jane believes it to have had a hard life.

(2) a. Jane believes that there are black swans in Brisbane.

   b. There are things which Jane believes {are/to be} black swans in Brisbane.

   c. There are black swans which Jane believes {are/to be} in Brisbane.

Sentences (1a) and (1b) differ in meaning, as do (2a), (2b), and (2c). Notoriously, Quine offered the following *Ur*-examples:

(3) I want a sloop

is ambiguous. Is there a particular sloop that I want or am I seeking "mere relief from slooplessness":

(3r) $(\exists x)(x$ is a sloop and I wish that I have x),

(3d) I wish $(\exists x)(x$ is a sloop and I have x)..

Suppose too that (the now world-famous character) Ralph is aware that espionage is prevalent and also thinks that no two people are of exactly the same height. Then, being a competent logician and a bit of a pedant, Ralph idly forms the redundant belief that the shortest spy is a spy, having no idea which person that might be. As Quine puts it, Ralph has no suspect; there is no one in particular whom Ralph believes to be a spy. That is, although

(4d) Ralph believes that $(\imath x)(x$ is the shortest spy) is a spy

is unexcitingly true,

(4r) $(\imath x)(x$ is the shortest spy) is a y such that Ralph believes that y is a spy

is false. Note that the singular term in (4r) occurs transparently; if the shortest spy *were* suspected or believed in particular by Ralph to be a spy and Tatiana is in fact the shortest spy, then Tatiana is Ralph's suspect whether he knows her name or not. We would claim also, although this is at least mildly controversial, that (4d) would be true whether there were any spies at all (much less a shortest spy), whereas (4r) entails the actual existence of a shortest spy and expresses a relation between Ralph and that person.

The relevance of all this to our proposed criterion of aboutness is that, although according to that criterion Ralph has a belief about Tatiana, there is an important sense in which his belief is not *about* Tatiana in particular at all. Intuitively, it is a fully *general* belief, tautologously inferred from the bare existence of espionage and the claim that any two people differ in height. Tatiana herself is related to Ralph by his belief *only* in that by sheer coincidence she uniquely satisfies the matrix of the description occurring in his representation. The representation seems a perfect instance of Russell's theory of descriptions: It is equivalent to the bare thesis that there exists a spy shorter than every other spy. Thus Ralph's belief could be true *whether or not Tatiana even existed*, so long as there are other spies and one of them is shorter than all the others. To put the point in possible-worlds jargon, Ralph's belief is true in any world containing *a* shortest spy, whether or not Tatiana herself inhabits that world. And it is at least in this sense that his belief is not *about* her.

Quine speaks of "relational" as opposed to merely "notional" belief and assimilates this difference to the medieval distinction between modalities *de re* and modalities *de dicto*. Just as

(5d) Necessarily, all tall spies are tall

fails to imply

(5r) All tall spies are necessarily tall

(since any actual tall spy you mention might have been short instead of tall),

(6d) Ralph believes that all tall spies are tall

fails to imply

(6r) All tall spies are {believed by Ralph to be/such that Ralph believes that they are} tall,

since none of the actual tall spies is an object of Ralph's attention; he has never heard of any of them. These data seem both hard and significant. The problem is to say what is needed for *de re* formulations, such as (1b), (2b), (2c), (3r), (4r), (5r), and (6r), to be true in addition to their bland *de dicto* counterparts.[3]

It should be noted that one recent philosophical tradition, inaugurated by Ernest Sosa and Mark Pastin among others[4] and called latitudinarianism, repudiates the stronger sort of aboutness illustrated here and emphasizes the weaker sort that we have already granted. Indeed, latitudinarians have spent a good deal of energy defending aboutness of the weaker sort *as* aboutness, unnecessarily in our opinion. What is more distinctive and remarkable about their position is that they want to deny the falsity of our *de re* formulations in the circumstances imagined. If they are to make this denial convincing they must somehow explain away the appearances, i.e., they must show why the *de re* formulations seem false and would be expected to seem false even though in reality they are true. The most obvious way of doing this is to appeal to independently justified principles of conversation à la Grice, but we have seen no very convincing instance of this strategy. Note too that

(7) Ralph believes that espionage is prevalent, but he does not suspect anyone in particular

is noncontradictory, so there must be *some* stronger belief relation than the latitudinarian is willing to grant.[5] For these reasons we presume the falsity of latitudinarianism for the purposes of this chapter, though we advert to the view from time to time.

Investigators have supposed that some one factor or complex of factors is required for *de re* belief over and above minimal aboutness, though they have admitted both that no such factor stands uncontroversially in view and that the correct one, whatever it is, may well turn out to be messy and perhaps highly interest relative. We think instead that there is a sequence of discriminable *grades* of aboutness; we distinguish and discuss them in section 3 below, but first let us say how our paratactic construal of attitude ascriptions extends to explicitly *de re* attributions.

2 De Re Attitude Ascriptions and "Knowing Who"

Consider

(8) John believes, of Tom, that he is a fool.

Here we face two obstacles. The paratactic strategy bifurcates belief and knowledge attributions at the level of logical form and thus raises the question of how an anaphoric pronoun in the display component (e.g., "he" in (8)) can be semantically related to its grammatical antecedent in the assertive component (e.g., "Tom" in (8)). Then too there is the problem of representing the vaunted "*de re* connection" between subject and object in a way that accommodates as comfortably as possible the diversity of intuitions that philosophers have expressed about where to draw the line that marks this connection. (Again, a critical review of these intuitions and general advice about drawing the line follow in section 3.)

2.1 Parataxis and Anaphora: Expanding Earlier Definitions and Postulates
To implement our paratactic strategy in the case of *de re* attitude ascriptions, it is necessary to make a modest assumption about anaphoric pronouns, such as "he" in (8), and a small retroactive modification in our earlier treatment of **BELIEVE** and **KNOW**. Since our account treats (8) as the parataxis ⟨"John believes, of Tom, that", ⟨"he is a fool"⟩⟩, we cannot take the usual route of regarding "he" as the reflection of a variable v that is bound by "Tom" (e.g., after the fashion of $(\exists v)(v = \textbf{Tom} \ \& \ \ldots v \ldots)$ or $(\textbf{Tom}_v)(\ldots v \ldots)$ or the like). Accordingly, we take such "dangling" anaphoric pronouns as reflections of *free* variables in logical form. (If we were including deictic pronouns in logical form, they would have to be represented by expressions other than ordinary free variables, and we would add an extra coordinate to indices that fixes their denotation at those indices.) Our earlier convention about regimentation ensures that "he" in "he is a fool" reflects x_1. (Purely for convenience we do not bother to distinguish among "he," "she," and "it.") Consequently, we can represent the logical form of "he is a fool" as it occurs in (8) by $\textbf{Fool}(x_1)$.

What about the logical form of "John believes, of Tom, that"? Our provisional, dyadic rendering of **BELIEVE** and **KNOW** provides no room for any analog of "of Tom." For this reason we retroactively stipulate that

BELIEVE and **KNOW** are (and always were) *triadic* predicates and that the logical forms of "John believes that" and "John believes, of Tom, that" are (9) and (10), respectively:

    (9)   **BELIEVE(John, $\langle$ $\rangle$, THAT$_1$)**,

    (10) **BELIEVE(John, $\langle$Tom$\rangle$, THAT$_1$)**.

($\langle$ $\rangle$, of course, names the empty sequence; we assume that the canonical idiom employs set-theoretic term-forming operators and that the truth theory specifies the appropriate sets as denotata of such terms.) To make sense of (9) and (10) we obviously must adjust our earlier, provisional account of the denotations of **BELIEVE**, **THAT**, and **FACTTHAT**. Let us begin with **THAT**.

In order to provide room for varying opinions on the minimum "grade" of involvement required for having a "genuine" *de re* attitude, let us employ "relation R obtains between an occurrence of term T (in a formula A) and the object a for utterer u at t" as a dummy phrase ultimately to be filled in by the reader's own choice of options from section 3 below. In the interim, and purely for the sake of definiteness, we officially unpack the dummy phrase as follows: An occurrence $/T/$ of a term $T \in \mathbf{T}^+$ in a formula $A \in \mathbf{F}^+$ *bears R to object a for u at t* iff T is a closed term such that either (i) $/T/$ lies in A outside the scope of any tense operator and $\mathbf{T}^+\mathrm{DEN}_I(z, T) = a$ for any denumerable sequence z and index I in which $u_I = u$ and $t_I = t$; or (ii) $\mathbf{T}^+\mathrm{DEN}_{I'}(z, T) = a$ for any denumerable sequence z and index I' in which $u_I = u$. (As we see in section 2.3 below, even this weak denotational construal has interesting consequences within our framework; the reader who is willing to take the technical adjustments on faith should skip to the penultimate paragraph of section 2.2.)

Now we may retroactively insert at stage 2 the following definition:

> DEFINITION. Where g is an n-ary sequence ($n \geqslant 0$), b is a person, A, $A' \in \mathbf{F}^+$, $T_1, \ldots, T_k$ are closed terms in $\mathbf{T}^+$ ($n \leqslant k \leqslant n + 1$), and I is an index, A' is a (g, b)-*substitution instance of A at I under* $T_1, \ldots, T_k$ iff (i) A contains free exactly the first k canonical variables $\mathbf{x}_1, \ldots, \mathbf{x}_k$; (ii) if $k = n$, no variable in A is starred, and if $k = n + 1$, then the star operator is applied in A to all and only occurrences of the $(n + 1)$th variable; (iii) $A' = A(T_1, \ldots, T_k/\mathbf{x}_1, \ldots, \mathbf{x}_k)$; and (iv) each term occurrence $/T/$ in A' answering to an occurrence $/\mathbf{x}_j/$ of the jth free variable in A is such that, for u_I at t_I, $/T/$ in A' bears R to b if $j = n + 1$ and to $g(j)$ if $1 \leqslant j \leqslant n$.

In practice, we treat "A' is a (g, b)-substitution instance of A at I" as shorthand for "There are closed terms $T_1, \ldots, T_k$ such that A' is a (g, b)-substitution instance of A under $T_1, \ldots, T_k$." Using this definition, we can adjust the stage 3 account of **THAT** along the following lines:

For any denumerable sequence z and index $I = \langle u, t, C, D, E, P \rangle$ in which $D = \langle \langle M_1, A_1 \rangle, \ldots, \langle M_i, A_i \rangle, \ldots \rangle$, if $M_i = \mathrm{CON}$, then $\mathbf{T}^{++}\mathrm{DEN}_I(z, \mathbf{THAT}_i) =$ that function d^i_{CON} from pairs of utterer–time pairs $\langle u', t' \rangle$ and n-ary sequences g $(n \geqslant 0)$ to sets of closed $\mathbf{F}^+$-formulas such that

$d^i_{\mathrm{CON}}(\langle \langle u', t' \rangle, g \rangle) = \{A \in \mathbf{F}^+ \colon A$ is a (g, u)-substitution instance at $\langle u', t', C, D, E, P \rangle$ of some $A' \in \mathbf{F}^+$ that plays for u' the same conceptual role modulo C that A_i plays for $u\}$; and

if $M_i = \mathrm{SEM}$, then $\mathbf{T}^{++}\mathrm{DEN}_I(z, \mathbf{THAT}_i) =$ that function d^i_{SEM} from pairs of utterer–time pairs $\langle u', t' \rangle$ in which $t' = t$ and n-ary sequences g $(n \geqslant 0)$ to sets of closed $\mathbf{F}^+$-formulas such that

$d^i_{\mathrm{SEM}}(\langle \langle u', t' \rangle, g \rangle) = \{A \in \mathbf{F}^+ \colon A$ is a (g, u)-substitution instance at $\langle u', t', C, D, E, P \rangle$ of some $A' \in \mathbf{F}^+$ that plays for u' at t' the same semantical role as $A_i\}$.

The appropriate adjustment to the stage 3 account of **FACTTHAT** follows suit; thus

For any denumerable sequence z and index $I = \langle u, t, C, D, E, P \rangle$ in which $D = \langle \langle M_1, A_1 \rangle, \ldots, \langle M_i, A_i \rangle, \ldots \rangle$, if $M_i = \mathrm{CON}$, then $\mathbf{T}^{++}\mathrm{DEN}_I(z, \mathbf{FACTTHAT}_i) =$ that function f^i_{CON} from pairs of utterer–time pairs $\langle u', t' \rangle$ and n-ary sequences g $(n \geqslant 0)$ to sets of closed $\mathbf{F}^+$-formulas such that $f^i_{\mathrm{CON}}(\langle \langle u', t' \rangle, g \rangle) = \{A \in \mathbf{F}^+ \colon A$ is a (g, u)-substitution instance at $I' = \langle u', t', C, D, E, P \rangle$ of some $A' \in \mathbf{F}^+$ that plays for u' the same conceptual role modulo C that A_i plays for u & $\mathbf{F}^+\mathrm{TRUE}_{I'}(A)\}$, *provided that* $\mathbf{F}^+\mathrm{SAT}_{I'}(z', A_i)$ for every denumerable sequence z' such that g is an initial segment of z' and $z'(n + 1) = u$ if the $(n + 1)$th free variable is starred in A_i, and $f^i_{\mathrm{CON}}(\langle \langle u', t' \rangle, g \rangle) =$ the empty set, otherwise; and if $M_i = \mathrm{SEM}$, then $\mathbf{T}^{++}\mathrm{DEN}_I(z, \mathbf{FACTTHAT}_i) =$ that function f^i_{SEM} from pairs of utterer–time pairs $\langle u', t' \rangle$ in which $t' = t$ and n-ary sequences g $(n \geqslant 0)$ to sets of closed $\mathbf{F}^+$-formulas such that $f^i_{\mathrm{SEM}}(\langle \langle u', t' \rangle, g \rangle) = \{A \in \mathbf{F}^+ \colon A$ is a (g, u)-substitution instance at $I' = \langle u', t', C, D, E, P \rangle$ of some $A' \in \mathbf{F}^+$ that plays for u' at t' the same semantical role as $A_i\}$, *provided that* $\mathbf{F}^+\mathrm{SAT}_{I'}(z', A_i)$ for every denumerable sequence z' such that g is an initial segment of z' and $z'(n + 1) = u$ if the $(n + 1)$th free variable is starred in A_i, and $f^i_{\mathrm{SEM}}(\langle \langle u', t' \rangle, g \rangle) =$ the empty set, otherwise.

(If A_i is not n-ary, then our definitions ensure that the set in question is empty; this need not worry us in practice, since our account of the satisfaction conditions of PSUAs, together with our amended account of **BELIEVE** and **KNOW** below, forces us to look only at indices assigning an A_i with the appropriate number of free positions.)

The amended account of triadic **BELIEVE** can be formulated as follows, leaving a blank for those extra psychological conditions that do not concern us here:

> For any denumerable sequence z and index I, $\mathbf{P}^{++}\mathrm{DEN}_I$ $(z, \mathbf{BELIEVE}) = \lambda xyv[x$ is a person & y is a finite sequence & v is a function from pairs of utterer–time pairs and finite sequences to sets of closed $\mathbf{F}^+$-formulas & for some L and $\mathbf{F}^+$-SUA $\langle S, A \rangle$ of L, x at t_I tokens $\langle S, A \rangle$ in foro interno & $A \in v(\langle \langle x, t_I \rangle, y \rangle)$ & ...].

The amended account of triadic **KNOW** follows the same pattern.

2.2 Truth Conditions and Dot Glosses

Without sloshing through the details, it should be clear that the generalized account includes the earlier one as a special case, i.e., the former reduces to the latter where empty sequences and closed $\mathbf{F}^+$-SUAs are concerned. The truth condition at an index of

(11) John believes that Tom is a fool

(= (1a) of chapter 4) is unchanged by the switch to triadic **BELIEVE** and the generalized denotation rules. What matters for present purposes is the effect on (8) above. Given what we have said so far, the appropriate reading for (8) *qua* English sentence is the PSUA $w = \langle \langle$ "John believes, of Tom, that", $\langle$ "he is a fool" $\rangle \rangle$, $\langle \mathbf{BELIEVE} \ (\mathbf{John}, \langle \mathbf{Tom} \rangle, \mathbf{THAT}_1)$, $\langle \mathbf{Fool}(\mathbf{x}_1) \rangle \rangle \rangle$. Let us quickly run through our revised semantics to see what truth condition for (8)/w emerges.

(8)/w is true at an index $I = \langle u, t, C, D, E, P \rangle$ iff w is true$_I$, i.e., iff every denumerable sequence z satisfies$_I$ w. By our new definitions and revised postulates, we have:

> [For all z, z satisfies$_I$ w] iff
> [For all z, $\mathbf{F}^{++}\mathrm{SAT}_{I'}(z, \mathbf{BELIEVE} \ (\mathbf{John}, \langle \mathbf{Tom} \rangle, \mathbf{THAT}_1))$ for each I' differing from I only in that $D_{I'}(1) = \langle M_1, \langle$ "he is a fool", $\mathbf{Fool}(\mathbf{x}_1) \rangle \rangle$, where M_1 is fixed as in $D(1)$] iff
> [For every such I' and z, $\langle \mathbf{T}^{++}\mathrm{DEN}_{I'}(z, \mathbf{John}), \mathbf{T}^{++}\mathrm{DEN}_{I'}$ $(z, \langle \mathbf{Tom} \rangle), \mathbf{T}^{++} \ \mathrm{DEN}_{I'}(z, \mathbf{THAT}_1) \rangle \in \mathbf{P}^{++}\mathrm{Ext}_{I'}(z, \mathbf{BELIEVE})]$ iff
> [$\langle$ John, $\langle$ Tom $\rangle$, $d_{M_1}^1 \rangle \in \{\langle x, y, v \rangle: x$ is a person & y is a finite sequence & v is a function ... & for some L and $\mathbf{F}^+$-SUA $\langle S, A \rangle$ of L, x at $t_{I'} \ (= t)$ tokens $\langle S, A \rangle$ in foro interno & $A \in v(\langle \langle x, t \rangle, y \rangle)$ etc.$\}$] iff
> [For some L and $\mathbf{F}^+$-SUA $\langle S, A \rangle$ of L, John believes-true $\langle S, A \rangle$ at t & $A \in d_{M_1}^1(\langle \langle$ John, $t \rangle, \langle$ Tom $\rangle \rangle)$].

Now if $M_1 = \mathrm{CON}$, then

$d^1_{M_1}(\langle\langle\mathrm{John}, t\rangle, \langle\mathrm{Tom}\rangle\rangle) = d^1_{\mathrm{CON}}(\langle\langle\mathrm{John}, t\rangle, \langle\mathrm{Tom}\rangle\rangle) = \{A \in \mathbf{F}^+:$ A is a $(\langle\mathrm{Tom}\rangle, u)$-substitution instance at $\langle\mathrm{John}, t, C, D, E, P\rangle$ of a unary open $\mathbf{F}^+$-formula A' that plays for John the same conceptual role modulo C that $\mathbf{Fool}(\mathbf{x}_1)$ plays for $u\}$.

And if $M_1 = \mathrm{SEM}$, then

$d^1_{M_1}(\langle\langle\mathrm{John}, t\rangle, \langle\mathrm{Tom}\rangle\rangle) = d^1_{\mathrm{SEM}}(\langle\langle\mathrm{John}, t\rangle, \langle\mathrm{Tom}\rangle\rangle) = \{A \in \mathbf{F}^+:$ A is a $(\langle\mathrm{Tom}\rangle, u)$-substitution instance at $\langle\mathrm{John}, t, C, D, E, P\rangle$ of a unary open $\mathbf{F}^+$-formula A' that plays for John at t the same semantical role as $\mathbf{Fool}(\mathbf{x}_1)\}$.

Consequently (and mercifully simplifying matters a bit), where I is an index marking conceptual role as salient,

(8)/w is true at I iff there is a formula $A(\mathbf{x}_1)$ whose behavior in John's language game is functionally equivalent to that of $\mathbf{Fool}(\mathbf{x}_1)$ in u_I's language game and John believes-true at t_I a sentence whose logical form is $A(T/\mathbf{x}_1)$ for some T whose occurrences therein bear R to Tom (for John).

And, where I is an index marking semantical role as salient,

(8)/w is true at I iff there is a formula $F(\mathbf{x}_1)$ which at t_I plays for John the same semantical role as—i.e., is extensionally isomorphic to— $\mathbf{Fool}(\mathbf{x}_1)$ and John believes-true a sentence whose logical form is $F(T)$ for some T whose occurrence therein bears R to Tom (for John).

Using dot quotes, we can give the following brief gloss:

(8) is true at I iff John believes-true at t_I a $(\langle\mathrm{Tom}\rangle, u_I)$-substitution instance at $\langle\mathrm{John}, t_I, C_I, D_I, E_I, P_I\rangle$ of a $\cdot$he is a fool.$\cdot$

Or, for short,

(8) is true at I iff John believes-true a $^{(\langle\mathrm{Tom}\rangle, u_I)}\mathrm{Sub}_{\langle\mathrm{John}, t_I\rangle}(\cdot$he is a fool$\cdot)$.

Given our minimal construal of R, the semantical properties of the $^{(\langle\mathrm{Tom}\rangle, u_I)}\mathrm{Sub}_{\langle\mathrm{John}, t_I\rangle}(\cdot$he is a fool$\cdot)$ in question are fixed but its conceptual role for John is not, since (apart from further constraints on R) there is no guarantee that John's predicating a conceptually individuated $\cdot$he is a fool$\cdot$ of Tom by means of some term whose occurrence in the relevant logical form bears R to Tom (for John at t_I) amounts to John's believing-true a conceptually individuated $\cdot$Tom is a fool$\cdot$ or anything of the sort.

What has been said regarding *de re* belief ascriptions extends mutatis mutandis to *de re* knowledge ascriptions. In glossing the truth conditions of the latter with colon quotes, however, we need to extend the device to open sentences in a way that harmonizes with our revised postulate for **FACTTHAT**. Accordingly, we stipulate that—where $a_1, \ldots, a_n$ are any objects, $\langle u, C, A \rangle$ is a partial utterance context for an open sentence "S," and $A \in \mathbf{F}^+$ contains free at least the first n and at most the first $(n + 1)$ canonical variables, the star operator being applied in A to all and only occurrences of the $(n + 1)$th variable (if any)—something is a $[a_1, \ldots, a_n]$:S: for u' at t' iff it is a ·S· for u' at t' such that $\mathbf{F}^+\mathrm{SAT}_I(z, A)$ for any index I in which $u_I = u'$ and $t_I = t'$ and any denumerable sequence z such that $\langle a_1, \ldots, a_n \rangle$ is an initial segment of z and $z(n + 1) = u$ if the $(n + 1)$th canonical variable is starred in A. Then we can say, e.g., that "John knows, of Tom, that he is a fool"—understood as having the paratactic logical form $\langle \mathbf{KNOW} \ (\mathbf{John}, \ \langle \mathbf{Tom} \rangle, \ \mathbf{FACTTHAT}_1), \ \langle \mathbf{Fool}(\mathbf{x}_1) \rangle \rangle$—is true at an index I iff John knows-true at t_I a $^{(\langle \mathrm{Tom} \rangle, u_I)}\mathrm{Sub}_{\langle \mathrm{John}, t_I \rangle}([\mathrm{Tom}]$:he is a fool:).

2.3 Flexibility and Neutrality

Our provisional requirement—that the underlying term occurrences should denote the object for the subject at the indicated time (in temporally rigid fashion if within the scope of a tense operator)—has immediate implications for latitudinarianism. In our weak, denotational construal there is nothing semantically special about *de re* attitude ascriptions, at least where semantical roles are at issue. Our theory dictates that (11) and (8)—given their obvious readings—are *truth-conditionally equivalent* at any index marking semantical role as salient, *provided* that R is equated in the foregoing way with denotation. At such indices, John's believing-true a ·Tom is a fool· and his believing-true a $^{(\langle \mathrm{Tom} \rangle, u_I)}\mathrm{Sub}_{\langle \mathrm{John}, t_I \rangle}(\cdot$ he is a fool·) come to exactly the same thing under our definition of sameness of semantical role! Of course our theory also provides for the truth-conditional divergence of (11) and (8) at indices marking *conceptual* role as salient, since, as we remarked two paragraphs back, the weak reading of R does not guarantee that a conceptually individuated $^{(\langle \mathrm{Tom} \rangle, u_I)}\mathrm{Sub}_{\langle \mathrm{John}, t_I \rangle}(\cdot$ he is a fool·) is a conceptually individuated ·Tom is a fool·. At such indices, (8) might be false, whereas (11) is true. Our two-schemes approach thus has the advantage of accommodating the latitudinarian's intuition that (11) and (8) sometimes seem to come to the same thing while simultaneously providing for the *contrary* intuition that sometimes (11) and (8) impose inequivalent conditions on the subject, and all this is accomplished relative to the weak, denotational reading of R! Similarly, our approach captures the latitudinarian feeling about the likes of (12) and (13) while at the same time accommodating opposing views:

(12) John believes that the shortest spy is a spy.

(13) John believes, of the shortest spy, that he is a spy.

If, at the common belief- and utterance-time, "the shortest spy" denotes someone, then, at indices marking semantical role, (12) and (13) impose the same condition on John; they may, however, diverge in truth value at indices marking conceptual role as salient, since, e.g., John may believe-true a conceptually individuated · The shortest spy is a spy · even if there are no spies at all.

The rapprochement effected by our minimal construal of R may seem excessively liberal to philosophers who fail to detect *any* sense in which mere facts about denotational convergence could warrant the move from (11) to (8) or from (12) to (13). We can accommodate them too. The domain of R might be restricted to occurrences of demonstrative terms and a special "demonstrated objects" coordinate added to indices and so defined that a demonstrative term denotes an object just in case the object is present and directly acting on the subject in certain ways. True *de re* ascriptions could thus be limited to cases in which the subject is in some sense "directly acquainted" with the object at the time in question,[6] or we might confine the domain of R to occurrences of terms that have in the subject's mouth a special sort of causal ancestry leading back to a successful dubbing of the object or perhaps to ancestral confrontations with the object itself; more on these options in section 3 below. Such a condition might be superadded to denotation or even made a part of the truth theory's account of denotation.

The availability in our theory of considerations of conceptual role permits even richer constraints. The domain of R might be restricted to occurrences of terms that not only denote the object for the subject but that also play some special sort of computational role in the subject's inner language game, either a role paralleling the ascriber's words or specified independently thereof. A "description theorist" might insist that the subject's term be computationally associated (if not identical) with some canonical definite description that denotes the object and that guides the subject's behavior in certain ways. Or, finally, one might adopt a view like Kaplan's, which incorporates restrictions of all these kinds: denotation (Kaplan's "resemblance"), special causal ancestry (Kaplan's "of-ness"), and special computational role (Kaplan's "vividness"). We hope that it is clear from these examples that our paratactic framework is compatible with virtually all the suggestions that have been made about the relative strength of the "*de re* connection" between subject and object. Since our account commits us to no particular understanding of R, we leave it to the reader to blend in his or her favorite extra ingredients.

2.4 *De Re Ascriptions of "Knowing Who"*

Two final points before we unleash our apparatus on *de re* ascriptions of "knowing who." We have avoided entanglement in the issue of the proper treatment of *empty* terms by supposing that the truth theory incorporates some device for dealing with them—e.g., the logic of the semantical metalanguage may be a free logic of the sort described by Burge ("Truth and Singular Terms"), allowing the truth theory to make nontoxic use of descriptions such as "the object assigned by z at I to **Zeus**" without generating unwanted entailments. The need for some such device is pressing in the present content, since, e.g., we want instances of "X believes, of N, that he/she/it is F" to be false when "N" is an empty singular term like "Santa Claus" or "the King of Alaska." This means that $\langle$**Santa Claus**$\rangle$ in, say, **BELIEVE** (**John**, $\langle$**Santa Claus**$\rangle$, **THAT**$_1$) must be interpretable in the truth theory by means of some metalinguistic phrase such as "the unary sequence whose only term is the object assigned by z at I to **Santa Claus**" and that the logic of the truth theory must enable us to show that the formula **BELIEVE** (**John**, $\langle$**Santa Claus**$\rangle$, **THAT**$_1$) is false when there is no object assigned by z at I to **Santa Claus**. Since all this can be accomplished by following a strategy like Burge's, we do not pursue the matter further here. In requiring such assistance, our paratactic approach is no worse than any other.

It is also noted that we have taken no special pains to provide for sentences of the form "X knows/believes, of $N_1, \ldots, N_k$, that Q," where "Q" contains more or less than k anaphoric pronouns. If we took such sentences seriously, we could make the obvious provisions for contracting sequences that are too long and for prolonging sequences that are too short. But we do not; so we take instead the short line that such sentences are simply ungrammatical and that a paratactic logical form such as $\langle$**BELIEVE** (**John**, $\langle N_1, \ldots, N_k \rangle$, **THAT**$_1$), $\langle A \rangle\rangle$ is ill-formed unless A contains exactly k distinct free variables (not counting starred variables, which—as we see later—do not correspond to anaphoric pronouns).

Finally we are able to formalize *de re* ascriptions of "knowing who." (As before, the reader concerned only with the upshot should skip to the final paragraph of this section.) Since triadic **KNOW** expresses a relation between a person, a sequence of objects, and a SUA (which is open in the appropriate number of places if the sequence is nonempty), we must somehow relate that sequence of objects to the structure of the SUA. Let us use the notation "$\hat{\mathbf{x}}_{m+1} \ldots \hat{\mathbf{x}}_{m+n}(A(\mathbf{x}_1 \ldots \mathbf{x}_m))$" to represent the general case of a regimented n-ary abstract containing free the first m (≥ 0) variables and having the next n (≥ 1) variables capped in the prefix and thereby internally bound. Our original definition of the set $Z[q, I]$ of n-ary "satisfying" sequences of persons for a regimented abstract q presupposed that q was closed; hence that definition must be extended to cover open abstracts when a particular sequence of objects provides the values of the free variables. When I is an index, g an m-ary sequence of objects ($m \geq 0$), and $q = \hat{\mathbf{x}}_{m+1} \ldots \hat{\mathbf{x}}_{m+n}(A(\mathbf{x}_1 \ldots \mathbf{x}_m))$, let

$Z[q, I, g] = \{\langle b_1, \ldots, b_n \rangle : b_1, \ldots, b_n$ are persons & for some denumerable sequence z, $z_i = g_i$ $(1 \leqslant i \leqslant m)$ & $z_{m+j} = b_j$ $(1 \leqslant j \leqslant n)$ & $\text{FSAT}_I(z, A)\}$.

Because of the possibility (heretofore deliberately ignored) that one of the free variables in A may be starred, receiving as its value some object b specified by the index in question rather than by the sequence g, we must extend the preceding definition as follows. When I is an index, g a finite sequence, b an individual, and q as above, we stipulate that

$$Z[q, I, \langle g, b \rangle] = \begin{cases} Z[q, I, g] \text{ if } q \text{ is } m\text{-ary and } A \text{ contains no starred variable;} \\ Z[q, I, \langle g(1), \ldots, g(m-1), b \rangle) \text{ if } m > 0, q \text{ is } (m-1)\text{-ary, and } \mathbf{x}_m \text{ is starred in } A; \\ \text{the empty set otherwise.} \end{cases}$$

Our original definition of $Z[q, I]$-formulas was designed to accommodate the eventual move from $Z[q, I]$ to $Z[q, I, \langle g, b \rangle]$: by the simple expedient of replacing mention of the former by mention of the latter in both definiendum and definiens, we have a ready-made definition of the set of $Z[q, I, \langle g, b \rangle]$-*formulas*. Our previous account of **THE-WHO-OF-IT** was in terms of a function from utterer–time pairs to sets of answer-formulas defined by means of $Z[q, I]$-formulas. The obvious emendation involves appeal to a function from utterer–time pairs *and* finite sequences to sets of (closed) answer-formulas, the latter now defined by means of $Z[q, I, \langle g, b \rangle]$-formulas, for $b = u_I$. We may thus take the following as our extended denotation postulate for **THE-WHO-OF-IT** (for simplicity, we ignore the complications occasioned by "promiscuous" abstracts): When z is any denumerable sequence, $I = \langle u, t, C, D, E, P \rangle$, and $E(h) = \langle M_h, q_h \rangle$ for some n-ary regimented abstract $q_h = \hat{\mathbf{x}}_{m+1}, \ldots, \hat{\mathbf{x}}_{m+n}(B(\mathbf{x}_1, \ldots, \mathbf{x}_m)) \in \mathbf{P}^+$ containing m free variables $(h, n \geqslant 1; m \geqslant 0)$: If $M_h = \text{CON}$, then

$\mathbf{T}^{++}\text{DEN}_I(z, \textbf{THE-WHO-OF-IT}_h) =$ that function W^h_{CON} from pairs of utterer–time pairs $\langle u', t' \rangle$ and finite sequences g to classes of $\mathbf{F}^+$-formulas such that $W^h_{\text{CON}}(\langle \langle u', t' \rangle, g \rangle) = \{A \in \mathbf{F}^+$: for some $J, A' \in \mathbf{F}^+$ and closed $T_1, \ldots, T_m \in \mathbf{T}^+$, J is a $Z[q_h, I', \langle g, u \rangle]$-formula for $I' = \langle u', t', C, D, E, P \rangle$, and A' plays for u' the same conceptual role modulo C that J plays for u, and A is a (g, u)-substitution instance of A' at I' under $T_1, \ldots, T_m$, and each F^i_j in J is in $P(\mathbf{x}_{m+1}, \ldots, \mathbf{x}_{m+n}(B(T_1, \ldots, T_m)))\}$;

and if $M_h = \text{SEM}$, then

$\mathbf{T}^{++}\text{DEN}_I(z, \textbf{THE-WHO-OF-IT}_h) =$ that function W^h_{SEM} from pairs of utterer–time pairs $\langle u', t' \rangle$ in which $t' = t$ and finite sequences g to classes of $\mathbf{F}^+$-formulas such that $W^h_{\text{SEM}}(\langle \langle u', t' \rangle, g \rangle) =$

$\{A \in \mathbf{F}^+$: for some regimented n-ary abstract $q = \hat{\mathbf{x}}_{m+1}, \ldots, \mathbf{x}_{m+n}$ $(B'(\mathbf{x}_1, \ldots, \mathbf{x}_m)) \in \mathbf{P}^+$, $A' \in \mathbf{F}^+$ and closed terms $T_1, \ldots, T_m \in \mathbf{T}^+$, q plays for u at t the same semantical role as q_h, and A is a $Z[q, I', \langle g, u \rangle]$-formula for $I' = \langle u', t', C, D, E, P \rangle$, and A is a (g, u)-substitution instance at I' of A' under $T_1, \ldots, T_m$, and each F_j^i in A' is in $P(\mathbf{x}_{m+1}, \ldots, \mathbf{x}_{m+n}(B'(T_1, \ldots, T_m)))\}$.

As expected, the original postulate for **THE-WHO-OF-IT** emerges as the special case in which g is the empty sequence, thus allowing us to treat *de dicto* knowing-who ascriptions as the limiting case.

We now see how our apparatus captures the intuition mentioned in section 3.5 of chapter 4 that (15) is more tendentious than is (14) regarding a linguistically impoverished being like Bertie (whose language lacks any singular terms save pure demonstratives):

(14) Bertie knows who Quine is.

(15) Bertie knows, of Quine, who he is.

The logical forms of (14) and (15) are, respectively, the paratactic structures

$$\langle \mathbf{KNOW\ (Bertie,} \langle \rangle, \mathbf{THE\text{-}WHO\text{-}OF\text{-}IT}_1), \langle \hat{\mathbf{x}}_1(\mathbf{x}_1 = \mathbf{Quine}) \rangle \rangle$$

and

$$\langle \mathbf{KNOW\ (Bertie,} \langle \mathbf{Quine} \rangle, \mathbf{THE\text{-}WHO\text{-}OF\text{-}IT}_1), \langle \hat{\mathbf{x}}_2(\mathbf{x}_2 = \mathbf{x}_1) \rangle \rangle,$$

where $\mathbf{x}_1$ in the latter is the free variable underlying the occurrence of the anaphoric pronoun "he" in (15). Sparing the reader the derivations and assuming the obvious readings for (14) and (15) in terms of the proffered logical forms, we can briefly state the upshot of these revisions as follows. When $I = \langle u, t, C, D, E, P \rangle$,

(14) is true at I iff Bertie knows-true at t a $:G!(Quine)$: for "G" reflecting a P important predicate.

and, where I' is like I except that $u_{I'} = $ Bertie,

(15) is true at I iff, for "G" reflecting an important predicate relative to P, Bertie knows-true at t a $^{\langle\langle Quine\rangle, u\rangle}Sub_{I'}([Quine]:G!(he):)$.

Unless Bertie can "demonstrate" Quine, she has no $(\langle Quine \rangle, u)$-substitution instances of $[Quine]:G!(he):$'s in her truncated idiom; hence (15) is false at every index regardless of whether semantical or conceptual roles of $\cdot G!(he) \cdot$'s are at issue. Barring a chance encounter, Bertie cannot know, *of* Quine, who he is—even in the weak, latitudinarian sense, let alone in any stronger sense. Nevertheless our account of the *de dicto* ascription (14) has provided it with a reading on which it may well be true. Bertie may know-true a *conceptually* individuated : G!(Quine): of the appropriate sort even though she is incapable (owing to Quine's elusiveness) of entertaining a semantically individuated : G!(Quine). :

3 Six Grades of De Re Involvement

As we have said, we intend to distinguish several different sorts of aboutness arranged in ascending order of strength, beginning with our bare *de dicto* or latitudinarian aboutness and ending with a virulently paradigmatic grade of aboutness, a sort of arch-aboutness. Let us get on with the enumeration.[7]

3.1 Grades 1 and 2: Flaccid versus Rigid Designation

Our initial complaint about Ralph's purely general belief and its effete relation to Tatiana is that Tatiana herself did not figure in its truth condition. For all that it mattered, Ralph's description, "the shortest spy," might as well have been dissolved in Russell's way, leaving no *genuine* singular term behind; indeed, if we think of Ralph's language of thought as a fully disambiguated logical idiom admitting no further analysis, *it* contains no Russellian descriptions at all, only the corresponding quantifiers and general terms. This underscores the anemia of the "relation" between Ralph's belief state and the living, breathing Tatiana. As a first step in the direction of full *de-re*-ness, let us require that Tatiana herself figure in the truth condition of any belief that is (more) strongly about her—that such a belief cannot be true in a possible world unless Tatiana herself exists in that world, and, more specifically, that even if there is a shortest spy in that world who is other than Tatiana, that spy's spyhood is irrelevant to the truth of (4r); the belief reported by (4r) is true in a world if and only if Tatiana is a spy in that world. If we recast this description to the vernacular of "propositions," the proposition believed by Ralph according to (4r) is a "singular" proposition,[8] a proposition containing Tatiana herself as a constituent rather than any description of her.

There are at least two different ways, however, in which Tatiana might "figure in" a belief's truth condition. (In some of our earlier writings on this topic[9] we did not distinguish them.) We think of *de re* belief as involving *contact* of some sort between the believer and the subject of his belief, but this need not hold of our current grade of aboutness as defined, for we have ways of dragging particular individuals into the truth conditions of both inner and outer utterances without "contact" of any sort occurring. As David Kaplan pointed out,[10] expressions such as "actual" and "in fact" serve to tie the truth a conditions of sentences to this-worldly referents even when the sentences are evaluated relative to other worlds. Ralph's belief that *the actual* winner of the 1980 election is nice but subnormal is true in a world *w* if and only if Ronald Reagan is nice but subnormal at *w*, regardless of the personality or intelligence of whoever won the 1980 election at *w*. (Alvin Plantinga pointed out[11] that the same rigidifying effect can be achieved by "world-indexing" one's descriptions, as in "the winner of the 1980 election *in our world/in the real world*.") In this way we can have a belief *about* the person who will be the first woman President— a belief in whose truth condition *she* figures regardless of her presidency or even of her womanhood—despite the total lack of contact between her and us and, needless to say, without our having the slightest idea who she will be. This grade-2 aboutness appeases the latter key intuition regarding *de re* belief, but it falls short of full-fledgedness in at least two respects: (i) the lack of contact itself and (ii) the fact that the relevant "singular term" appearing in the believer's representation achieves its reference only by exploiting its descriptive content—Reagan "figures in" Ralph's belief about the actual winner only because he satisfies the description "won the 1980 election in the actual world," and the first woman President figures in our belief about "the first woman President" only in virtue of her actually being President (which is not—n.b.—to deny that the belief's truth value is determined in another world by *that* woman's properties rather than by those of whomever is woman-President first in that world). If we accept Plantinga's formulation and allow his world-indexed descriptions to be Russellized away (as he does), we see that the only genuine singular term left in our representation is some name of the actual world, our world, itself; this encourages the idea that there is some still more intimate way in which a belief could be about someone: Though we believe about her that she is both intelligent and lucky, she is not such that we believe *her in particular* to be intelligent and lucky; probably she will not even be born until after our deaths. (The use of the apparently scope-specifying phrase "in particular" is beginning to seem relative to grade of aboutness; this needs investigation.)

3.2 Grade 3: Rigidity and Causal Grounding
There is still another grade of aboutness to be captured, one that involves "contact" and that is not essentially mediated by purely descriptive Russellian denotation. The idea of "contact" more than suggests causality, and this suggestion comes as no surprise to any fan of *de re* belief. Some theorists, such as Kaplan,[12] have proposed outright that a believer's representation(-token) must contain a singular term *causally grounded in* Tatiana if it is to be genuinely *de* Tatiana. Others have proposed epistemic requirements, such as that the believer "know who" Tatiana is, have her somehow "in his ken,"[13] be "acquainted" or "en rapport" with her, or at least know some key things about her. The epistemic requirements seem to presuppose the initial causal condition, since (on our view) one could not bear any

such relation to Tatiana unless one were causally connected to her—unless she had brought herself or been brought to one's attention. A further motivation for the minimal causal requirement is that one feels *de re* belief of grade 3 to be a *real relation*, so to speak, a real relation in nature, between the believer and the subject of the belief. Cognate with this is the idea that my believing *de re* of someone that she is F suffices for its being a *real property* of that person that she is believed by me to be F. It is in no way natural to say on the basis of (4d) alone that Tatiana is suspected by Ralph of being a spy, or even believed by Ralph to be a spy (just as (5d) attributes no property to any individual, whereas (5r) says that every tall spy has not only the property of being tall but that of being necessarily tall). Thus let us say that a belief has grade-3 aboutness if and only if the believer's representation contains a singular term whose occurrence is causally grounded in[14] the object that figures appropriately in the representation's truth condition. It is this requirement that is unsatisfied by our belief about the first woman President, and it is nicely underwritten by causal theories of *genuine reference* for natural languages.

Even here, dramatic distinctions are available, for causal contact can be made under what are epistemically the most discouraging of circumstances. Recall a justly famous case presented by Keith Donnellan,[15] in which we discover the horribly savaged body of Smith and judge on the spot that Smith's murderer is insane. We maintain that this judgment is so far ambiguous. We could (and probably do) mean that *whoever* murdered Smith is insane. But we could also mean that whoever *actually* murdered Smith is insane, so that our belief would be true if Tatiana (the real murderer) is insane even though we have never heard of her and even though we might even have someone else—Yuri, say—tentatively in mind at the same time. Note that Tatiana does here satisfy our causal requirement for grade-3 aboutness, since our belief that Smith's murderer is insane is the last member of a causal chain whose earlier links include the perceptual state that produced it, the hideous condition of Smith's body that produced the perceptual state, and Tatiana, who produced the hideous condition. Yet this is still not a case in which we feel that Tatiana herself is believed by us to be insane. Why not?

Several answers come to mind. Perhaps the most popular is that we lack the proper sort of *epistemic* contact with Tatiana, mentioned above, even though the bare minimal causal condition is satisfied. By the same token, the causal chain is too indirect; Tatiana's getaway, disguise, prepared alibi, etc. serve as a screen that prevents us from *following* the causal chain backward in pursuit of the culprit, at least without extraordinary detective skill and effort on our part. Third, the description under which we think of Tatiana (insofar as we are thinking *of* her at all) still feels too officey, *even though it is rigidified*. It seems—almost as if it were not rigid—to specify a role rather than an occupant; we know it denotes the same individual in any world (and so in that sense specifies an occupant), but we still have to add, "whoever that may be."

This last point, or feeling, can be spelled out a little more precisely, as follows. How is the valuation function for our language of thought computed when it takes our mental token of "Smith's murderer" as argument? That is, how is the referent of that token determined? Clearly, by reference to the property of having murdered Smith, our token has conceptual content that is contingently true of Tatiana and denotes her by exploiting that content even though in our rigidified interpretation the description as a whole is necessarily true of her. Note that although an appropriate causal chain exists, it plays no role in the determination of reference: If we had tokened the rigidified description "Smith's murderer" even *without* having seen the grisly evidence, the token would have denoted Tatiana just as surely and in just the way as it does now. In this sense, it does not *designate* or *refer to* Tatiana even though it denotes her *and* is causally grounded in her.

3.3 Grade 4: Direct Reference plus Causal Grounding

We have (at least) two choices: to give our causal-chain requirement more prominence in the determination of reference or to revert to an epistemic requirement that subsumes the causal chain. For reasons that become clear later, we prefer the former option, and at this point we re-emphasize the causal chain by tying it to Kaplan's notion of "direct reference."

In a public natural language, ordinary proper names refer without expressing contingent properties of their bearers, or so Kripke, Kaplan, and others[16] have persuasively argued. Contrary to Russell's view, names are not semantically equivalent to descriptions of the form "whoever or whatever is the so-and-so." Semantically they refer directly, and their referents are determined *solely* by the (appropriately shaped) causal chains that ground them in their referents. (Note with care: This is not to say that a speaker's use of such a name is unaided by what Frege called a "mode of presentation" as a matter of psychology; it is only to deny that the name *semantically expresses* the content of that mode of presentation. As we see below, this distinction between psychological and semantic contributions is crucial. Note also that for some singular terms, such as indexical pronouns like "you" and "I," the "appropriately shaped causal chains" are so short and direct as to be degenerate cases.) Now, we suggest that direct reference of this sort occurs in languages of thought as well. Mental tokens are causally grounded in objects and thereby refer to those objects without expressing contingent information about them. A mental utterance containing a referring term of this sort expresses a "singular proposition," i.e., one that has the referent itself as a constituent rather than any conceptual representation of that referent. Now we can define a fourth grade of aboutness: A thought is about a thing just in case some element of the thought *directly* refers to that thing. This condition is unsatisfied by us vis-à-vis Tatiana as we view all that is mortal of Smith.

Objection   The referent *itself* is supposed to figure in the content of a thought if that thought is to count as *about* it in the fourth sense. But this is absurd. The referent itself is not inside my head, nor does a bit of brain extend itself from my eyeball and touch the referent ever so lightly. (If one did, Tatiana would doubtless be surprised.)[17] What is in our heads is at best a representation of Tatiana and one that is directed toward her from a point of view; it seems undeniable that we can think of her only under some mode of presentation or another. Does this not deep-six the "direct reference" theory *um einen Schlag*?

No—though it is plainly true, it does not. When we said that a mental token could refer without *expressing* any contingent property of its referent, we meant that no such property figured in the truth condition of the containing judgment, even though the mental name is of course associated at any given time with one or more perspectival modes of presentation that account for the name's own causal powers and computational role within the believer's psychology. The key point here is the nature of this "association." Traditionally it has been thought a semantical matter; the name has been thought to incorporate the mode of presentation as part of its meaning. But this is a mistake, born of failure to distinguish our two schemes for individuating belief contents. Indeed, it is born of uncritical use of words such as "content." As is easily shown by indexical examples such as those discussed at length above, there is no single notion of "content" that accommodates all our intuitions concerning sameness of belief. The traditional notion must be cracked in two. As we have maintained, it splits into *propositions expressed* in the truth-conditional sense and *inferential/computational roles*, an inner-causal notion.[18] Beliefs can differ in expressed propositions despite their sameness of inferential role ("I am in danger"), and vice versa ("Yes, you are in danger"). This, we contend, is what happens in the case of direct reference. The mode of presentation exists (indisputably) but figures in inferential role rather than in truth condition. Mental names do not abbreviate descriptions (nor are they equivalent to them in any other semantical way); they merely share their inner functional roles from time to time.[19] And this defuses the objection; our fourth mode of aboutness is secure.[20]

3.4 Grade 5: Direct Reference plus "Ken" Relations

Even grade-4 aboutness does not always live up to our paradigm of *de re* belief, for a believer may make direct reference to something even under epistemically impoverished circumstances. We can refer directly to Tully, in speech or in thought, without knowing anything about him other than that he is said by Quine to be identical with the Roman orator Cicero. For some people that would be insufficient to warrant a heartfelt ascription of *de re* belief. They want a tighter causal connection that (as David Lewis[21] puts it) carries important *information* about Tully; they want epistemic contact, *intimate* contact—perceptual contact if they can get it. Thus we might define a fifth grade of aboutness, characterized by direct reference *plus* some "ken" relation, an epistemic intimacy requirement. (This is one way of understanding Kaplan's proposal in "Quantifying in"; Lewis and others have since defended such a view of the *de re*.) Here things get fuzzy, in part because no clear "ken" relation has ever been settled on by fans of grade-5 aboutness and in part because the intimacy requirement seemingly carried by the *de re* locutions of ordinary language are themselves interest relative and controlled by social and other features of conversational context,[22] but there are some uncontroversially clear cases. Direct visual contact is one; direct visual contact plus manual grabbing accompanied by shouts of *"This guy! THIS VERY PERSON!!"* is perhaps the clearest.

3.5 Grade 6: Unmediated Acquaintance
We suppose that there is conceivably a *sixth* grade of aboutness: that which Russell himself had in mind throughout his discussions of the present topic. This grade requires so diaphanous, direct, and *epistemically unmediated* acquaintance with one's referent that one cannot be thus acquainted with one object in two ways at the same time, at least without being aware that the two acquaintings have the same object. (Failure of the latter condition would entail the existence of an interposed representation of the object.) Thus we cannot be acquainted with ordinary physical objects in this Russellian way; with physical objects there is always the possibility that we might bear each of two perceptual relations to one, no matter how intimate, without realizing that the objects of these relations are one and the same. The only sort of entity that we could think about in our sixth way would be a sense datum. If we believe in sense data, as Russell did, we have a truly *ultimate* grade of *de-re*-ness, not just $99\frac{44}{100}\%$ pure, and can regard grade-5 aboutness as a cheap imitation (Russell himself did not countenance aboutness of any but the first and sixth kinds).[23] If, on the other hand, we reject sense data as we rejected spookstuff, grade-5 aboutness is the nearest fuzzy approximation.

3.6 Prospects for Drawing the Line
Perhaps it is time we recapitulated all six grades of aboutness in one spot. In grade 1 the believer's representation contains a singular term (of any sort) that semantically denotes X. In grade 2, X itself figures in the representation's truth condition; the relevant singular term designates X

rigidly. In grade 3 *X* figures in the representation's truth condition, and the relevant singular term is causally grounded in *X* in addition to being rigid. In grade 4 the representation directly refers to *X* by way of an appropriate causal chain. In grade 5 there is direct reference to *X* and there is also a ken relation between the believer and *X*. In grade 6, in holding his belief, the believer is directly acquainted with *X* without benefit of mediation by any *representation* at all.

Is there, now, a single distinction between attitudes *de dicto* and attitudes *de re*? Or has that distinction shattered into fragments corresponding to our various grades of aboutness? We introduced the notion of the *de re* in terms of a logical scope distinction and the permissibility of exportation or quantifying in. But logical properties alone will not help us mark anything like the traditional distinction, for intuitively, existential generalization is valid whenever an extensional relation holds between thought and object, and even our first grade of aboutness establishes *an* extensional relation between believer and semantic denotatum (this is the latitudinarian's initial insight). To mark the traditional distinction in a well-motivated way we must look for a natural break in the series of grades of aboutness. And such a break is there—between grades 3 and 4. We saw that despite the causal connection that obtains in a case of type three ("Smith's murderer" rigidly understood), the *mechanism* of reference in that case involves descriptive material and role filling *rather than* the causal chain. Moreover, as we saw, a thought of grade 3 does not express a singular proposition (except insofar as it may refer to the actual world, @, itself), i.e., not a singular proposition involving the thought's denotatum as a constituent. For these reasons, grade-3 aboutness differs in no theoretically significant way from grade-2 aboutness.

It might be argued that the grade-4/grade-5 distinction is more salient and important than the grade-3/grade-4 distinction. Indeed, this would have been the dominant view if direct-reference theories had not come into vogue a decade ago. We do not think it can be sustained, however; the grade-4/grade-5 distinction is *in*distinct, fuzzy, and interest relative, whereas the grade-3/grade-4 distinction is clear as a bell. Moreover, grade-4 thoughts express "singular propositions" just as grade-5 ones do; and it is hard to think of a case of direct mental reference that intuitively falls on the *de dicto* side of the traditional distinction.[24] We conclude that our natural break is between grades 3 and 4; if so, it is best to identify *de-re*-ness with (and to unpack "/*T*/ bears *R* to *a* for *u* at *t*" in terms of) aboutness of grade 4 or higher.[25]

What, then, of scope? That is a question about belief *ascription*, not about belief itself.[26] Yet we can say this: *De re* belief in our sense is paradigmatically well reported by existential, universal, or individual quantification into a doxastic context, such as (1b), (2b), (2c), (4r), or (6r), since the referent of the belief appears in propria persona in the belief's truth condition, rather than being represented by a descriptive proxy. Belief in a singular proposition *relates* the believer to the individual constituent of the proposition precisely for that reason, and the relation is nicely explicable in terms of the believer's hosting a representation that refers directly to that constituent.

As the latitudinarians argue, this excellent basis for quantifying in is not the only possible basis; and as we pointed out earlier, one *can* perform existential generalization any time a belief relates an object extensionally to the believer. So (to take the most extreme case) there is *a* sense in which even the first grade of aboutness licenses quantifying in, a sense in which Tatiana is believed by Ralph to be a spy even though he has never heard of her and could not conceivably suspect her. But this sense is uninteresting, for the *relation* between Ralph and Tatiana under which existential generalization holds is uninteresting: (i) The relation is not secured by Ralph's proposition alone; an extraneous contingent fact about Tatiana is needed to complete the connection. (ii) Though genuine and extensional, the relation is not a "real relation in nature"—this, we think, lies behind our feelings about "contact"—but a composite relation one element of which is semantical (Tatiana's satisfying the matrix of Ralph's description). This is why latitudinarian quantification is unnatural even though it can be interpreted.[27]

4 The De Re and "Knowing Who"

With all the foregoing in place, we pause to note a few features of our view in relation to the standard literature, and to correct certain misconceptions that are harmful and widespread.[28]

(i) Though aboutness of grade 5 requires epistemic activity of some sort, belief *de re* has little if anything to do with "knowing who," despite everyone's (theoretically curious) tendency to express intuitions of *de-re*-ness or non-*de-re*-ness by mobilizing indirect-question clauses. The notion of "knowing who" is as highly context dependent as is whatever epistemic notion figures in the analysis of grade 5 aboutness, and this may encourage identification of the two.[29] But in fact the interest relativity of "knowing who" far outruns that of grade-5 aboutness, and its parameters are controlled in quite different ways.[30] We argued this at some length in our article, "Knowing who," but here we can also present some quickie examples to illustrate the point: (a) Perry White has Clark Kent by the throat and is berating him for his timidity in chasing down stories. "Useless chicken**** milquetoast!!" he howls. This is a clear case of grade-5 aboutness, and certainly White believes *of* Kent that he is a milquetoast; but he does not thereby *know who Kent is* for any but the most obvious and crude immediate purposes such as that of backhanding him. He has a belief *de*

Kent, period, but he knows who Kent is and knows of Kent who he is only for some purposes and not for others. (b) Jones is a rich man of great worldly power who happens to enjoy slumming. He has a beat-up old Maverick and likes to drive around seedy neighborhoods. One day, in the very worst of these neighborhoods, he runs over Gonzo's foot. Enraged (and hopping on his other foot), Gonzo chases after Jones' car and manages to catch it. He drags Jones from behind the wheel, looks at him long and carefully, and says, "Now I know what you look like. If I catch you in this neighborhood again I'll rip your ****ing lungs out." Then he slaps Jones around a bit and lets him go. Here Gonzo certainly has some attitudes *de* Jones. But Zonker, standing by, observes sardonically and correctly that Gonzo does not know who it is that he has been slapping around. (c) You are a police detective investigating a murder and talking flaccidly or attributively about "the murderer." You prove that whoever did the murderer is (again attributively) the person who lives at such-and-such an address. Then for present purposes (that of laying hands on the culprit and throwing him in jail), you do know who the murderer is, but we may suppose that you have no attitudes *de* him in the sense of grade-5 aboutness, since you have not yet tracked him down at the address in question. Thus in some contexts there is "knowing who" without *de re* belief. The moral is again that the parameters of "knowing who" are far less tightly circumscribed than are those of grade 5 aboutness.

(ii) It is currently fashionable to deny that *de re/de dicto* is a distinction between *beliefs*: "There aren't two kinds of belief, but only two kinds of belief *ascription*."[31] We applaud this as an attempt to separate thoughts from their ascription, but it is not quite right as it stands. What is true is (a) that there are not two *mutually exclusive* kinds of belief, since on our view the *de re* is but a special case of the *de dicto*, and certainly (b) that the word "believe" is not ambiguous as between "relational" and "notional" *senses*,[32] and (c) that in Dennett's words, there are not "two different sorts of mental phenomena," if by that he means psychologically different sorts. There are (nevertheless) two kinds of belief: *de dicto* beliefs that are also *de re* and *de dicto* beliefs that are not. The difference lies in the different sorts of truth condition they have and in the differential impact of "methodological solipsism" on them, respectively.

(iii) We explicate the *de re* as a special case of the *de dicto*.[33] This is sharply at variance with the view presented by Tyler Burge in his paper, "Belief *de re*."[34] He insists that both the *de dicto* and the *de re* are mutually exclusive and that the *de re* is psychologically if not conceptually prior to the *de dicto*.

We find Burge's initial conception of the traditional distinction peculiar (no doubt he finds ours reciprocally peculiar). For him the root idea of the *de dicto* is that of a *fully general* belief whose truth value is entirely context independent. Accordingly, he defines *de re* belief simply as *deictic* belief, where what is believed is in effect an open rather than a closed sentence or proposition. We agree that a deictic belief most likely is *de re* in our sense as well, since all the indexical pronouns, etc. that make for deixis are devices of direct reference and create grade-4 aboutness (though tense may be an exception if it does not involve reference at all). But it does not follow that a *de re* belief is not also *de dicto*; a deictic belief is a belief *de* an indexical dictum. If there were no indexicals in the language of thought there would be no problems about indexical attitudes and no solutions to those problems either.[35] Nor does it follow, by the same token, that the *de re* is irreducible to *or* conceptually prior to the *de dicto*—though Burge does not claim that this follows, and we grant his contention that if we did not begin with *de re* beliefs we would almost certainly never acquire any *de dicto* beliefs.

(The reason we find Burge's initial conception peculiar is that it is not directly suggested either by Quine's original data (3) through (4r) or by the medieval distinction applying to the alethic modalities. Burge shows himself well aware of these historical antecedents and argues that his own distinction is philosophically more crucial than the traditional one, but his argument is on its face unconvincing.)[36]

(iv) It follows from our view that one cannot have a *de re* attitude toward a nonexistent. This is as it should be, or so we have argued independently elsewhere;[37] nonexistents can be known only by description. But some theories of believing allow beliefs *de* nonexistents,[38] and if we are right, they are wrong—or at least, their proponents' initial conceptions of the *de re* must be carefully distinguished from ours.

5 Interim Summary

Since we have come a long way from the shallow representations (1**) and (2**) of chapter 2, let us pause and take stock of what has changed in our account of "knowing who." Adoption of the two-scheme paratactic approach has enabled us to provide a single sort of logical form for instances of "S knows who N is," whereby much that was explicitly (and clumsily) represented in (1**) and (2**) is now absorbed into the interpretation of that logical form by means of our indexical semantics. And the same approach has been seen to generalize into a unitary account of knowing-who ascriptions in general. Our original account had two prominent features: (i) emphasis on teleological relativity, incorporated in the notions of classificatory purposes and corresponding important predicates, and (ii) reliance on a strong thesis anent the syntactic and semantic reality of referential/attributive ambiguity to handle opaque versus transparent "senses" of "knowing who." Our new account preserves (i) while obviating the need for (ii). As regards (ii), the existence of both opaque and transparent readings is now viewed from the standpoint of two-schemism, as a semantic consequence merely of the contextual ambiguity of deferred ostension between computational and truth-conditional schemes of individuation. As regards (i), the teleological parameter and the concomitant notion of an important predicate (for a given purpose) have both been exported from our original representations into our indexical semantics, where, though explicated in fancier ways, they continue to exercise much the same intuitive force. Purposes, as components of indices, are now viewed as selection functions that determine contextually salient classificatory vocabulary (and, where promiscuous predicates are concerned, salient "units" of discourse). In the end, the new and more adequate formal machinery is driven by essentially the same idea as before: To know who N is for purpose P is to know-true a sentence of one's language of thought which is *appropriately equivalent (i.e., computationally or—in a restricted way—semantically, as the case may be) to* a true answer to the query "Who is N?" in which N is uniquely classified in P-admissible vocabulary. What has been added—viz., the italicized two-schemist qualification—merely sharpens the picture with which we began.

III

Chapter 6
Self-Knowledge and Identity

Some philosophers have held that *self*-knowledge occupies a special place in epistemology and the philosophy of mind. And it might be thought, particularly by those of a Cartesian bent, that one's knowledge of one's own identity has a special, privileged status not shared by one's knowledge of anyone else's identity or by anyone else's knowledge of one's own.[1] "I am transparent to myself: My self-knowledge is mediated neither by inference nor by any teleological element such as a passing purpose or project. I know my own identity directly and completely, whereas others know it only inferentially and relative to certain sets of purposes." This sort of claim might be the product of a metaphysics featuring Cartesian egos and/or intrinsically subjective facts; alternatively, it might stem simply from the linguistic observation that "I am *me*" expresses purely trivial information no matter who utters it and when.

If some version of this contention is correct, i.e., if there is some objective asymmetry between knowing one's own identity and knowing others', then our theory of "knowing who" is inadequate. For one thing, the theory predicts no such asymmetry. For another, it would inevitably saddle S's self-knowledge with the usual teleological element and with mediation by the knowledge of a (presumably empirical) facts.[2] Thus two questions present themselves: Is our view indeed damaged by the special case of "S knows who N is," where N = S? And what is it for S to know who N is in virtue of knowing simply that *he*, S, is N?

If we revert to the crude referential/attributive terminology of chapters 1 and 2, we see immediately that things are not so awful as they might appear. Only some of the instances of the allegedly troublesome schema

    (1) S knows who S is

seem to generate a problem of the sort envisioned. If we replace both occurrences of "S" in (1) by "the only person in town to have a distant cousin who is both a disk jockey and a criminal lawyer," reading at least the second occurrence attributively, the resulting sentence would ascribe substantive a posteriori knowledge acquired inferentially if at all and clearly would be true only relative to a purpose or project in the way we have examined. For that matter, if we replace both occurrences of "S" by "Ronald Reagan" and imagine that Reagan suffers from severe amnesia, the same is true: He would know who Reagan was only inferentially and for some purposes but not for others.

Of course, these instances of (1) are not the sorts of examples that our potential opponent has in mind, and they are certainly not ones that we would paraphrase by producing the far more troublesome

(2) S knows who he himself is.

The now notorious "he himself" construction, immortalized by Castaneda as "he*," codifies what philosophers had in mind when they supposed that self-knowledge is a special sort of cognition asymmetrically distinguished from knowledge of the identity of others. To evaluate its impact on our theory of "knowing who," we must advert to an account of self-regarding attitudes in general.

1   The Nature of First-Person Attitudes

Among the various propositional attitudes a person might have, there is undeniably something special about those that are explicitly first person, self-regarding, or *de se*, i.e., attitudes whose content would be formulated by the subject using the equivalent in his or her language of the first-person singular pronoun "I." The special character of these attitudes manifests itself in the much-discussed peculiarity of ascriptions of self-regarding attitudes to others.[3]

1.1   Data and Puzzles
Consider, e.g., (3a−c):

(3) a. John believes that N is in danger,

    b. John believes that *he himself* is in danger,

    c. John believes, of John, that he is in danger

(where "N" in (3a) is any nonreflexive singular term denoting John). Curiously, the *de se* ascription (3b) resists assimilation to both *de dicto* ascriptions of the form (3a) and *de re* ascriptions such as (3c). On the one hand, (3b) seems to imply (3c), but not the converse. Suppose that John sees a man in a dangerous situation and comes immediately to believe of that man, demonstratively or under some description, that he is in danger; but unbeknownst to John, it is actually *himself* that he is viewing in a cleverly placed mirror. Then (3c) is true (since that man = John) but it seems that (3b) might well be false (John smugly says to himself, "I'm glad I'm not in that sucker's shoes"). On the other hand, (3b) neither implies nor is implied by (3a). This can be illustrated by simple cases involving amnesia or selective ignorance. Cringing in fear, John may believe that he himself is in danger but may fail to believe that N is in danger simply because he is unaware that he himself = N; or as before, he may believe that N is in danger without believing that he himself is in danger. In sum, then, though *de se* attitude ascriptions seem to entail their *de re* counterparts, they are not equivalent to either their *de re* or *de dicto* counterparts.

The upshot of these considerations for knowing-who ascriptions is obvious. Parallel to (3a–c), we have:

(4) a. John knows who N is.

    b. John knows who *he himself* is.

    c. John knows, of John, who he is.

Castaneda's well-known example of the amnesiac war hero serves to show that the relations among (4a–c) mirror those among (3a–c). John, now a famous war hero, awakes in a hospital as an anonymous amnesia victim. Relative to any interesting purpose, he does not know who he himself is. (Of course, there are trivial purposes for which he does know who he himself is. He can, e.g., distinguish himself *qua* physical object from the other patients in the ward, but he cannot remember his own past and hence cannot make use of any of the *autobiographical* predicates that would be important relative to standard purposes.) Hearing of a famous war hero named "John" who vanished in battle (and who is, of course, none other than himself), John reads up on the case to the point where he has amassed a huge body of biographical information about the missing hero. Given his possession of this information, it seems reasonable to concede that for most standard purposes he knows who John/the war hero is, and he may also know *of* John/the war hero, who he is; but alas, he does not yet know that *he himself* is John/the war hero. So we seem to have a clear case in which (4a) and (4c) are true relative to standard purposes while (4b) is false relative to those same purposes. Conversely, we can easily alter the example so that John remembers enough of his past to count as knowing who he himself is (relative to those purposes) without counting as knowing who N (e.g., the war hero) is. He might awake with full memory of his past up to but not including his adult military adventures and subsequently never hear about anyone's heroic deeds.

1.2 The Irreducibility Thesis: Some Proposals
In our previous essay, "Who, me?," we took a hard line against the alleged irreducibility of self-regarding attitudes and maintained that all the foregoing appearances are sleazily deceptive and that self-regarding attitudes are only a slightly special case of *de re* attitudes after all. In particular, we

defended the following theses:

> (i) The *object* of a self-regarding attitude, viz., the proposition believed, as identified by a set of possible worlds, is precisely the same as that of the corresponding *de re* belief.
>
> (ii) Moreover, *ascriptions* of attitudes *de se* and the corresponding *de re* ascriptions have the same truth conditions; any implication apparently carried by *de se* ascriptions but not by *de re* ascriptions is pragmatic at best, not semantic.

The argument for (i) is substantially just that John's belief about himself and someone else's corresponding *de re* belief about him have the same truth condition—they are true under precisely the same conditions and in exactly the same possible worlds; if a "proposition" is or corresponds to a set of worlds, then John and his corresponding *de re* believer believe the same proposition.

Thesis (i) taken out of context is not likely to be controversial. Thesis (ii) is controversial. Indeed, (ii) strikes many people as preposterous (though after they have read our article they usually soften this verdict to merely "still false"). Our argument for (ii) was as follows: We have at least two rather strong motives for accepting (ii), viz., (a) to respect intuitions about another kind of case that offset Castaneda's intuitions about his,[4] and (b) to shun the surds in semantics and the surds in nature that (we contend) are entailed by denying (ii).[5] Moreover, none of the standard arguments against (ii), based on the familiar data reviewed above, comes close to succeeding; in each case, either an equally plausible interpretation of the data supporting (ii) is available or the argument in question turns out to prove too much.[6] Nor could we anticipate any convincing further objection to (ii). Thus we were left with strong reason to accept (ii) and no good reason not to, despite the feeling on almost everyone's part that there is more to the irreducibility thesis than we were prepared to allow.[7]

We still insist on (i), but in light of the two-scheme theory of belief-content individuation we are now willing to compromise on (ii). When we wrote "Who, me?," we joined most of our colleagues[8] in being blind to one of the two schemes; we focused arbitrarily on the truth-conditional scheme at the expense of the functional or computational scheme (as witness our emphasis on (i)); we tacitly thought that (ii) followed from (i), as indeed it would if the truth-conditional scheme alone were in play. Our present view is that belief ascriptions are potentially ambiguous with respect to content individuation by truth condition and content individuation by functional or conceptual role. So we can allow a sense of attitude ascriptions for which (ii) is false. The resulting interpretation of (ii) seems to suit Castaneda's data perfectly.[9]

Castaneda's problem is exacerbated when we state it in terms of *change* of belief. Suppose John believes that *that* man whom he is ostending is about to be pounced on by a crazed, homicidal puma, but unbeknownst to John the man he is ostending is again himself reflected in a mirror. He proceeds on his way, unconcerned about his own safety, until he turns and sees the puma in the flesh and thereby suddenly acquires the belief that *he himself* is about to be pounced on, said change of belief prompting an immediate and striking change in behavior. Yet how is this apparent change in belief content expressed? John already believed that *that* (ostended) man was about to be pounced on; he already believed the singular proposition $\langle$John, $\lambda x(x$ is about to be pounced on)$\rangle$. So what he comes to believe on seeing the puma in the flesh is not that proposition. Yet what he does come to believe, that he himself is about to be pounced on, has exactly the same truth condition as that singular proposition and is true in just the same worlds. Thus, although we must agree that John has acquired a new belief, there is no clear sense in which the "new" belief differs in content from what John believed all along.

Perry ("The problem of the essential indexical") argues that our pre-theoretic notion of belief "content" is confused, and he proposes to split that notion into two, distinguishing John's belief "object," or proposition believed, from his "belief *state*," which is what is going on in John's head. It is the former that determines the truth value of John's belief and the latter that causally shapes John's behavior. In our case, John's belief object remains the same throughout the story, but his belief state changes; we might say he believed the proposition $\langle$John, $\lambda x(x$ is about to be pounced on)$\rangle$ all the while, but suddenly came to believe it in the first person way as well as in the third person way.

This bifurcation of the notion of a belief's "content" predicts an ambiguity in the question of whether two people have "the *same* belief." This ambiguity will already have been anticipated independently by any reader who appreciates the two-scheme hypothesis we defended in chapters 3 and 4, and it is readily discerned at the level of data as well: Suppose that Jones believes that he (himself) is underpaid, Smith believes that *he* (himself) is underpaid, and Brown agrees with Smith that Smith is underpaid. Which two of the three have *the same belief*? Surely in one sense Jones and Smith have the same belief—both go and threaten the chairman—but in another sense Smith and Brown do; conceptually, functionally, or computationally, the beliefs of Jones and Smith are the same, whereas truth conditionally the beliefs of Smith and Brown are the same. Which is the *correct* sense of "same belief"? That depends on whether one is more interested in causes and the explanation of behavior or in semantics, truth, and reliability; there is no further fact of the matter.[10]

This all sounds eminently sensible and right, as it did to us even at the time of writing "Who, me?"; indeed we distinguished therein between believing a given singular proposition "first-personishly" and believing that same proposition only "third-personishly." But it is only a schema for a solution, not a solution itself, so long as both the latter terminology and Perry's state/object distinction remain unexplicated.

1.3 The Solution

As we have broadly hinted, the sentential account of attitude ascriptions (supplemented by our two-scheme theory of content individuation), yields an explication. It is cognate with our solution to Kripke's Puzzle in chapter 4: Before seeing the puma, John believed what was both truth conditionally and computationally a · That man is about to be pounced on ·, but did not believe any · I am about to be pounced on · *computationally* speaking. His sudden belief change consists in his coming to token an · I am about to be pounced on ·, computationally individuated, in addition to his standing · That man is about to be pounced on ·, with the obvious resulting change in his behavior. This is the sense, neglected by us in "Who, me?" in which it is after all false that John early on believed that *he himself* was about to be pounced on.[11]

If the two-scheme theory is correct, is there not also a sense generated by the truth-conditional scheme in which John has believed all along that he himself is in danger? Semantically we think there is, though John would never have expressed his belief in the first-person way: What he was believing was in fact that he himself was about to be pounced on. Admittedly this sense is hard to hear, and there are two clear reasons why this should be. First, as we have said, the truth-conditional scheme is imposed when what concerns us is directly related to the truth values or other semantical aspects of beliefs; the computational scheme is imposed when what we care about are causes and effects. The case of John is clearly of the latter type—what interests us about it is the question of just what made John take sudden evasive action. Thus imposition of the truth-conditional scheme here is felt to be inappropriate. The second and far more powerful reason is that reflexive pronouns such as "he himself" are presumably *conventional signals* to the effect that the computational rather than the truth-conditional scheme is to be imposed. Drawing on the theory of "lexical presumption" that we developed elsewhere,[12] we argued in "Who, me?" that this is so.[13] A clear symptom is that, even though an informed hearer of "John believes that he himself is about to be pounced on" would object to the speaker's choice of the *lexical item* "he himself" before John's alarming realization, the hearer can see that that item picks out what is in fact the correct propositional component (John) and can be made to grant that there is a discernible though inappropriately lexicalized sense in which what was said is true—just as if we say "Joan is a professional philosopher but she's smart," a hearer can be made to grant that what we said is semantically true in that both its conjuncts are true, even though the hearer may object to our lexicalizing choice of the word "but" (assuming the hearer denies that being a professional philosopher tends to preclude being smart).

If these two reasons are sound, then it is no surprise that John's original mental analog of "That man is about to be pounced on" is not normally counted as a ·I am about to be pounced on·; plainly, the representation that John associates with "that man" and the one he associates with "I" play quite different computational roles and accordingly produce quite different behavior, which is exactly what our theory should predict.

2 "Knowing Who" in the First Person

Augmented as it has been by the two-scheme version of representationalism, our theory of "knowing who" is adequate as it stands to handle the facts of (3a–c) and (4a–c), but this needs to be shown.

2.1 De Se Attitude Ascriptions

The key ingredient of *de se* attitude ascriptions is our earlier notion of the *progenitor* of the display sample in a surface parataxis. Briefly, our proposal is this:

(i) The token reflexive **I** in logical form is the progenitor of surface occurrences of "he himself," "she herself," and "I myself."

(ii) An appropriate starred variable in logical form is the progenitor of surface occurrences of "I" (as distinct from "I myself").

Let us begin with (i). The logical form of the *de se* ascription (3b) is accordingly the canonical parataxis $\langle$**BELIEVE** (John, $\langle$ $\rangle$, **THAT**$_1$), $\langle$**In Danger** (**I**)$\rangle\rangle$, and the logical form of the *de se* ascription (4b) is the canonical parataxis $\langle$**KNOW** (John, $\langle$ $\rangle$, **THE-WHO-OF-IT**$_1$), $\langle\hat{\mathbf{x}}_1(\mathbf{x}_1 = \mathbf{I})\rangle\rangle$. In light of the foregoing, (3b) is true at an index I iff John believes-true at t_I a ·I am in danger·. Similarly, (4b) is true at I iff John knows-true at t_I a : G!(I): for "G" reflecting an important predicate of John relative to P_I.

Our use of "I" within dot quotes here calls for some comment. A conceptually individuated ·I am in danger· for John is a sentence of John's language, the behavior of whose logical form in his language game is functionally equivalent to that of **In Danger** (**I**) in the ascriber's (e.g., our) language game. But our definitions ensure that a *semantically* individuated ·I am in danger· for John is a sentence of John's language whose logical form is, in John's context, extensionally isomorphic to **In Danger**(**I**) as evaluated in *John's* context—*not* as evaluated in the ascriber's context! It is what **I** in **In Danger** (**I**) (which is the progenitor of the ascriber's words) denotes for

John, not for the ascriber, which is semantically relevant. A semantically individuated ·I am in danger· for John thus always has a subject term which, in John's mouth, denotes John himself, but this term could be a name, a demonstrative, or a description; it need not (though it might) be a token reflexive. In contrast, it is plausibly arguable—though we do not debate the matter here—that a *conceptually* individuated ·I am in danger· (indeed, any conceptually individuated ·I am F·) would have to have a logical form whose subject term obeys the same *semantical* rule as the underlying **I**, hence a subject term that we could, for practical purposes, simply identify with **I** in logical form. (This is cognate with the idea, prominent in recent literature,[14] that conceptual roles, though not determining specific truth conditions, may nonetheless determine something like "character" in Kaplan's sense.[15] A simplified version of this requirement is embedded in clause (iii) (chapter 3, section 3.3) of our definition of "playing the same conceptual role."[16]

Under our initial, liberal construal of the relation *R*, the upshot for our theory's treatment of (3a–c) and (4a–c) is as follows. At indices marking semantical role as salient, (3a–c) are mutually equivalent, as are (4a–c). If John believes-true, e.g., a semantically individuated ·John is in danger·, then he believes-true—given our remarks in the preceding paragraph—a semantically individuated ·I am in danger·, in which case he believes-true an ·N is in danger· wherein occurrences of the subject term in his mouth bear *R* to him, in which case he again counts as believing-true a ·John is in danger·. Similarly, if John knows-true a semantically individuated :G!(John):, then he knows-true what is for him a semantically individuated :G!(I):, hence knows-true a :G!(N): in which occurrences of the subject term in his mouth bear *R* to him, which in turn qualifies him as knowing-true a :G!(John):.

We observed in section 1.1 that there is a much-discussed sense in which the *de se* ascriptions are not equivalent to their *de re* or *de dicto* counterparts, though they do imply the former of these. Not surprisingly, this is just the "sense" provided by evaluation at indices which mark *conceptual* role as salient. At such indices, we have the following results. First of all, (3b) implies (3c), and (4b) implies (4c); conceptually individuated ·I am in danger·'s and :G!(I):'s are by definition ·N is in danger·'s and :G!(N):'s whose subject terms behave *semantically* (as well as computationally) like **I**—hence are sentences in which these terms in John's mouth bear *R* to John. Second, (3c) does not imply (3b), nor does (4c) imply (4b); conceptually individuated ·N is in danger·'s and :G!(N):'s whose subject terms are merely required to bear *R* to John (in John's mouth) clearly need not be conceptually individuated ·I am in danger·'s or :G!(I):'s for John. Third, (3a) neither implies nor is implied by (3b), and (4a) neither implies nor is implied by (4b), since first- and third-person sentences do not in general play the same conceptual roles. That these last three results anent (3a–c) and (4a–c) are the ones typically "heard" or "felt" is explained, as noted above, by facts about lexical presumption.

For working purposes, we have construed the dummy relation R weakly—in effect, as grade-1 aboutness in the sense of chapter 5. If R is identified with higher grades of aboutness, the connections between *de dicto* and *de re* attitude ascriptions threaten to attenuate, since extensional isomorphism (as characterized in chapter 3) preserves only grade-1 aboutness. If desired, lost connections could be restored in obvious ways by toughening the account of denotation for canonical terms and/or the conditions for extensional isomorphism. Inasmuch as we have informally urged construal of R by reference to aboutness of grade 4 or higher, we would naturally favor a causal account of term denotation and a tighter definition of extensional isomorphism (which would require matching modes of reference). Where *de se* attitude ascriptions are concerned, the intuitively desired implicative relation to the corresponding *de re* ascriptions is preserved in our favored construal of R, for self-regarding thoughts—whether computationally or (in the stricter way) semantically individuated—would clearly exemplify grade-4 aboutness. The underlying **I**, like other, less specialized demonstratives, is for its user a directly referential term.

2.2 The Ambiguity of "I"

Turning now to (ii) of our proposal, let us consider what our theory has to say about

(5) John believes that I am in danger.

The logical form of (5) is the canonical parataxis $\langle$**BELIEVE (John,** $\langle\ \rangle$, **THAT**$_1$), $\langle$**In Danger**$(x_1^*)\rangle\rangle$. Accordingly, (5) is true at an index I just in case John believes-true a $(\langle\ \rangle, u_I)$-substitution instance (at I) of a $\cdot$he* is in danger$\cdot$ ("he*" being the surface reflection of the underlying x_1^*)—in effect, iff John believes-true some $\cdot$N is in danger$\cdot$ for "N" denoting the hypothetical utterer of (5). Although this particular result seems perfectly in order, what happens when someone reports his or her *own* first-person beliefs, as in

(6) I believe that I am in danger.

It may come as a bit of a surprise that our theory regards (6) as *ambiguous*. On one reading, the utterer of (6) is indeed self-ascribing a first-person belief; let us call this the *de se* reading of (6). There is arguably, however, a second construal of (6) on which the self-ascribed belief may *not* be in the first-person; let us call this the *de re* reading of (6). Now it is admittedly difficult to hear the *de re* reading, but this is only because the main verb is in the present tense, which occasions cognitive interference from purely conversational considerations. Consider instead

(7) I *believed* that *I* was in danger.

Here is it easy to imagine that the utterer of (7) is reporting his or her discovery of one of the "trick mirror" examples deployed above. That is, we can imagine him or her saying, "Aha! The endangered person I was looking at was really myself, so, without realizing it, I believed that *I* was in danger!" Here the utterer is self-ascribing past possession of a *non*-first-person belief *about* himself or herself. Because of this duality of possible readings, we distinguish in (i) and (ii) (section 2.1) between "I" and "I myself," only the latter forcing the *de se* reading, as in (8a–b):

(8) a. I believe that I myself am in danger.

b. I believed that I myself was in danger.

According to (i), the logical form of (8a) is thus unequivocally $\langle \mathbf{BELIEVE}\,(\mathbf{I}, \langle\ \ \rangle, \mathbf{THAT}_1), \langle \mathbf{In\ Danger}\,(\mathbf{I})\rangle\rangle$. Sentence (8a) is true at an index I iff u_I believes-true an ·I am in danger·—which, if I marks conceptual role as salient (as "myself" conventionally signals), is always something in the first person. Sentence (6), we maintain, can be taken either as elliptical for (8a) or as having the logical form $\langle \mathbf{BELIEVE}\,(\mathbf{I}, \langle\ \ \rangle, \mathbf{THAT}_1), \langle \mathbf{In\ Danger}\,(\mathbf{x}_1^*)\rangle\rangle$. In the latter *de re* reading, (6) is true at I iff u_I believes-true an ·N is in danger· for "N" denoting u_I. It should be noted that "myself" can accompany "I" in the "that" clause only when the subject term of the attribution is "I"; sentence (9), unlike (8a), is ungrammatical:

(9) *John believes that I myself am in danger.

These facts suggest to us that there is an "I"/"I myself" distinction parallel to the "he"/"he himself" distinction. The second member of each pair has only a reflexive function (conventionally signaling the salience of conceptual roles), and the first member of each pair is ambiguous in use with respect to a reflexive and a directly referential function. Proposals (i) and (ii) codify this situation. Accordingly there is a counterpart duality in the interpretation of (10a), although, as before, it is easier to hear when the tense is shifted, as in (10b):

(10) a. I know who I am.

b. I knew who I was.

Our remarks about (5) carry over mutatis mutandis to (11), whose logical form is $\langle \mathbf{KNOW}\,(\mathbf{John}, \langle\ \ \rangle, \mathbf{THE\text{-}WHO\text{-}OF\text{-}IT}_1), \langle (\hat{\mathbf{x}}_2(\mathbf{x}_2 = \mathbf{x}_1^*))\rangle\rangle$:

(11) John knows who I am.

Briefly, (11) is true at an index I iff John knows-true a $:G!(N):$ for "N" denoting u_I and "G" reflecting a P_I important predicate of u_I.

2.3 De Se versus De Dicto Ascriptions of "Knowing Who"

This brings us, finally, to the connection between *de se* knowledge ascriptions and *de dicto* knowing-who ascriptions of the form "X knows who F'd." Any adequate theory should explain the intuitive attractiveness of unrestrictedly inferring (12b) from (12a):

(12) a. John knows that he himself (alone) shot Mary.

b. John knows who shot Mary.

It is important to realize, however, that we are *not* dealing with an entailment here. Sentence (12b) might be false when (12a) is true simply because the context specifies a purpose relative to which John's :I alone shot Mary: contains no important predicate of the culprit—i.e., there is no salient "G" answering to a predicate in $P(\hat{x}_1(x_1 \text{ shot } \textbf{Mary}))$ for which it follows that John knows-true a :One and only one thing shot Mary and G!(it):.

This raises the question of whether there *are* purposes for which the truth of (12a) would suffice for that of (12b). The only way to secure the inference is to appeal to purposes in which it is $\hat{x}_1(x_1 = \textbf{I})$ relative to $\hat{x}_1(x_1 \text{ shot } \textbf{Mary})$ that counts as an important predicate; only then is it guaranteed that John's :I alone shot Mary: is a nontrivial :One and only one thing shot Mary and G!(it):, since the former can be construed as a :One and only one thing shot Mary and *it* [uniquely, of course] *is* I:. But our explication of purposes by means of Form W(Rev.) clearly rules out taking $\hat{x}_1(x_1 = \textbf{I})$ as an important predicate for any but *non*-information-seeking purposes of a mere file-labeling sort. So our theory dictates that (12a) by itself implies (12b) only at specially chosen indices.

Does this restrictive result disbar us from satisfying the aforementioned adequacy condition? Can we still explain why the inference from (12a) to (12b) generally strikes people as correct even for fairly rich, information-seeking purposes? The answer is implicit in what we said above. The inference in question is so attractive simply because it is tacitly taken as an *enthymeme*—one whose expansion *is* (by the light of our theory) a correct inference whenever the suppressed premise is *not* redundant with respect to the purpose at hand, viz.,

(12a) John knows that he himself (alone) shot Mary.

[(12c) *John knows for P who he himself is.*]

Therefore

(12b) John knows for P who shot Mary.

In ordinary contexts, it is simply taken for granted on all hands that every normal person knows who he himself/she herself is for *many* garden-variety classificatory purposes—e.g., knows his/her own name, address, occupation, recent history, etc.—and so, barring some *special* reason for thinking that John is *not* a normal person, the suppressed premise automatically rides along for these "normal" purposes P. But, we submit, no one who consciously *denied* the suppressed premise (12c) for some information-seeking P *and who held P constant for (12b) as well* would suffer the least temptation to infer (12b) from (12a)! (One should be struck by the close parallel with, e.g., "knowing *where*": If we imagine that John, being hopelessly lost in Africa, stumbles into a cave and discovers what he recognizes from legend to be King Solomon's Mines, there should be no temptation to say that he knows *where* King Solomon's Mines are! His ability truly to assert "*Here* are King Solomon's Mines" is cold comfort, since he doesn't know where "here" is.)

Let us return to the two questions with which we began this chapter. First, is our view damaged by the special case of self-knowledge? Not that we have seen or can see. The alleged "asymmetry" derives from the idea that John's knowing *who he himself is* is fundamentally different from anyone's (even John's) merely knowing *who John is*—different in that the former piece of knowledge, unlike the latter, is absolute and effortlessly noninferential. That there is *some* difference between the two cases is undeniable, but it is not of the radical and exciting sort envisaged.

Consider the truth conditions that under our theory are assigned to (13) and (14):

(13) John knows who he himself is.

(14) X knows who John is.

Sentence (13) is true at I iff John knows-true a : G!(I): for some P_I important predicate "G"; and (14) is true at I iff X knows-true an : H!(John): for some P_I important predicate "H." That both are teleologically relative should, by now, go without saying; so let us turn our attention to the question of the epistemic status of what is alleged to be known-true in (13) and (14).

Relative to individuation by *semantical* roles, John's : G!(I): and X's : H!(John): could in principle be *type-identical* sentences regardless of whether X is John or someone else, in which case what makes each of his/their Mentalese sentences true would be the *same* fact about John in either case. No spooky "perspectival facts" are required here, nor, in light of the possible type identity, is there any reason to think that there is anything epistemically special about what *John*, as opposed to some distinct X, knows-true in such a case.

If a difference in what is known-true is wanted, we must obviously look to individuation by *conceptual* roles. Computationally, John's :G!(I): and X's :H!(John): are clearly not in the same line of work, even if X = John and the predicates are the same—which, of course, is why there is the sense of (13) and "John knows who John is" in which neither implies the other. This important computational difference by itself, however, entails no special epistemic status for John's :G!(I): which is not enjoyed by X's :H!(John):. No one would suppose, e.g., that John's knowing-true an :I am the richest man in America: must be epistemically easier for John than Mary's knowing-true a :John is the richest man in America:—neither can avoid entanglement with the a posteriori.

Indeed, where "knowing who" is concerned, it seems that the only candidate for such special status would be the likes of a (conceptually individuated) :I am I:, for there is at least some plausibility in the claim that *this* sort of thing could be known-true "noninferentially," is "self-evident" or "axiomatic" for its possessor, etc. Now John's "knowing true" such an :I am I: is just what is involved in the truth condition for

(15) John knows that *he himself is he himself.*

If there is a genuine epistemic asymmetry between (13) and (14), it presumably lies in an implicative tie between (15) and (13) that fails to hold between (15) and "John knows who John is" (let alone any other instance of (14)). Such a tie, however, would require that $\hat{\mathbf{x}}_1(\mathbf{x}_1 = \mathbf{I})$ count as an important predicate for the purpose at hand. But this, as we have seen, is impossible, since there is *no* P such that $\hat{\mathbf{x}}_1(\mathbf{x} = \mathbf{I}) \in P(\hat{\mathbf{x}}_1(\mathbf{x} = \mathbf{I}))$. Consequently, the fact (if it is a fact) that (15) attributes to John a special bit of nonrelative, noninferential knowledge has no tendency to show that (13) ever does likewise. The data regarding *de se* knowledge ascriptions can be adequately explained by our two-schemes paratactic approach without the need for positing any inferential/noninferential or relative/absolute asymmetries.

Thus, in passing, we obtain our reply to the second question with which we began this chapter, viz., What is it for S to know who N is [for purpose P] in virtue of knowing simply that he, S, [i.e., he himself] is N? To see the answer clearly, let us borrow an example from Perry. John is following a trail of spilled sugar in the supermarket and wondering, "Who is the slob who made the mess?" Suddenly he discovers a leak in the bag of sugar he put into his basket on entering the market and, mentally retracing his steps, comes to the realization that *he himself* is the slob who made the mess. Does John, with that piece of knowledge alone, now know *who* the slob is (for some salient purpose P)? Bearing in mind what we said earlier about (12a–b), we must beware of suppressed premises. If we avail ourselves of the overwhelmingly probable assumption that John *already* knows who he himself is, for garden-variety purpose P, then, unless he is a total moron, he obviously does know who the slob is for P. But the moment we entertain the hypothesis that John is not a normal person, that he does not know who he himself is *for purpose P*, we are prevented from concluding that he "must" know who the slob is for P. The only way to prevent the entertaining of this hypothesis is to specify that P is a mere file-labeling purpose that counts $\hat{x}_1(x_1 = I)$ as an important predicate, so that John *automatically* counts as knowing who the slob who made the mess is for P. As we have seen before, however, this fails to guarantee John's knowledge of who he himself is relative to P.)

We can now generalize and give our formal answer to the second question (in, of course, its teleologically relativized version). The question: What is it for S to know who N is [for purpose P] in virtue of knowing simply that he, S, [i.e., he himself] is N? Our answer: It is for P to be a minimal, non-information-seeking purpose of the file-labeling sort. That is what it is, but it marks nothing of particular interest: Assuming opaque readings, we would have gotten the same answer relative to the boring question, "What is it for S to know who Tully is in virtue of knowing simply that Tully = Cicero?"

3 One's Own Identity

We have been concerned with emphasizing the ultimately *predicative* character of "knowing who." To know who N is is to know-true a predication, an :F!(N): in which "F" is important for certain purposes. Even when "F" is allowed by those purposes to be of the sort "=M," knowing-true an :F!(N): is not to grasp a bare metaphysical essence or haecceity. Thus the fact that "knowing who" is usually expressed in English using what seems to be the "is" of *identity* must be taken lightly as a relatively superficial appearance.[17] But one cannot help noticing that the word "identity" itself figures prominently in discourse about "knowing who"; we have used it scores of times already in this book. "To know who someone is" and "to know someone's identity" are virtual synonyms. This indicates that if the connection between "knowing who" and identity is merely superficial, it is more robust and substantial than are most surface-grammatical appearances.

Oddly but happily for our theory, the word "identity" and its cognates as used in conversational English turn out to be even more obviously predicative than are the knowing-who locutions we have already examined. (In what follows we lapse into colloquial talk of a person's "important properties." With the technicalities now behind us, this language-neutral way of speaking, rather than a more exact discussion couched in terms of the roles played by Mentalese sentences containing important predicates, makes for smoother reading. We trust that no misunderstanding will result.) Consider the following representative examples.

(i) A person who is disoriented because his or her life has taken a completely unexpected and devastating turn or one who finds oneself performing an action very much out of character is sometimes said to experience "loss of identity." (Equally and in the same breath we say, he (she) is suddenly unsure of who he (she) is.[18]) But no one can *lose his (her) identity* (in the literal, numerical sense) save through death,[19] and no one in either of the circumstances we have mentioned suffers primarily from sudden *ignorance* of a (genuine) identity statement either. What has happened in these cases is, rather, precisely that either the subjects are unsure that they have such-and-such properties of a sort they consider important or that they have lost the sense that such-and-such properties they know they have *are* important. Such is *alienation* generally,[20] and such in particular is *self*-alienation: What seemed to matter most, or what would be taken by other members of the community to matter most, now matters not at all. (N.B., one may "lose one's identity" in some such way while gaining *another* identity or one may lose identity entirely and become no one, a nonperson.)

(ii) Dissociative amnesia victims[21] are said to have lost their identity in an even more radical and dramatic sense. Here again this usage cannot be literally (numerically) correct, nor can we charge the patient with traumatic forgetting of a genuine identity statement, a necessary truth. What the victim has forgotten is instead strikingly selective: not how to ride a bicycle, not how to buy a ticket to see a movie, not that $2 + 2 = 4$, not that metal objects sink when you throw them in water, not that snow in Ohio does not turn bright orange when it hits the ground, not that people like being told nice things about themselves—but rather virtually all *his or her own properties* that people universally consider important: name, address, spouse, children, occupation, interests, and so on.[22] Dissociative amnesia is precisely a *forgetting of one's important properties.*[23]

(iii) Teenagers have "identity crises," or at least they did in Erik Erikson's day. Yet (to coin a phrase) an interest in the law of identity can hardly be attributed even to the above-average college sophomore. What the sufferer seeks is rather meaning in life, a shouldering of important properties.

(iv) Not dissimilarly, with luck and perspicacity an aspiring writer or composer finds his or her identity *as* a writer or composer, i.e., finds the contribution that is most important for him or her to make. Note that in the numerical sense of "identity," the common expression "identity as an F" makes no sense at all (unless, irrelevantly, Geach's "relative identity" thesis is true).

(v) "Identity" talk is commonly engaged in by feminists and other champions of oppressed groups. A liberated woman seeks and perhaps finds her true identity ("who she is," "who she really is"); even an entire ethnic group may search for its identity. Again, to understand such talk as genuinely expressing numerical identity would make nonsense or at least drastic silliness of it (note in particular that the phrases *"true* identity" and *"really* is" make no sense if intended numerically). For a woman to discover her identity is for her to determine which of her properties are *truly* important, or at least important to *her,* as opposed to the properties that have been enforced, encouraged, or otherwise stressed by her parents, her husband, or society.[24] (Actually this cannot be the whole story, for not just any *truly* important properties will do.[25] The woman might be the niece of a wealthy shipowner, which is important to her because of her expectations, and she might have a uniquely odd-looking mole, which is important to her because it is precancerous, but these properties would have little to do with her "identity" in any feminist sense. We suppose that this is because the money she expects to inherit and the cancer she intends to avoid are only derivatively (even if urgently) important concerns; she needs in a general way to have ample means and to avoid fatal diseases in order to carry out the more distinctive projects that are more fundamentally important to her. Or perhaps "identity" talk of the feminist sort is conventionally restricted to matters of conflict between one's own predilections and stereotyped sex roles. In any case, it is *somehow* a matter of important properties.)

(vi) Other morally significant categories also are specified in terms of a predicative sense of "identity," e.g., the notion of a *violation of privacy*: Not every potentially unwanted observation of one's doings or possessions counts as a violation of one's privacy even if it is wrong. Stanley Benn has suggested that the narrower protection of "privacy" should be restricted just to observation of those doings or possessions that are counted by social convention as partly constitutive of one's "identity."[26] For another example, one useful theoretical definition of an "incest taboo" (wider than any strictly biological characterization) is the prohibition of sexual activity on grounds of one's partner's identity rather than of the nature of the act performed.[27]

(vii) People sometimes undergo "changes of identity" even for reasons other than the raising of political consciousness. A criminal who changes his identity to avoid capture or a courageous and honest witness who moves to a distant state and changes his identity to avoid mob retribution after testifying in an organized-crime case has not per impossibile falsified a genuine identity statement either. Rather, he has altered name, address, physical appearance, occupation, and perhaps even family connections—though probably not interests and preferences and other features of personality, for which reason we are inclined to grant a sense (over and above the strictly logical) in which he has not really changed his identity after all.

Various sorts of pronominal usages in English parallel these "identity" locutions in confirming our contention that "knowing who" is at bottom a predicative matter.

(viii) Dudley brings Lavinia flowers. "For me?" she exclaims, "Why these luxuriant blossoms?" "Because you're you," he replies fulsomely. As before, an interest in the law of identity can hardly etc. etc., nor is it Lavinia's (numerical) self-identity that has put Dudley in his hotly romantic mood. "Because you're you" here has to mean "Because you have the properties that are important to me in such-and-such crucial ways." (Though Dudley would never have gotten to first base with Lavinia if he had come around saying things to her like "You have the properties that are important to me in such-and-such crucial ways." There is a feeling among romantics that true love—and other morally charged regard for a particular person—cannot be based in any essential way on any accidental properties of the object of that regard. But we will see that this idea is a bunny-fur-minded myth; it can be taken literally, but when it is, it leads to absurdity—and what for the romantic is worse than a detached and scientistic view of the value of persons (see note 28). Note for now that romantics of the sort we have mentioned do *not* take the idea literally but commonly express it by saying that true love is based on the beloved's "identity" or on "who (s)he is"—i.e., according to us, on whatever properties of the beloved are counted as *important* for the purposes at hand.)

(ix) Teenagers complain that their parents do not know "the real me," or in the grip of identity crisis they search for "the real me." As always, this cannot mean a genuinely bare haecceity as opposed to a disguised or fake one; the teenagers are raising the question of what about them is important.[28]

(x) There is a feminist pronominal usage that parallels (v) above, as in the slogan "Free to be ... you and me."[29] In the numerical sense, everyone is *always* free, indeed logically compelled, to "be me"; what the feminist is *not* free to do, until the eventual success of women's liberation, is to choose to acquire the properties that are important to her without answering to a male-controlled establishment.

(xi) As we have noted, a person commonly wants to be loved or regarded "for oneself"; Sandra wants Walter to love *her*, not her money, her piano, her piano playing, or even her sparkling conversation (which she considers merely brittle). Superficially, these locutions are puzzling. Robert Kraut has offered an ingenious theory that posits nonstandard world lines as alternative "objects of affection" in such cases.[30] We prefer the more straightforward account that falls out of our view of such pronominal uses as predicative: "Love me *for myself,*" and "Love *me,* not my pearly teeth or my french fries or my sparkling conversation," mean "Love me for the properties *I* deem important," or (equivalently from the inside) "Love me for the properties that are *truly* important." It may seem odd to suppose that one who says "Love me for myself" could have any set of contingent properties in mind, since given any such set the person would probably want to be loved even if he or she were to lose those particular properties. But the notion of love is a causal notion—love is of necessity grounded in some of the beloved's properties or other, even if those properties are historical or otherwise relational—and the properties are invariably contingent. If Sandra's utterance is *not* a plea for attention to her important though contingent properties, it is incoherent and conceptually doomed to disappointment, for haecceities as such have no causal powers.[31]

(xii) Consider the puzzling but prevalent expression "If I were you." Taken as expressing numerical identity, this subjunctive antecedent is not merely counterfactual but counterlogical; distinct individuals are necessarily distinct. Notice too that whatever relation it does express is asymmetric:[32] "If I were you" and "If you were I/me" express different hypotheses:

(16) {If I were you/??If you were me} I wouldn't wear that racist sweatshirt to the game.

(17) If I were you, I wouldn't be able to take advantage of Smedley's weak backhand; but if you were me, *you* wouldn't be able to take advantage of it.

Here again, what is hypothesized is nothing about genuine identity, but rather the taking on by me of your contextually important properties (N.B., not necessarily the ones that currently seem important *to you*): if I were *about to go to the game*; if I were *opposing Smedley at tennis* or if you had *my characteristic inability to control the ball.* Similar remarks apply to subjunctive wishes and the like.[33]

The foregoing barrage of examples convinces us that our predicative analysis of "knowing who" fits not only "who" clauses themselves but related locutions couched explicitly in terms of "identity." In the next chapter, we address two closely related problems in current moral philosophy, each having to do with what has come to be called "the impartial point of view." Though we are mad-dog impartialists ourselves, we find, uncomfortably, that our theory of self-knowledge and identity lends some weight to the recent case against impartialism.

Chapter 7
Identity and Morality

Impartialist (in one sense Kantian[1]) ethical theory emphasizes the abstract formal deliberative features of the rational agent as such, the universalizability of moral reasons, and the rational unacceptability of making (unprincipled) exceptions in favor of oneself or one's friends. After all, it is truistic that, like civil and criminal law (conceived according to the American democratic ideal), moral law applies to everyone equally.[2] But moral philosophers have found this truism difficult to spell out in any way that bears substantively on conduct.

1 Impartialism and Its Problems

The classic and perennial attempt is of course the Golden Rule, which owes its universal appeal entirely to its never being taken literally. The *idea* behind the Golden Rule is that of impartialism—that one should make no exception in one's own favor. The rule implements this idea brilliantly by suggesting that one identify(!) with one's victim's interests or good by *hypothetically putting oneself in his or her shoes.* But the specific version of this implementation literally recommended by the rule is absurd: that one force one's own tastes and preferences on one's victim whether the victim likes it or not.[3] A more perspicacious understanding of "making another's good one's own" or "putting oneself in the other's shoes" is required. The obvious choice is to imagine oneself with the other's tastes and preferences instead of one's own—which leads (again assuming stark literalness) to the requirement that one gratify one's victim's tastes and preferences, whatever they may be and whatever relation they may bear to one's own.

This unexpected and drastic unclarity of what it is to "put oneself in another's place" or to "adopt another person's point of view" finds a more subtle manifestation in R. M. Hare's more sophisticated discussion of universalizability in moral reasoning.[4] In Hare's view, when we propose to ourselves a course of action based on a certain reason, we must ask ourselves whether we would be willing to exhort our victim to perform the same or corresponding action based on that reason if he or she were in our present (actual) circumstances. But the question naturally arises of just which, or whose, preferences are imputed to the victim as part of this again hypothetical supposition. Hare explicitly rejects the suggestion that our victim's own preferences control the hypothetical choice (p. 108); the distinctive form of moral argumentation for which Hare is famous requires that we consult *our own* present actual inclinations. But as he sees forthwith (p. 111), this leads directly to the well-known "fanatic" problem: If an agent's preferences are eccentric enough and particularly if the agent is willing to undergo great suffering in pursuit of some cherished but grossly misguided and (to us) evil ideal, Harean reasoning is powerless to convict this fanatic of immorality in acting on that ideal.[5]

John Rawls offers a still more powerful mechanism for putting oneself in another's place.[6] He casts the moral or social theorist as a member of a hypothetical group of choosers who are in the presocial "original position": They are concerned with deciding (collectively) on the basic principles that will regulate their eventual society. Though the choosers are "mutually disinterested," each is concerned with maximizing self-interest (and each is perfectly rational). What keeps the deliberations from simple degeneration into squabbling is that the choosers are behind a "veil of ignorance": Though any number of "positions," roles, or careers will be available for occupancy in the social structure that the choosers end up regulating, no chooser knows which position he or she will occupy; none *knows who he or she will be.* For Rawls, this means that if I am a chooser I will know neither my social status, my occupation, my particular talents and abilities, my preferences (except for the "primary goods," more on which below), nor even my conception of the good or my overall life plan. Thus Rawls ensures fairness, for my ignorance of these bits of detail—my ignorance of *my identity*—prevents me from engaging in any sort of special pleading and from making any exception in my own favor. All I can do in the name of rational self-interest is to make sure that no "position" in the society-to-be is too lowly or degraded or otherwise undesirable, lest I unluckily turn out to be its occupant.[7] Since all choosers in the group are blinded by the veil of ignorance and are thus necessarily impartial, the basic rules of the society they choose are likewise blind to the identities of its individual members and is thus necessarily fair.

This ingenious fusion of contractarian, utilitarian, and Kantian ideas nonetheless inherits the aforementioned problem for impartialism.[8] If while behind the veil of ignorance I know neither what my tastes and preferences nor what my conception of the good will be, what basis have I for choice? I have hypothetically relinquished everything that, to me, makes me *me*; this is impartiality or selflessness with a vengeance.[9] Presumably Rawls has in mind a Sidgwickian conception of utility as satisfaction of desire, neutral with respect to specific desires (so that, e.g., a masochist's pain counts as positive utility); thus as a chooser I am to assume the conative cloak of whatever generic individual it is whose "position" I am considering. Happily this does not put me back in the business of simply gratifying the desires of some particular recipient or victim, whatever they may be, for I now have a large number of generic recipients to consider, and I must balance their interests against each other, since inasmuch as I have done anything unto the least of these my brethren, I might well turn out to have done it unto me. Yet without having any idea a priori what desires and preferences the denizens of a purely hypothetical society might have, I cannot look out for those preferences in conducting my deliberations.[10]

Rawls' solution (pp. 62, 90–95) is to posit certain basic interests had by all choosers—what he calls the "primary goods"—on the grounds that they are as nearly universal as it matters among humans and are in any case practical preconditions of satisfying any other desires at all; he claims that they are what any person has reason to seek independently of that person's more specific preferences: first liberty, then income or wealth, and self-respect. This seems reasonable enough if we are theorizing about creatures very like ourselves, but it does not take us very far in specifically moral decision-making as opposed to Rawls' own primary concern, the choice of a society's most basic institutions. For even if (indeed, especially if) we grant it universal that human beings value liberty and the other primary goods, that in no way helps us take account of differences in preference across persons, the prevalent differences of which are just what created our initial problem of impartialism considered as a substantive aid to moral decision. Nor are we any further ahead in our attempt to understand what it is to "put oneself in another's place."[11] (We do not mean to imply that Rawls himself claimed to shed light on that notion, nor do we intend any criticism of Rawls' own project as *he* conceives it.)

2 Identifying with Others: Teleological Relativity Again

What can our theory of "knowing who" contribute to the present aspect of the universalizability issue? We claim to offer a correct analysis, but it is a disappointing one for those who would make empathetic thought experiments the cornerstone of moral decision-making.[12] To put oneself into another's place is to "identify with" that person, to step into that person's actual niche instead of one's own: in short, we submit, hypothetically to become *who that person is.* It would perhaps be more natural to speak more simply of becoming *that person,* thus assimilating the empathetic hypothesis to our vaunted subjunctive "If I were you"; but we have seen that the appearance of a genuine identity locution here is entirely misleading. "If I were you" already means "If I were in your position," which according to our theory can also be expressed by saying "If I were who you are."

Our theory also predicts a teleological relativity in all three formulations. All three are short for, "If I had those properties of yours that are important for P [the purpose highlighted by contextual features]." And in the case of empathetic moral argument, we must ask, which of one's recipients' properties *are* important? Unfortunately, that is just what our best-known empathetic theories either leave open or prejudge.[13] When in the course of deciding whether I should lie to your spouse about where I did or did not see you last night, I say "If I were in your shoes" or (more pedantically) "If I were who you are," I do not mean, "If I had a great-grandfather whose half-sister served with Crazy Horse at Little Big Horn" or "If I were the first person in this room to have used the word 'crabgrass' within the past hour." Why not? Because those properties are not *morally relevant* in the context. Which are the morally relevant properties? That depends on the moral reasons that might be given in the context for either decision—which in turn depends on what background moral theory one already holds. What I take to be my recipient's "place," "shoes," or "position" and what I take to be "becoming who" he or she is, requires a judgment (on my part) of moral relevance, and a judgment of moral relevance in turn requires a theory that tells us what properties of people are the truth-makers of moral judgments themselves, i.e., and to wit, a moral theory, a normative ethics. In order to perform an empathetic thought experiment—in order to employ the device of "putting myself in another's place"—I must already have and mobilize an antecedently justified background normative theory.[14]

If we are right about this, the upshot is that the empathetic device cannot stand as a fundamental moral armament, and a criterion of right action based on such a device cannot be the fundamental principle of morality. This should come as no surprise to anyone who has seriously tried to formulate a literal and empirically adequate version of the Golden Rule or who has wrestled with Hare's theory or tried to separate Rawls' formal mechanism from Rawls' own substantive views on fairness and on what is good. The only empirically adequate formulation of the Golden Rule is something like, "Do unto others what you would think was right if you were in relevantly similar circumstances"; Hare's universalizability principle expressly and ineliminably alludes to relevant similarity as well.[15] No such principle can be applied unless one already has a criterion of moral relevance, and no one who does not already accept some moral theory can defend a criterion of relevance. To see that the same objection applies to Rawls' view, consider sets of hypothetical choosers whose ideas of prudence or self-interest are vastly different from our own and sets of hypothetical members of one's created society whose moral views and "conceptions of the good" are radically different from our own (actual current) views. Given these two arrays of possible if farfetched alternatives, it would be hard to motivate settling on any definite judgment of the form, "I wouldn't want *that* to happen to me at any cost."

The point, we should emphasize, constitutes an *objection* only to those theories according to which (i) a principle or method of empathetic identity transfer is *fundamental* to morality and/or (ii) such a principle can by itself or in conjunction with a body of purely factual information yield a substantive moral judgment. We are far from denying that the Golden Rule or the methods of Hare and Rawls have practical value in moral decision-making. But we think that this value is only marginally cognitive. Properly understood, the Golden Rule, the universalizability principle, and Rawls' method considered as a means of moral choice are "morally significant tautologies," to use a phrase of Alan Gewirth's in a way he did not intend;[16] they have neither normative nor factual content by themselves, but they have their uses nonetheless in that they remind us of our standing moral priorities, enforce logical consistency, and warn us against rationalization—compare "Do the right thing," "First things first," "Business is business," "Duty is duty," and "You gotta do what you gotta do." The enforcement of priorities, of consistency, and of honesty with oneself are functions of great importance in our practical moral life even though they are not part of substantive theory construction; since most people do not at least consciously engage in substantive moral theory construction anyway, it is not surprising that the Golden Rule looms so much larger in the history and the psychology of popular ethics than does any theoretical pill or confection created by professional philosophers.

Let us move on to the second aspect of impartialism that we think we can illuminate.

3 Reflexive versus Impersonal Reasons and Universalizability

Since the publication of Thomas Nagel's *The Possibility of Altruism*,[17] it has been customary to distinguish "subjective" from "objective" moral reasons on the basis of indexicality. An agent's reason for acting is "subjective" iff it contains what Nagel calls a "free agent-variable," i.e., an unbound variable taking the agent himself as value. (To avoid the many irrelevant connotations of the subjective/objective terminology, we speak simply of *reflexive* as opposed to *impersonal* reasons.) The distinction is best illustrated by considering several types of ethical egoist on the basis of the reasons that motivate their ostensibly selfish actions.[18] Suppose that Hud pushes his way to the head of the line, viciously elbowing an old lady and trampling a two-year-old, in order to get the last remaining portion of ice cream. His reason for acting in that way is *to get the ice cream*, and as in any complementizing occurrence, "to" here is a lexical variant of "that NP" (NP = noun phrase): Hud acts in order *that he* get the ice cream. But there are three different further reasons that might ground this proximate one, corresponding to three different attitudes toward universalization. (i) Hud may think that he, Hud, is a uniquely privileged character and that everyone should help Hud get what he wants. (ii) He may think that the world would be a better place in the end if everyone acted selfishly at all times instead of going around trying (often misguidedly) to benefit others. On the other hand, (iii) he may not be willing to universalize at all; he may care only that *he* get the ice cream and have no views about what anyone else is obligated or permitted to do. In this last case, the reflexive pronoun "he" occurs ineliminably; it cannot be replaced by "Hud" or by any other designator (flaccid or rigid) of Hud. A puzzle here: The ineliminability of this reflexive is not due to the tired old possibility of amnesia, etc., for Hud's reasons are as they are regardless of his beliefs about anyone's identity.

In cases (i) and (ii) Hud's reasons are impersonal even though his *actions* systematically benefit himself; we may disagree with his background moral theories (particularly in (i)), but we cannot fault him on Harean grounds. Only in (iii) is his reason ineliminably self-regarding.[19] Note that this distinction can be generalized to reasons that one might have for unselfish, even heroic acts as well, so long as *group* egoism or tribal morality of some sort is envisioned: A man runs back into the proverbial burning house to save his child; this may be because he thinks everyone should protect the interests of that child, Melinda Snarf, or because he thinks everyone should protect the interests of Ephraim Snarf's children, or because he thinks every person should protect the interests of his or her own children, but also (very likely[20]) for none of these general reasons but simply because Melinda is *his* child. Or consider patriotism. We may make great sacrifices for our country but for reasons of the same different sorts—because the USA is the best country and everyone (including America's enemies) should support it, because everyone should support his or her own country (loyalty being a good thing), or simply because it is *our* country (right or wrong) and that is that.[21]

As we remarked, the apparent irreducibility of these Nagelian reflexives is puzzling since the identities of persons are not in question. But the two-scheme theory comes to the rescue. The reflexives occur within complementized clauses that state reasons, and such locutions are lexical variants of "that" clauses and thus are subject to individuative-scheme disambiguation. Hud's reason, e.g., is *to get the ice cream*, i.e., it is an ·I get the ice cream·. Now if the truth-conditional scheme were imposed, this reason would receive a purely impersonal interpretation: Any extensionally isomorphic reason formulation—i.e., any "X F's Y" such that "X," "F," and "Y" denote Hud, $\lambda xy(x$ gets $y)$, and the ice cream, respectively—would be counted as equivalent, and the singular-term positions would be transparent. Thus Hud could be understood only as acting on *some* policy—not necessarily an egoistic one—that would result in Hud's getting the ice cream. But this interpretation would obliterate our apparently sound distinction between impersonal and reflexive reasons, leaving us with another puzzle.

Fortunately, truth-conditional dot individuation is independently forbidden here because we used "to" as a complementizer in the first place. "To" as opposed to "that" generally forces computational rather than truth-conditional interpretation; we presume that is what it is for. (Just as Castañeda's "he himself" is. John the amnesiac war hero may intend *that* John claim a Bronze Star but cannot intend *to* claim the Bronze Star—i.e., that *he himself* should do so—until he recovers from his amnesia.) If this is right, then standardly formulated reason clauses are always type individuated computationally, since they are complementized using "to" rather than "that." There is an obvious explanation for this: When we discuss reasons, we do so as a means of understanding and predicting action; normally we are not interested in the truth values of the propositions expressed in the reasons (until we begin to consider whether the action will be or has been successful). Thus Nagel's distinction is saved; Ephraim's reason for rushing into the burning house may be to save *his* child, per se, rather than to save Melinda impersonally considered or even to be a one's-own-child-saver among other one's-own-child-savers; it may thus be a reason that only he can have with respect to Melinda, just as the self-regarding belief that his own child is in danger is one that only he can have with respect to her.[22] Moreover, we have explained Andrew Oldenquist's well-known conclusion: that "real" or reflexive egoism, loyalty, or patriotism can be practiced only by a creature that possesses "a concept of self."[23]

We need, however, to consider the connection between the reflexive/impersonal distinction and universalizability, particularly since universalizability has recently become a bone of contention between "impartialists" (which unexpectedly comprehends utilitarians of all sorts, and even some ethical egoists, along with Kantians; cf. note 2) and moral philosophers of a comparatively new breed, loosely called "personalists." The personalists, who include Oldenquist, Bernard Williams, Michael Stocker, and Lawrence Blum,[24] argue roughly that my pursuit of my own "life plan" (in Rawls' phrase) or "projects" (in Williams') and/or my attachment to my family, my friends, or my neighborhood often overrides the strictly impartial concern that I may have for the rights or welfare of others, as a matter of human nature; furthermore (and much more to the point), the personalists contend that this is often entirely as it should be—that in many cases, normal, intelligent, decent people would not approve of or respect us for taking the lofty impartialist line and for sacrificing our own or our friends' interests. Notably, the sorts of interests that are thus thought to override considerations of impartial application of maxims, respect for persons, or utility are those that (so to speak) give meaning to the protagonist's life and so figure centrally in his or her self-conception—those interests that are part of the protagonist's identity, in short.[35] Thus universalizability, although useful and required for some moral purposes, is limited by the personal and seldom extends or *should* extend to people or other creatures remote from us[26]—especially when our "ground projects" or our marriages or close friendships are at stake—even when those remote others are in as "relevantly" similar circumstances (impersonally described) as one likes.

Our three sorts of reasons differ psychologically (though not truth conditionally) in a way that is cognate with our three attitudes to universalizability. Take for simplicity the case of the three egoists. Hud_1 believes for some reason that he is a privileged character; he is not selfishly motivated even though his action is designed to benefit him. Accordingly, the practical reasoning that drives his rush to the ice-cream table contains the generalization "Everyone (similarly situated) should help H get the ice cream," where "H" is replaced by some representation of Hud_1—not necessarily a first-person representation—containing whatever descriptive material is involved in his belief that he is an *Übermensch* of some sort and a premise to the effect that he himself is H. Hud_2 holds a less eccentric view—that everyone should always act out of self-interest (for only in this way is the greatest overall good achieved, etc.). Representing himself merely as one person among others in a public world, as Nagel would say, Hud_2 infers that he therefore must hurl himself at the ice-cream table; there is no getting out of it.

Each of these two characters has "one thought too many," in Williams's now celebrated phrase.[27] Each is acting on principle; neither is thinking personalistically in the manner of a "real" egoist. Contrast Hud_3. He does not have the extra, general thought, but sees the ice cream, thinks only "I want the ice cream and the overall best way to get it is to grab it," and grabs it. He does not think in the same mental breath that each of the other, similarly situated revelers should defer to him, but no more does he think that they should lunge for the ice cream too (that would hardly suit his purpose, as Hare emphasizes). He is committed to no moral judgments about others. He just grabs and hopes for the best (payoff for him).

So much the worse for Hud_3, we think; Hud_1 and Hud_2 may be misguided but at least they are principled; their impersonalism is (comparatively) a virtue, not the slavish lack of self-respect that the impartialists warn us against. But the personalists score better against the impartialists when the talk turns to altruism based on tribal loyalty. My wife wants me to treat her well and to make her good my good, not because everyone should treat everyone well or even because everyone is obligated by the marriage contract to treat his or her spouse well, but (i) because she is *Mary Ann*,[28] *herself* rather than under an accidental description (cf. our earlier discussion of identity-related pronominal usage),[29] and (ii) because she is *my* wife (not because she is my *wife*), if any description is wanted. To confine my concerns to the impersonal demands of morality would be unuxorious at best, perhaps monstrous. So goes, in part, the personalist critique of universalizability.

We disposed of (i) in chapter 6. Although there are *de re* attitudes and transparent attitude ascriptions, there is no such thing as love or regard that is directed purely and simply to a haecceity, nor would a love that is grounded in a (metaphysically genuine) nonhaecceitist, qualitative essence (such as her unique genetic code) be the sort of love that is sought by romantics like Lavinia or (here) Mary Ann. There is only love that is grounded in the beloved's truly (or designatedly) important properties. As for moral reasons, we have argued that in virtue of the role reasons play in our explanatory economy, standard characterizations of reasons are computationally individuated, and consequently there is no such thing as a reason that entirely lacks descriptive content.

Yet Mary Ann's demand (ii) is harder to ignore, for as we have seen (indeed, as according to our own theory we have insisted), there *is* such a thing as an irreducibly reflexive reason. And as we have also seen, it can be distinguished even from the general obligations implicit in a moral marriage contract; it is the sort of reason that only one other person can have vis-à-vis a given individual, and it is not universalizable. Let us pursue this last point.

It is sometimes complained that the "sporting egoist" or the "sporting patriot"—an egoist or patriot who contends that every person or every nation should seek to maximize its own welfare, and let the best person or nation win—cannot deliver a coherent ought-to-be or a deontically perfect world, as opposed to a collection of mutually inconsistent ought-to-do's. It is impossible by definition that everyone win, and thus impossible by definition that everyone live up to their obligations; thus there is no world in which everyone does live up to them. On this ground, egoism has been charged with incoherence.[30] A similar charge can be laid against marital altruism of the universalized variety if we suppose a conflict of interest between two different wives. Suppose that Lavinia, who has finally married Dudley sometime since we mentioned her last, badly needs a copy of *Logic, Semantics, Metamathematics* by the weekend and that Mary Ann badly needs one too, but that there is only one copy at the store. Lavinia and Mary Ann are both too busy to fare forth, so Dudley and I head for the bookstore, each hoping to obtain the book before the other does. Each of us believes himself obligated to get the book for his own wife, as a matter of marital loyalty and support. But we cannot both fulfill these altruistic obligations. Thus a critic of universalized marital altruism asks, "How *should* things turn out?" There is (the critic responds to his own rhetorical question) no answer; universalized altruism no more provides a coherent ought-to-be than does universalized egoism.

We do not accept this criticism. If we are true "sporting egoists" or "sporting tribal altruists," we *do* have a vision of an ideal state of affairs: It is the vision precisely of a game well played. Of course only one player wins and of course the other loses, but if the loser has played well and has done his best, all's right with the game (and the world), particularly since the emergence of at least one loser is a conceptual truth and to complain about a conceptual truth would be both irrational and mean of spirit. In the case of an egoistic individual sport, the players smile and have some beers together after the game. In the case of *Logic, Semantics, Metamathematics,* Lavinia may think the less of the handless and bootless Dudley for losing the race to me, but she does not fault his regard for her or his husband-liness; he did his best, even though his best is not that of a seasoned competitive book-shopper.[31]

Whether or not this defense of the universalizing egoist/altruist succeeds, we may try to contrast impersonal morality based on principle with the kind that disdains the "thought too many." Suppose that Mary Ann has been reading the personalist critics of universalizability and quite specifically demands behavior on my part that is based on irreducibly reflexive and nonuniversal reasons. We may be hard put to understand this demand as *moral* or (not to beg the question against Williams' and Wolf's alternative terminology (cf. note 26)) to understand it as worthy of respect and as properly overriding impartialist moral concerns; and we are tempted to dismiss it, as traditional impartialists have tended to do, by simply writing it off as unintelligible—the *moral* point of view, it has been said, is impartial trivially and by definition. But we think the current popularity of personalism and its treatment as a live and nonnegligible competitor by impartialists militate against its mere unintelligibility or trivial falsity. A significantly extended argument would be needed to show it to be defective. Furthermore, our two-schemist account of reflexive reasons seems to show that the personalist concept of a moral reason is coherent, contra traditional impartialists.[32]

4   *The Inviolability of Persons*

We expect that our theory could throw other sorts of light as well on the moral concept of personhood, or rather on one or more of the distinct concepts that have variously gone under that rubric. To conclude this chapter let us make one further illustrative suggestion regarding what Rawls and Nozick have called the "inviolability of persons."[33] This inviolability or "separateness" of persons supposedly balks utilitarianism in that it forbids actions that would otherwise be morally recommended on grounds of utility increase; but to our knowledge no one has ever cashed the metaphor and so explained what precisely *is* wrong with the actions thus forbidden.[34] Combining Williams' notion of a "ground project" with our own theory of "identity" and with an independently suitable understanding of utility, we can explicate one sense of "inviolability" (though surely not the only sense that figures in moral theory); and on the conception that results, we see that the inviolability of persons in that sense is a consequence of utilitarianism rather than a barrier to happiness, though the conception is of little or no use in confounding fanatics or utility monsters.

No utilitarian worth two hedons in a bucket conceives of utility as *pleasure* in the sense of a psychological magnitude at a time; "eudaimonistic" utilitarianism, which prizes human flourishing in some more general sense, is far more plausible in the light of obvious counterexamples to the hedonistic variety. Now, it should also be clear that Williams' "ground projects" are closely connected to flourishing in this sense: Insofar as it is plausible to think that such projects play the central role in human life that Williams envisions for them, it is plausible to understand flourishing and hence utility by reference to them; utilities attaching to one's ground project are given far greater weight than are utilities of more jejune sorts; thus (for the sort of utilitarianism we have in mind) respect for people's ground projects has significant moral priority, though presumably not the impartiality-threatening force that Williams himself seems to see for it. And the properties of a person that relate directly to that person's ground project are therefore, from a moral point of view, that person's *most important* properties. Hence they are the properties that for moral purposes our theory of "knowing who" counts as constitutive of that person's *identity*, just as Williams intends. Thus on the eudaimonistic notion of utility and our view of "identity" it comes out true that any good utilitarian will think twice before trespassing his own or another's identity or separateness as a person, as measured by weighty, because ground-project-related, utilities; and in this sense, at least, the utilitarian grants with enthusiasm that persons are inviolable in a way that bars appeal to utilities of lesser gravity. (Though, as we mentioned above, fanatics and utility monsters cannot be expected to agree, precisely because their ideas of *importance* do not match yours or ours.)[35,36]

Chapter 8

"Knowing Who" and Epistemic Logic

Since the publication of Hintikka's *Knowledge and Belief*, notions of "knowing who"—both formal and informal—have figured centrally in foundational investigations of quantified epistemic logic. So we may well ask what light our theory of "knowing who" has to shed on standard disputes and puzzles in that area.

Putting aside questions of strict logical form (and ignoring tense), the shallow representations arrived at in chapter 2 can be modified in light of chapters 3–5 to yield the following unified paraphrase schema for "S knows who N is" in a suitable first-order language **L**:

(1) $(\exists\phi)(\text{Imppred}(\phi, S', P, \ulcorner N' \urcorner) \ \& \ \mathbf{K}:\mathbf{M}(S', \langle \ \rangle, \ulcorner \phi!N' \urcorner))$.

Here "$\mathbf{K}:$" is interpreted as "knows that" (where "$\mathbf{M}$" goes proxy for a role marker, SEM or CON); "Imppred" is understood as in chapter 2; the quantifier ranges over predicates of a suitably restricted fragment **L'** of **L** (which, for convenience, can be identified with S's language of thought); and "S'" and "N'" are appropriate translations of "S" and "N" into **L'** (see (i) below).

1 The Tradition in Epistemic Logic

The main differences between the formal treatment of "knowing-who" adumbrated in our schema (1) and that with which Hintikka began are as follows:

> (i) We make a Russellian distinction that Hintikka does not: We take the primitive singular terms of the paraphrase language **L** to be of two sorts: individual constants and iota-terms. Only natural-language expressions that function referentially (as semantically unstructured rigid designators) are translated by us into individual constants of **L**. Superficially singular terms functioning attributively (as semantically equivalent in the context to flaccid descriptions) are represented by appropriate iota-terms of **L**. The identities of "S'" and "N'" in paraphrase (1) thus depend on a prior decision about the contextual workings of "S" and "N" in any given instance of "S knows who N is," and

questions about the opacity or transparency of "N" are absorbed into that of whether "**M**" in the paraphrase schema should be replaced by "SEM" or by "CON." (In this way we provide a place for any genuinely semantic referential/attributive ambiguity that may attach to "N," while upholding our official view that two-schemism per se holds the key to puzzles about opacity.)

(ii) We represent our teleological parameter explicitly rather than submerging it as Hintikka does in the background pragmatics.

(iii) As the form "$\mathbf{K} : \mathbf{M}(S', \langle \ \rangle, \ulcorner \phi ! N^\urcorner)$" in (1) attests, we think of propositional-attitude ascriptions as relational, by way of the Sellarsian/Davidsonian theory of ostended exemplars.[1]

(iv) In particular, we advocate two-schemism with respect to the type individuation of the exemplars, as recorded in (1) by the schematic flag "**M**."

(v) We regard the provision of a theory in **L** of the $(\mathbf{L} - \mathbf{L}')$-predicates "$\mathbf{K} : \text{CON}$," "$\mathbf{K} : \text{SEM}$," "Imppred," etc., as riding piggyback on a previously given truth theory θ in **L** for $\mathbf{L}'$,[2] augmented by suitable explications in **L** of direct reference and certain functional-psychological notions (see the next paragraph). Thus we think of our formal idiom **L** as a syntactic and semantical metalanguage for that part **L'** of itself reserved for the transcription of ostended **L'**-exemplars. (Purely for expository convenience, we assume that in addition to the familiar semantical vocabulary "DEN," "SAT," and "T," **L** contains restricted variables of the following sorts: "τ^n," "π^n," and "σ^n" (for a given numeral n) range over **L'**-formulas in which just the alphabetically first n variables occur free and in which no variable has both free and bound occurrences; "α" and "β" range over **L'**-terms; "μ" ranges over **L'**-variables; "Ω" and "Σ^n" range over denumerable sequences and n-ary sequences ($n > 0$), respectively; and "Γ^n" ranges over n-ary sequences of terms of **L'**. We also assume the presence in **L** of the following useful vocabulary: "$\Sigma^n \times \Gamma^n$" as shorthand for "$\langle \langle \Sigma^n(1), \Gamma^n(1) \rangle, \ldots, \langle \Sigma^n(n), \Gamma^n(n) \rangle \rangle$" and "$\Gamma^n | \pi^n$," read as "the result of simultaneously substituting $\Gamma^n(1), \ldots, \Gamma^n(n)$ for the n free variables of π^n taken in their alphabetical order.")

We think of "$\mathbf{K} : \mathbf{M}$" as a *defined* predicate in **L** whose representationalist definition is—subject to the small emendation made below—expressed in **L** by the following biconditional, in which "$R(\alpha, x)$" and "$\approx \mathbf{M}(\sigma^n, x, \pi^n)$" are antecedently defined theoretical constructions, read respectively as "α directly refers to x" and "σ^n plays for x the same **M**-role as π^n," and "$W(\tau^0, x)$" goes proxy for the appropriate account of the characteristic functional role played in x's inner economy by a closed formula τ^0 when x knows-true τ^0:

(2) $\mathbf{K}:\mathbf{M}(x, \Sigma^n \overset{.}{\times} \Gamma^n, \sigma^n) \leftrightarrow (\exists \pi^n) \{ \approx \mathbf{M}(\pi^n, x, \sigma^n) \ \& \ \{(i)[1 \leqslant i \leqslant n \rightarrow R(\Gamma^n(i), \Sigma^n(i))] \ \& \ (\exists \tau^0)\{\tau^0 = \Gamma^n|\pi^n \ \& \ W(\tau^0, x) \ \& \ T(\tau^0)\}\}\} \ \& \ (\Omega)\{(i)[1 \leqslant i \leqslant n \rightarrow \Omega(i) = \Sigma^n(i)] \rightarrow \mathrm{SAT}(\Omega, \sigma^n)\}.$

Though we do not attempt full characterization of "R" and "$\approx \mathbf{M}$," we suppose them so defined that the likes of (2) and (3) can be proved:

(3) $(\Omega)[\mathrm{DEN}(\alpha, \Omega) = \mathrm{DEN}(\beta, \Omega)] \rightarrow [\approx \mathrm{SEM}(\sigma^n, x, \pi^n[\alpha/\mu] \leftrightarrow \ \approx \mathrm{SEM}(\sigma^n, x, \pi^n[\beta/\mu])],$

(4) $R(\alpha, x) \rightarrow (\Omega)[\mathrm{DEN}(\alpha, \Omega) = x].$

Officially our interests crisscross Hintikka's. His main concern apropos quantified epistemic logic is to avoid latitudinarianism by restricting quantification into epistemic contexts to cases in which the knower "knows who" the object of his belief is; this is precisely how "knowing who" entered discussion of epistemic logic in the first place. By contrast, we have already provided in chapter 5 for restriction of quantifying in in terms of direct reference of representations without alluding to "knowing who"—either directly or indirectly (and perhaps circularly) by way of our understanding of direct reference in turn. In our current notation, "S knows, of someone, who (s)he is" is paraphrased by

(5) $(\exists \alpha)(\exists y)(\exists \phi)[\mathrm{Imppred}(\phi, S', P, \alpha) \ \& \ \mathbf{K}:\mathbf{M}(S', \langle\langle y, \alpha \rangle\rangle, \ulcorner \phi!x \urcorner)].$

But this very provision affects the related issues in epistemic logic, and there are several further standard questions that we can illuminate also. For reasons of fatigue we do not construct an entire formal system that embodies all these contributions, but we address the issues and questions seriatim, suggesting appropriate postulates as the need arises. In some cases the effects are deflationary rather than expansive and exciting; so be it.

2 The Impact of Our Theory

(i) Epistemic logicians have not challenged Hintikka's suggestion that "knowing who" serve as the appropriate restricting criterion for quantifying epistemic contexts; even the late Gail Stine,[3] Hintikka's sharpest critic within the standard literature, granted it. We do challenge it; indeed, we think it is easily shown false by the sorts of examples we adduced in section 4 of chapter 5. As we observed there, the interest-relative propriety of quantifying in and the purpose-relative truth of knowing-who ascriptions are controlled by different contextual parameters, the relativity of "knowing who" ranging far more widely than that of *de-re*-ness. In some contexts (for some purposes) "knowing who" may obtain but only *de dicto*; in others a knower may have an attitude *de* someone without knowing who that person is. (If the parameters of "knowing who" and *de re* knowledge did track together, Hintikka's suggestion would of course make perfect sense intuitively as well as formally, especially given his formal explication of "knowing who" as we discussed it in chapter 1: To know who N is for purpose P is to know of N modulo purpose P that N is X, where X is someone known to us for purpose P. We surmise that the suggestion has been accepted so readily in the epistemic-logic literature (despite its evident falsity) because writers and readers simply have not noticed the differences in teleological relativity. This inattention is due particularly to Hintikka's quickness in granting such relativity *tout court*.) Our policy of representing the parameter of "knowing who" explicitly helps to correct its confusion with the much better confined parameter (however it works exactly) of quantifying in.

(ii) Much ink has been spilled over Hintikka's justly controversial dual reading of the quantifiers. Because of his knowing-who restriction on quantifying in (combined, as Stine points out, with his eschewing of free variables[4]), a quantifier in his system that binds a variable across an epistemic operator cannot have its normal range but must be restricted to a domain of individuals "known to" the operator's subject. This "dual" treatment gives rise to any number of oddities and objections (though many of these are fairly easily circumvented).[5] By contrast, we avoid such problems entirely, since we handle quantifying in antecedently and independently and avoid reliance on "knowing who" in particular. For the same reason we have no trouble quantifying negated knowledge statements of the sort noted by Castaneda ("On the logic of self-knowledge"),[6] and we accommodate the consistency of Sleigh's sentence "There is someone such that *a* knows that he exists but not who he is"[7] (whose paraphrase in our notation is "$(\exists x)(\exists y)\{\mathbf{K}:\mathbf{M}(a, \langle\langle y, \alpha\rangle\rangle, \ulcorner(\exists z)(z = x)\urcorner)$ & $\sim(\exists\phi)[\text{Imppred}(\phi, a, \mathrm{P}, \alpha)$ & $\mathbf{K}:\mathbf{M}(a, \langle\langle y, \alpha\rangle\rangle, \ulcorner\phi!x\urcorner)]\}$").

(iii) One may ask, what is the correct (or the best) *analysis* of "knowing who" within a quantified epistemic logic? Every practitioner seems to agree with Hintikka's original proposal to represent "S knows who N is" as "$(\exists x)\mathbf{K}_S(x = \mathrm{N})$", where the quantifier is restricted to individuals known to S. And no wonder, since (as we argued in chapter 1) the restriction nicely trivializes Hintikka's proposal considered as an analysis. If we thus *presuppose* a notion of "knowing who," Hintikka's formula is perfectly serviceable because it is trivially correct. If we do not presuppose it, we see no interesting or illuminating analysis of "knowing who" within the fairly shallow vocabulary of epistemic logic; assuming the correctness of (2) above, (1), (5), and their variants are the simplest expressions that can do even minimal formal justice to the everyday notion of "knowing who." On the other hand, our own theory (by means of its incorporation of two-schemism) at least reveals the effect that the pragmatic ambiguity of knowing-who ascriptions can have on transparency of term occurrences—a feature that is masked by Hintikka's fully opaque use of singular-term letters—for it affords, e.g., a sense of "a knows who b is" and "a knows who c is" in which either expression together with "$b = c$" implies the other (viz., when the truth-conditional scheme is in play; cf. (3)).

(iv) In response to a criticism by Sleigh,[8] Hintikka at one point augmented his original system with a new rule, (C.ind $=$),[9] which has been accepted by later writers (including Stine (p. 132)) at least for cases not involving self-regarding attitudes. The rule requires in effect that "$b = c$", "$(\exists x)K_S(x = b)$", and "$(\exists x)K_S(x = c)$" jointly imply "$K_S(b = c)$". If this implication did not hold and if we continued to read the second and third premises as knowing-who ascriptions, then S's knowing who b and c are and knowing that b is F would imply S's knowing that c is F even when S is unaware that b and c are identical, which is agreed by all sides to be counterintuitive. Yet (we would say) the cure is hardly better than the disease, since the thesis codified by (C.ind $=$) is a strong one, inviting obvious counterexamples. Hintikka ("Individuals, possible worlds," p. 59) rightly dismisses some of these as exploiting parameter shift, but it seems plain that counterexamples enough are afforded by suitable choices of a firmly fixed parameter (even without recourse to self-regarding attitudes). For example, a mystery fan may know who Emma Lathen is for the purpose of recommending choices of mystery novels to a neophyte and may know who R. B. Dominic is for the very same purpose and yet be unaware that Lathen and Dominic are one and the same (in the sense, appropriate to this example, of hosting no computational equivalent of "Emma Lathen = R. B. Dominic"). More generally, so long as the purpose in question is relatively *undemanding* and the computational scheme is in force, there is no reason to suppose that the respective bodies of information involved in knowings who modulo that purpose are rich enough to validate (C.ind $=$).[10,11]

What all this suggests, given the undisputed formal utility of (C.ind $=$) in Hintikka's system, is that the ordinary notion of "knowing who" as captured by our theory simply does not correspond to the much stronger notion of the identity of a "genuine individual" throughout a subject's set of epistemic alternatives that drives Hintikka's entire approach to quantified epistemic logic.[12] This is, of course, no embarrassment to that approach or to any particular logical system that results; it only blocks the reading of Hintikka's formulas in terms of "knowing who" in the ordinary sense and confirms our earlier contention that "knowing who" in that sense must be divorced permanently from issues of quantifying in and the identity of indiscernibles.[13]

(v) Castaneda has repeatedly and notoriously wielded *self-regarding* attitudes against Hintikka.[14] His original charge was that Hintikka offers no adequate representation of statements of self-knowledge, such as "Jones knows that he himself is Jones." Contrary to Hintikka's proposal in *Knowledge and Belief*, "$(\exists x)(x = j \;\&\; K_j(x = j))$" does not do, for its English translation, "Someone known to Jones is known by Jones to be Jones," might be true of the amnesiac war hero even though the hero precisely does not know that he himself is Jones.[15] After an exchange of accusations of missing the point,[16] Hintikka[17] distinguished two modes of transworld individuation or "methods of cross-identification." John, the war hero, knows who John the war hero is, so to speak, by description, but in his amnesia he "cannot place the hero into any cognitive *Lebenswelt* of his own, nor can he help anybody else to place the hero into *his* sphere of personal acquaintance, except perhaps inadvertently" (Hintikka, "On attributions of 'self knowledge,'" p. 79); he cannot individuate the hero "by acquaintance." (On this usage, the peculiarity of dissociative amnesia is that its victim loses acquaintance with himself.) Thus Hintikka maintains that quantifiers binding variables within the scope of epistemic operators are ambiguous with respect to interpretations according to these two methods of cross-identification and introduces an appropriately disambiguating notation. And, just as we take the "he himself" locution to enforce (by means of lexical presumption) deployment of the computational scheme of role individuation, Hintikka suggests that that locution requires deployment of the "personal cognitive" or "first-hand acquaintance" reading of the quantifier (pp. 80–81).

We do not buy Hintikka's distinction between individuation by description and individuation by "first-hand acquaintance." Unless the object of our acquaintance is a sense datum or some other object that is diaphanously present to us, unmediated by mental representation, our seeming "acquaintance" is always to some extent descriptive. (This point is a psychological, not a semantical one, and so is compatible with our rejection of the Millian/Russellian dichotomy in section 2 of chapter 4 and section 3.3 of chapter 5.) Some descriptions are more likely than others to be useful to us immediately in laying hands on our victim, but the difference is only of degree.[18]

Castaneda would presumably concur and maintain that anything less than a *fully diaphanous*, unmediated "acquaintance" leaves room for counterexamples of his sort.[19] Moreover, if the security and infallibility of first-person reference is underwritten by an epistemically special sort of acquaintance with oneself (which to our knowledge Castaneda does not clearly insist on), this same special sort of acquaintance is not shared between one person and another, even though each of us can be acquainted in a looser and more familiar sense with another person. So Castaneda is unlikely to be impressed by Hintikka's concluding reply or to relinquish his view of the distinctive status of self-regarding attitudes and its unrepresentability in

Hintikka's system. The issue is at a stalemate. What can our own theory contribute?

On our view as expounded in chapter 6, for Jones to know that he himself is Jones is for Jones to know-true a computationally individuated : I am Jones: (invocation of the computational scheme being enforced by the surface reflexive). This is (we agree with Castaneda) something that only Jones can do, because of the success grammar of "knows"; since only Jones is Jones, only Jones can be related by *knowing* to the singular proposition $\langle \lambda u(u = u), \text{Jones} \rangle$ under a first-person representation. Hintikka's original notation affords no way of marking anything like the distinction between our two schemes, so it would seem that one should be introduced. Castaneda himself proposed to add both a special reflexive operator[20] and an indexing system to identify the antecedents of referentially ambiguous reflexive pronouns,[21] though he offered no accompanying semantic proposals.[22] Hintikka pooh-poohed these efforts,[23] mainly on the basis of his contention that his system can already represent self-knowledge unaided once we enforce the distinction between individuation "by acquaintance" and less demanding forms of picking-out. But (straining our instinctive reluctance to grant that self-regarding attitudes are sui generis in any way whatever) we have defended Castaneda against that contention. Thus on the grounds of our two-schemism, we too contradict Hintikka: Quantified epistemic logic needs a distinctive way of representing attitude complements whose computational as opposed to truth-conditional individuation is mandated by surface grammar.[24]

In our current notation, where individuative scheme is explicitly marked by "CON" or "SEM," a metalinguistic variant of Castaneda's proposal can be made to serve. Briefly, suppose that $\mathbf{L}'$ contains an *individual parameter* "$\$$"—in effect, a dummy name, i.e., an expression that functions syntactically as an individual constant but semantically like some designated free variable—and that $\mathbf{L}$ employs *starred* versions of its formula-variables to range over formulas of $\mathbf{L}'$ containing "$\$$." Then, treating (2) as defining "$\mathbf{K} : \mathbf{M}(x, \Sigma^n \dot{\times} \Gamma^n, \sigma^n)$" for the case in which "σ^n" ranges over n-ary formulas *not* containing "$\$$," we can introduce a predicate "SELFDEM(α, x)," read as "α is a *self-demonstrative* for x," and use it together with some syntactic notions to define "$\mathbf{K} : \mathbf{M}(x, \Sigma^n \dot{\times} \Gamma^n, \sigma^{n*})$." The requisite syntactic vocabulary is "$(\Gamma^n, \alpha) | \pi^{n*}$" (read as "the result of simultaneously substituting $\Gamma^n(1)$, ..., $\Gamma^n(n)$ for the n free variables of π^{n*} taken in their alphabetical order and substituting α for each occurrence of "$\$$" in π^{n*}") and "VAR$\$(\sigma^{n*})$" (read as "the result of substituting the alphabetically $(n + 1)$th variable for each occurrence of "$\$$" in σ^{n*}"). "SELFDEM," of course, is intended to capture the special role of the terms that replace "$\$$"; we take it to be defined in such a way as to ensure the following theorems among others:

(6) $\text{SELFDEM}(\alpha, x) \rightarrow R(\alpha, x)$.

(7) $[\text{SELFDEM}(\alpha, x) \ \& \ \text{SELFDEM}(\beta, x) \rightarrow \{ \approx\mathbf{M}(\sigma'', x, \pi''^*[\alpha/``\$'']) \leftrightarrow \approx\mathbf{M}(\sigma'', x, \pi''^*[\beta/``\$'']) \}$.

The definition of "$\mathbf{K}:\mathbf{M}(x, \Sigma'' \dot{\times} \Gamma'', \sigma''^*)$" can now be given in two parts, by [SEM* ⊢1] and [CON* ⊢1]:

[SEM* ⊢1] $\mathbf{K}:\text{SEM}(x, \Sigma'' \dot{\times} \Gamma'', \sigma''^*) \leftrightarrow (\exists\pi''^*) \{ \approx\text{SEM}(\pi''^*, x, \sigma''^*) \ \& \ (\exists\alpha)\{(i)[1 \leqslant i \leqslant n \rightarrow R(\Gamma''(i), \Sigma''(i))] \ \& \ (\Omega)[\text{DEN}(\alpha, \Omega) = x] \ \& \ (\exists\tau^0)\{\tau^0 = (\Gamma'', \alpha)|\pi''^* \ \& \ W(\tau^0, x) \ \& \ T(\tau^0)\}\} \ \& \ (\tau^{n+1})\{\tau^{n+1} = \text{VAR\$}(\sigma''^*) \rightarrow (\Omega)\{[(i)[1 \leqslant i \leqslant n \rightarrow \Omega(i) = \Sigma''(i)] \ \& \ \Omega(n + 1) = x] \rightarrow \text{SAT}(\Omega, \tau^{n+1})\}\}$.

[CON* ⊢1] $\mathbf{K}:\text{CON}(x, \Sigma'' \dot{\times} \Gamma'', \sigma''^*) \leftrightarrow (\exists\pi''^*) \{ \approx\text{CON}(\pi''^*, x, \sigma''^*) \ \& \ (\exists\alpha)\{(i)[1 \leqslant i \leqslant n \rightarrow R(\Gamma''(i), \Sigma''(i))] \ \& \ \text{SELFDEM}(\alpha, x) \ \& \ (\exists\tau^0)\{\tau^0 = (\Gamma'', \alpha)|\pi''^* \ \& \ W(\tau^0, x) \ \& \ T(\tau^0)\}\} \ \& \ (\tau^{n+1})\{\tau^{n+1} = \text{VAR\$}(\sigma''^*) \rightarrow (\Omega)\{[(i)[1 \leqslant i \leqslant n \rightarrow \Omega(i) = \Sigma''(i)] \ \& \ \Omega(n + 1) = x] \rightarrow \text{SAT}(\Omega, \tau^{n+1})\}\}$.

Finally, we could adopt the following as a schematic translation rule:

If "N knows that ... N ..." translates as "$\mathbf{K}:\mathbf{M}(\text{N}', \langle \ \rangle, \ulcorner$——N' ——$\urcorner)$," then "N knows that ... he himself ..." translates as "$\mathbf{K}:\text{CON}(\text{N}', \langle \ \rangle, \ulcorner$——\$——$\urcorner)$," and "N knows who he himself is" translates as "$(\exists\phi)$ (Imppred $(\phi, \text{N}, \text{P}, \ulcorner\$\urcorner)$ & $\mathbf{K}:\text{CON} (\text{N}', \langle \ \rangle, \ulcorner\phi! \$\urcorner))$".

Beyond proposing the likes of

(8) $[\mathbf{K}:\text{CON}(x, \langle \ \rangle, \sigma^{0*}) \ \& \ \mathbf{K}:\text{CON}(x, \langle \ \rangle, \pi^{0*})] \rightarrow [\mathbf{K}:\text{CON}(x, \langle \ \rangle, \ulcorner\sigma^{0*} \ \& \ \pi^{0*}\urcorner)$,

(9) $\mathbf{K}:\text{CON}(x, \langle \ \rangle, \ulcorner(\exists\mu)(\mu = \$)\urcorner)$,

and

(10) $[\mathbf{K}:\text{CON}(x, \langle \ \rangle, \sigma^{0*}) \ \& \ \mathbf{K}:\text{CON}(x, \langle \ \rangle, \ulcorner\$ = \alpha\urcorner)] \rightarrow \mathbf{K}:\text{CON}(x, \langle \ \rangle, \sigma^{0*}[\alpha/``\$''])$,

we cannot go into further detail here about the nature of the axioms required to capture self-demonstratives' distinctive contribution, but we mention some applications of this impressionistically sketched apparatus to a few sample inferences as a token of good faith:

(a) Castaneda points out, and Hintikka agrees,[25] that "Jones knows that he himself is wise" implies "Jones is wise." Hintikka proposes to represent the premise as "$(\exists x)(x = j \ \& \ K_j(x \text{ is wise}))$" (the quantifier flagged for individuation "by acquaintance"), which straightforwardly implies "j is wise" in Hintikka's system. But we have agreed with Castaneda that Hintikka's quantifier restriction does not suffice to forestall counterexamples of the amnesiac sort; for example, Jones might be perceptually acquainted with Jones as intimately as one likes, say by way of a mirror or by grasping one of his own limbs, and still not know that he himself is Jones. Rather than attempt to patch Hintikka's system (with its vastly different presuppositions), let us see how matters proceed in our own formalism. In our augmented notation, "Jones knows that he himself is wise" translates as "$\mathbf{K}:\mathrm{CON}(j, \langle\ \rangle, \ulcorner\mathrm{Wise}(\$)\urcorner)$," from which "Wise($j$)" follows from [CON* ⊢1] and the ingredient truth theory for **L'**, which jointly ensure the provability of

$$\mathbf{K}:\mathrm{CON}(j, \langle\ \rangle, \ulcorner\mathrm{Wise}(\$)\urcorner) \to T(\ulcorner\mathrm{Wise}(j)\urcorner)$$

and

$$T(\ulcorner\mathrm{Wise}(j)\urcorner) \leftrightarrow \mathrm{Wise}(j).$$

(In effect, then, (2), [CON* ⊢1], and [SEM* ⊢1] jointly provide our meta-linguistic analog of Hintikka's rule (C.K) for inferring "p" from "K_ap.") Likewise, "Jones knows that $a = b$" (and hence "$a = b$") can be shown to follow from (our representations of) "Jones knows that he himself $= a$" and "Jones knows that he himself $= b$"—i.e., from the two premises

$$\mathbf{K}:\mathrm{CON}(j, \langle\ \rangle, \ulcorner(\$ = a)\urcorner)$$

and

$$\mathbf{K}:\mathrm{CON}(j, \langle\ \rangle, \ulcorner(\$ = b)\urcorner),$$

we can derive (by means of (10))

$$\mathbf{K}:\mathrm{CON}(j, \langle\ \rangle, \ulcorner(a = b)\urcorner).$$

(b) The *de-re*-ness of all knowledge *de se* is automatically guaranteed on our account. For example, "Jones knows that he himself is wise" can be shown to yield "{Someone/Jones} is known by Jones to be wise": both

$$(\exists\alpha)(\exists y)\mathbf{K}:\mathrm{CON}(j, \langle\langle y, \alpha\rangle\rangle, \ulcorner\mathrm{Wise}(x)\urcorner)$$

and

$$(\exists\alpha)\mathbf{K}:\mathrm{CON}(j, \langle\langle j, \alpha\rangle\rangle, \ulcorner\mathrm{Wise}(x)\urcorner)$$

follow from

$$\mathbf{K}:\mathrm{CON}(j, \langle\ \rangle, \ulcorner\mathrm{Wise}(\$)\urcorner).$$

And, in general,

$$(\exists\alpha)\mathbf{K}:\mathrm{CON}(x, \langle\langle x, \alpha\rangle\rangle, \mathrm{VAR}\$(\sigma^{0*}))$$

follows from

$$\mathbf{K}:\mathrm{CON}(x, \langle\ \rangle, \sigma^{0*}).$$

(c) In Hintikka's representation, "*a* knows that he himself is *b*" implies "*a* knows who *b* is," and "*a* knows that he himself is self-identical" implies "*a* knows who he himself is." But neither implication is unconditionally acceptable. As is entailed by our proposed axiom (9), every normal person presumbly knows that he himself is self-identical—even the vauntedly vatted brain, all of whose extracerebral inputs are manufactured by the Evil Deceiver, is usually supposed to know *that* much—but surely it is a contingent and empirical matter of fact whether he can individuate himself in any interesting way at all. And *a*'s knowing that he himself is *b* does not amount to knowledge (for purpose P) of who *b* is unless P is a trivial, label-seeking purpose. Our own proposals do yield the desirable result that, for so trivial a purpose,

$$\mathbf{K}:\mathrm{CON}(x, \langle \ \rangle, \ulcorner \$ = b \urcorner)$$

implies

$$(\exists \phi)\,[\mathrm{Imppred}(\phi, x, \mathrm{P}, \ulcorner b \urcorner) \ \& \ \mathbf{K}:\mathrm{CON}(x, \langle \ \rangle, \ulcorner \phi ! b \urcorner)].$$

But our account of purposes in chapter 2, as applied in chapter 6, clearly blocks the inference in all other cases. And those same considerations ensure that it is *never* correct to infer

$$(\exists \phi)\,(\mathrm{Imppred}(\phi, x, \mathrm{P}, \ulcorner \$ \urcorner) \ \& \ \mathbf{K}:\mathrm{CON}(x, \langle \ \rangle, \ulcorner \phi ! \$ \urcorner)]$$

from

$$\mathbf{K}:\mathrm{CON}(x, \langle \ \rangle, \ulcorner \$ = \$ \urcorner).$$

We have applied our theory of "knowing who" to some otherwise disparate issues in philosophy of language, philosophy of mind, ethical theory, and philosophical logic—to good effect, we hope, in each case. We await still further opportunities.

Notes

Chapter 1

1. See, e.g., Jaakko Hintikka, *Knowledge and Belief* (Ithaca: Cornell Univ. Press, 1962); Arthur Prior, "*Oratio obliqua*," *Aristotelian Society Supplementary Volume* 37 (1963), 115–126; Anthony Kenny, "*Oratio obliqua*," *Aristotelian Society Supplementary Volume* 37, (1963), esp. 139–140; Keith Donnellan, "Reference and definite descriptions," *Philosophical Review* 75 (1966), 281–304; Hector-Neri Castaneda, "On the logic of attributions of self-knowledge to others," *Journal of Philosophy* 65 (1968), 439–456; Saul Kripke, "Naming and necessity," in *Semantics of Natural Language*, D. Davidson and G. Harman, eds. (Dordrecht: D. Reidel, 1972), 293; Michael Lockwood, "Identity and reference," in *Identity and Individuation*, M. K. Munitz, ed. (New York: New York Univ. Press, 1971), 199–211; Gail Stine, "Quantified logic for knowledge statements," *Journal of Philosophy* 71 (1974), 127–140; and subsequent theorists some of whose works we discuss in this book.

2. We conflate use and mention in this harmless way throughout, avoiding cumbersome goings-on about the replacement of schematic letters.

3. The multiple ambiguity thesis is held widely, if casually. Occasionally it finds its way into print; see, e.g., Prior ("*Oratio obliqua*," 124), who speaks of "different senses" of "knowing who."

4. Though regrettable, this standard failure of logical analyses to secure syntactic advantages is to be expected. Linguistic theory itself is currently riven by internecine disputes and fragmented into numerous formats and programs; it would be unreasonable to require that philosophers choose and cozy up to one faction rather than another, much less that they adjudicate these differences and reconcile their proposals to the winner's particular way of doing things. The requirement of syntactic plausibility, however, has a useful corollary regarding the relative degree of explanatory burden. Let us explain.

   A *grammar* for a natural language L is a formal mechanism that associates strings of expressions of L with interpreted formulas of some stipulated symbolic calculus in such a way as to yield a criterion of well-formedness in L for such strings; we would also want the grammar to provide for the eventual semantic interpretation of the well-formed strings by means of some sort of semantic component attaching to the symbolic calculus. The details, of course, vary crazily from one linguistic program to another, but a rough criterion of explanatory burden emerges regardless: The greater or lesser the superficial dissimilarity between a target sentence S of L and its proposed symbolic regimentation A, the greater or lesser the prima facie burden of explaining how to incorporate the pairing $\langle S, A \rangle$ into a workable grammar for L, hence the lesser/greater the prima facie plausibility of regarding A, in a genuinely principled way, as the (or a) logical form of S in L. In default of a reasonably complete and agreed-on formal grammar for English, this intuitive test at least serves to distribute the onus of justification in a fairly smooth way. For a defense of a similar precept and an encapsulating metatheory for linguistic semantics, see W. Lycan, *Logical Form in Natural Language* (Cambridge: Bradford Books/MIT Press, 1984).

Surprisingly, linguists have had little to say about "knowing who." C. L. Baker mentions the notion in passing in his work on embedded questions ("Notes on the description of English questions," *Foundations of Language* 6 (1970), 197–219), but he offers no special theory of "S knows who N is." The treatment of "knowing who" in Montague grammar has been explored to some extent by Hintikka in "On the proper treatment of quantifiers in Montague semantics" (in *Logical Theory and Semantic Analysis*, S. Stenlund, ed. (Dordrecht: D. Reidel, 1974), 45–60; see also M. J. Cresswell, *Logics and Languages* (London: Methuen, 1973), 236–238; L. Karttunen, "Syntax and semantics of questions," *Linguistics and Philosophy* 1 (1977), 3–44; P. Hirschbühler, *The Syntax and Semantics of Wh—— Constructions* (Bloomington: Indiana Univ. Linguistics Club Publications, 1979); and J. Groenendijk and M. Stokhof, "Semantic analysis of Wh—— complements," *Linguistics and Philosophy* 5 (1982), 175–234. Another pertinent contribution is R. D. Hull, "A semantics for superficial and embedded questions," in *Formal Semantics of Natural Language*, E. L. Keenan, ed. (Cambridge: Cambridge Univ. Press, 1975), 39ff.

5. Pages 131ff. Other page references to this work are inserted parenthetically in the text.

6. Actually, Hintikka uses schematic letters "*a*," "*b*," ... for personal variables; we replace them throughout without further comment.

7. Hintikka goes on to wield this analysis against Quine's claim that we can intelligibly quantify across an epistemic operator only if that operator is on that occasion being construed transparently.

8. The restriction also accords nicely with the common feeling that one cannot have knowledge or beliefs *about* a particular person unless one knows who that person is (see, e.g., Prior, "*Oratio obliqua*," 122). We argue in chapter 5, however, that that feeling is badly misguided.

9. His comment here is echoed in his "Individuals, possible worlds, and epistemic logic," *Nous* 1 (1967), 43.

10. See W. Lycan, "The paradox of naming," in *Analytical Philosophy in Comparative Perspective*, B. K. Matilal and J. L. Shaw, ed. (Dordrecht: D. Reidel, 1985), 81–102.

11. In *Words and Objections: Essays on the Work of W. V. Quine*, D. Davidson and J. Hintikka, eds. (Dordrecht: D. Reidel, 1969); reprinted in *Reference and Modality*, L. Linsky, ed. (Oxford: Oxford Univ. Press, 1971), 112–144. Page references in the text are to the latter version. We again replace quoted schematic letters with our own.

12. Our use of the word "final" here is not quite fair; Kaplan closes his paper by acknowledging his awareness of "obscurities and difficulties" (p. 144).

13. "Language of thought" is not Kaplan's term; we borrow it ultimately from Gilbert Harman, *Thought* (Princeton: Princeton Univ. Press, 1973), 54. This notion has come in for merry and derisive criticism in the past few years. We believe that the standard criticisms are misguided in that they rest on a crass caricature of the representationalist view; see chapter 4.

14. To see more adequately what "clarity and detail" might come to, let us marshal a few further remarks by Kaplan ("Quantifying in," 136): (a) S's *knowing* or *being acquainted with* N suffices for S's having a vivid name of N. (b) If S has a vivid name of N, then S must believe that the name has a referent. (c) A vivid name "robustly and clearly delineates" its referent's nature. (d) A vivid name represents a person who plays a "major role" in S's inner story. However, (e) in order to have a vivid name of N, S need neither believe himself to have perceived the name's referent nor have any "means of locating" that referent physically. Finally, (f) in general, the more detailed ("complete") a name is, the more vivid (or likely to be vivid) it is, though of course the harder it will be for the name to denote.

15. From Kaplan's point of view, this is just as it should be; we argue in chapters 4 and 5 that

the parameters that control the legitimacy of quantifying in are different from and more narrowly restricted than those that figure in "knowing who."

16. Kripke, "Naming and necessity," 270. (Further page references are included parenthetically in the text.) Kripke does not suggest, of course, that a rigid designator could not have denoted some object other than that which it in fact denotes; he means just that "in *our* language, it stands for that thing, when *we* talk about counterfactual situations" (p. 289), no matter what counterfactual situations we are talking about. The designator thus picks out its referent independently of any of the referent's contingent properties.

17. The reader may be skeptical of this, thinking that S's acquaintance with N *must* be mediated (psychologically speaking) by some "mode of presentation" featuring one or more contingent properties of N. The latter claim is true without question, but we argue in chapters 4 and 5 for a radical separation of psychological from semantical aspects of thought; what is psychologically mediated may nevertheless be semantically immediate. The notion of rigid designation is semantical.

18. Peter van Inwagen has understandably suggested that our use of the notion of a referential designator might make our analysis circular in that referentiality is sometimes explained in terms of someone's "knowing who" the referent is (see, e.g., Donnellan, "Reference and definite descriptions," and Lockwood, "Identity and reference," 208–209). However, (i) we have not characterized referentiality in this way, and (ii) we believe it is a serious mistake to do so, since a description may be used referentially even when no one knows who the referent is and attributively even though everyone knows who the (*de facto*) referent is. For considerably more on this point, see chapter 5.

19. See Hintikka, *Knowledge and Belief*, 148–149.

20. Donnellan expresses doubt that the ambiguity he discusses under the heading "referential/attributive" is a real syntactic/semantic one, believing it to be merely pragmatic. We take the opposite tack, for reasons that we cannot state in full without digressing through a welter of Donnellan exegesis. (The *main* reason is that Donnellan's distinction affects truth conditions, and on our view that suffices for semantical significance.)

21. See, e.g., Kripke, "Speaker's reference and semantic reference," in *Contemporary Perspectives in the Philosophy of Language*, P. French, T. E. Uehling and H. Wettstein, eds. (Minneapolis: Univ. of Minnesota Press, 1979), 6–27; Michael Devitt, "Donnellan's distinction," *Midwest Studies in Philosophy* 6 (1981), 511–524; Rod Bertolet, "The semantic significance of Donnellan's distinction," *Philosophical Studies* 37 (1980), 281–288.

22. This was pointed out to us by George Schumm (Ohio State University).

23. See Michael Devitt, "Singular terms," *Journal of Philosophy* 71 (1974), sec. 2; and S. Boër, "Attributive names," *Notre Dame Journal of Formal Logic* 19 (1978), 177–185.

24. John Pollock offers an interesting hybrid example: A detective who thinks he has encountered another victim of Jack the Ripper might say, "I know who did this, but I still don't know who he is" (*Language and Thought* (Princeton: Princeton Univ. Press, 1982), 198).

25. We find this principle immensely useful for semantics. For elaboration on it and an excellent example of its use, see Donald Davidson, "Truth and meaning," *Synthese* 17 (1967), 304–323, and "On saying that," in *Words and Objections*, D. Davidson and K. J. J. Hintikka, eds. (Dordrecht: D. Reidel, 1969), 158–174.

Chapter 2

1. An example might be useful here. The name "Ronald McDonald" belongs to whichever actor is currently playing the clown who does advertisements and promotions for McDonald's hamburgers. Suppose that Fred St. John is currently filling that role, and

suppose that S asks, "Who is Fred St. John?" (knowing that Fred St. John is a television personality and desiring to know which one in particular). Then the reply "Fred St. John is Ronald McDonald" may well be final. We would explain this finality by saying that "Ronald McDonald" is in this case a *title*, shorthand for the attributive description "the actor who plays the clown in McDonald's advertisements" or the like. So the response "Fred St. John is Ronald McDonald" is equivalent to "Fred St. John (alone or currently) plays the clown ...," which *is* a final answer to S's question, given S's purposes as hypothesized.

2. Cf. Lockwood, "Identity and reference," and Dennis Stampe, "Attributives and interrogatives," in *Semantics and Philosophy*, M. K. Munitz and P. K. Unger, eds. (New York: New York Univ. Press, 1974), 159–196. Lockwood hints (pp. 207–208) at the asymmetry we mean to establish here. Stampe (pp. 165–166) explicitly notes the asymmetry but does not seem to appreciate its full force.

   In "Answers to Questions," Hintikka joins us in evaluating knowing-who ascriptions by reference to questions, and seems to move toward our teleological view.

3. Cf. Stampe, "Attributives and interrogatives," 166.

4. Cf. the exchange in *Exodus* 4:11–12 between Moses and God, where the relevant property of Moses is "being a messenger of God"; this property gives him the authority to give orders to the Pharaoh.

5. We note in passing that there are what might be called "mentioning" uses of definite descriptions in "who" questions, uses that are neither attributive nor (purely) referential. "Who is the F?" can be a material-mode surrogate for "What is an 'F'?," or "What does 'the F' mean?"; and the appropriate reply is a dictionary definition of "the F" couched in the material mode. For example, "Who is the Pope?" if asked by the teacher of a course on world religions may invite not "He's John Paul II" but "The Pope is the head of the Roman Catholic Church" or "The Pope is the designated successor of St. Peter, the Vicar of Christ." In this sense "knowing who the Pope is" has nothing to do with anyone's identity; it is simply knowing what a Pope is or knowing what "the Pope" means. Failure to appreciate this can lead to confusions; Stampe ("Attributives and interrogatives") falls into several. Since our concern is identity of individuals, we ignore "mentioning" uses of descriptions in setting out our prototheory. We return briefly to the topic in section 4.6 of chapter 4.

6. Cf. C. Chastain, "Reference and context," in *Minnesota Studies in the Philosophy of Science, Vol. 7: Language, Mind, and Knowledge*, K. Gunderson, ed. (Minneapolis: Univ. of Minnesota Press, 1975), 194–269.

7. In Chapter 6 we show that this primacy of the attributive goes a long way toward solving the well-known puzzles of *self*-knowledge and self-regarding attitudes.

8. Ontologically, we incline toward the view of fictional characters defended by Peter van Inwagen in "Creatures of fiction," *American Philosophical Quarterly* 14 (1977), 299–308. However, see also W. Lycan and S. Shapiro, "Actuality and essence," *Midwest Studies in Philosophy* (to be published).

9. The latter conception underlies Lycan's discussion of languages of thought in "Toward a homuncular theory of believing" (*Cognition and Brain Theory* 4 (1981), 139–159) and in "The paradox of naming"; cf. J. McCawley, "A program for logic," in *Semantics of Natural Language*, D. Davidson and G. Harman, eds. (Dordrecht: D. Reidel, 1972), 498–544; by contrast, Gilbert Harman champions the idea that each of us thinks *in* an undisambiguated natural language such as English. But it is important to resist the temptation to take sides here and the idea that a person has just *one* mental language in which all thought is carried out; representation of all sorts occurs in different parts of the brain and at different levels of functional organization. Our references to "*the* language of thought" throughout this chapter are merely a colloquial convenience.

10. See our discussion of attitudes *de re* in chapter 5.

11. For that matter, there is no obvious reason to admit that ambiguous constructions, such as definite descriptions or "is," infest the language of thought at all; perhaps it is only the paraphrases that are there in the first place.

Chapter 3

1. Donald Davidson, "On saying that." Davidson's theory is a younger sibling within the inscriptionalist family of Wilfrid Sellars' well-known proposal involving dot quotation. We have expounded and defended versions of the latter in previous writings (Lycan, "The paradox of naming"; Boër, "Names and attitudes," in *The Philosophy of Logical Mechanism: Essays in Honor of Arthur W. Burks*, M. Salmon, ed. (Dordrecht: D. Reidel, to be published); and elsewhere), but for present expository purposes we find it more convenient to begin with Davidson.

2. See Lycan, "Davidson on saying that," *Analysis* 33 (1972–1973), 138–139; and S. Blackburn, "The identity of propositions," in *Meaning, Reference, and Necessity*, S. Blackburn, ed. (Cambridge: Cambridge Univ. Press, 1975), 182–205; however, for various replies to this criticism, see C. McGinn, "A note on the Frege argument," *Mind* 85 (1976), 422–423; M. Platts, *Ways of Meaning* (London: Routledge and Kegan Paul, 1979), 888; and J. McDowell, "Quotation and saying that," in *Reference, Truth and Reality*, M. Platts, ed. (London: Routledge and Kegan Paul, 1980), 456. For a survey of possible refinements and residual problems for Davidson's account, see Platts, *Ways of Meaning*, chap. 5; and R. Arnaud, "Sentence, utterance, and samesayer," *Nous* 10 (1976), 69–96.

3. We engage throughout in the practice of designating vocabulary items of the unseen canonical idiom by their boldfaced English counterparts.

4. The word "pragmatics" has unfortunately acquired two different technical senses recently. In older usage, pragmatics is distinguished from syntax and semantics. To pragmatics in this sense belong the theory of speech acts, the theory of conversational implicature, etc., which presuppose rather than affect the assignment of determinate truth conditions to target sentences of one's object language. In more recent usage (due largely to Richard Montague), pragmatics is a *part* of semantics, sometimes called indexical semantics, that deals with the effect of contextual considerations on denotation, satisfaction, and truth in languages with context-sensitive expressions such as deictic pronouns, token reflexives, and the like. In what follows, we use "pragmatic" and its cognates in the second of these two senses, for, as will become clear, we regard the "pragmatic ambiguity" inherent in deferred ostension as something that bears on the truth conditions of sentences such as (3); and the formal implementation of our strategy for exploiting this ambiguity is a straightforward piece of indexical semantics.

5. Hilary Putnam, "The meaning of 'meaning,'" in *Minnesota Studies in the Philosophy of Science*, vol. 7 (Minneapolis: Univ. of Minnesota Press, 1975), 131–193.

6. Putnam, "The meaning of 'meaning,'" and J. A. Fodor, "Methodological solipsism considered as a research strategy in cognitive psychology," *Behavioral and Brain Sciences* (1980) 63–73. Note that the notion of conceptual role is not always construed solipsistically; see G. Harman, "Nonsolipsitic conceptual role semantics," unpublished.

7. Hilary Putnam, "Philosophy of physics," in his *Mathematics, Matter and Method: Philosophical Papers*, vol. 1 (Cambridge: Cambridge Univ. Press, 1975), 88.

8. For (considerable) elaboration of this point, see chapter 11 of Lycan, *Logical Form in Natural Language*. Actually we believe that there are reasons for identifying sentence

meaning in the traditional sense with truth condition rather than with conceptual role if we are forced to choose (see chapter 10), but when we turn from public natural languages to inner thoughts, these reasons evaporate, and (as we emphasize below) our two individuative schemes endure as noncompeting alternatives.

9. See Montague's *Formal Philosophy*, R. Thomason, ed. (New Haven: Yale Univ. Press, 1974). We would like our discussion to generalize to any semantical format that associates sentences of a natural language on some principled grounds with formulas of a logical calculus, which are themselves semantically interpreted by explicit truth definition, though the details of our treatment may happen to end up favoring some such formats over others. (In *Word Meaning and Montague Grammar* (Dordrecht: D. Reidel, 1979), David Dowty showed that generative semantics and the present versions of Montague grammar are special cases of universal grammar; see also R. Cooper and T. Parsons, "Montague grammar, generative semantics and interpretive semantics," in *Montague Grammar*, B. Partee, ed. (New York: Academic Press, 1976), 311–362.)

10. Taking these rules as purely formal—i.e., not as parasitic on the semantical interpretation of the canonical idiom—simplifies matters by allowing noncircular talk about such rules in the specification of that interpretation. Admission of semantically conditioned transformations does not in principle prevent such talk; it merely forces us to engage in elaborate stratification of transformations to match the "stages" of semantic interpretation, discussed later in the text.

11. A (much) fuller exposition and defense of such a program for natural-language semantics was undertaken by Lycan in *Logical Form in Natural Language.*

12. Since we are dealing with only a small and manageable array of contextual features, we here prefer the Montague-Scott method of indices to the more general method of assignment functions defended in chapter 3 of Lycan's *Logical Form in Natural Language.*

13. For all we care, SEM and CON might be 0 and 1, respectively. All that really matters is that SEM be distinct from CON, though it is useful to think of them as necessary existents, such as numbers or pure sets, to which we are ontologically committed in any case. Alternatively, we could think of "M" as ranging over any nonempty set Y of items, each of which is somehow intimately connected with either semantical or conceptual roles, provided that the notions of semantical and conceptual role do not figure essentially in the specification of Y. We could then bring out the connection with particular sorts of roles in the course of specifying the denotation of **THAT** by invoking some background theory about what makes a member of Y salient to one sort of role rather than another. In light of our earlier, informal remarks, Y might be thought of as a set of explanatory purposes or interests. Rather than complicate matters, we stick by the "arbitrary marker" ploy.

14. Here and throughout we treat a sequence as a function from the *positive integers* (or an initial segment thereof) so as to bring our notation into line with the ordinary English practice of counting objects beginning with the first rather than the zeroth.

15. Treated in this way, formulas containing abstracts do not semantically record certain syntactic scope distinctions. For example,

   (a) **PAST**$[G(\imath xFx)]$

is not *semantically* distinguished from

   (b) $\hat{y}(\mathbf{PAST}[G(y)])(\imath xFx),$

despite the syntactic differences vis-à-vis the scope of the description with respect to the tense-operator, since proviso (i) views (b), in effect, as a stylistic variant of (a). The intuitively desired semantic distinction would, in any event, arise between (a) and the independently available formula

   (c) $(\exists y)(y = \imath xFx \ \& \ \mathbf{PAST}[G(y)]).$

Given the limited role that abstracts are called on to play for us, we regard the foregoing wrinkle as a "don't care." If, however, a richer expressive role for abstracts were needed, then we could easily use the present apparatus to define a derivative notion of the "extension" of an abstract (at an index, etc.). This would ensure that (b) works semantically like (c) rather than like (a).

16. There are well-known ways of doing this. For a particularly attractive suggestion, see T. Burge, "Truth and singular terms," *Nous* 8 (1974), 309–325.

17. For example, compare David Lewis' "meanings" ("General semantics," in *Semantics of Natural Language*, D. Davidson and G. Harman, eds. (Dordrecht: D. Reidel, 1972), and M. J. Cresswell's "structured meanings" in his book *Structured Meanings* (Cambridge: Bradford Books/MIT Press, 1985).

18. We beg the reader's indulgence for the two use/mention conflations in our formulation of the postulate: the one concerning numerals and numbers involved in our use of "**THAT**$_i$" and the other concerning our employment of "$T^{++}DEN_i$" both as a functor of the truth theory and as an external designation for the function ultimately specified by the theory. Both lapses are remediable but at the cost of tedious circumlocution. In what follows, we continue to fudge in both these ways, choosing brevity over rigor.

19. If semantically conditioned transformations were allowed, this postulate would remain noncircular, given the plausible assumption that any semantical fact presupposed by talk of S's being derivable from A in L (where $A \in F^+$) can be adequately expressed in terms of the interpretation of the fragment F^+.

Chapter 4

1. See W. G. Lycan, "Toward a homuncular theory of believing," *Cognition and Brain Theory* 4 (1981), 139–159, and "Psychological laws," *Philosophical Topics* 12 (1981), 9–38.

2. In particular, of course, to "believe-true" an inner token is not to believe *that* the token *is* true. It is for the token to perform the sort of job within in its host's internal bureaucracy that distinguishes beliefs from desires, intentions, and other attitudes.

3. Particularly, Lycan, "Toward a homuncular theory of believing," and "The paradox of naming"; also, see note 7 below.

4. See, e.g., M. J. Cresswell, *Logics and Languages* (London: Methuen, 1973), 167–169, and Cresswell's own references. For a contrasting though compatible view according to which expressions such as "the fact" are "deleteable" head nouns rather than complementizers, see S. Munsat, "WH——complementizers," *Linguistics and Philosophy* (to be published).

5. For example, Cresswell, *Logics and Languages*.

6. Boër and Lycan, *The Myth of Semantic Presupposition*, (Bloomington: Indiana Univ. Linguistics Club Publ., 1976) sec. 3.3; see also Lycan, *Logical Form in Natural Language*, 96n.

7. There is considerable terminological slack here. Seemingly no two philosophers agree on precisely what is required for something to count as a "language." Our own criterion here is minimal and quite inoffensive: that a language be some system of physical tokens type-individuated according to truth condition on the basis of internal referential structure. In particular, we do not require (i) that the other "sentences" entailed by a given sentence also be its immediate parts or other mereological relatives (cf. Brian Loar, "Must beliefs be sentences?" *PSA* 1982 (Lansing: Philosophy of Science Association, 1982)), or (ii) that formulas of the internal system of representation be inscribed either

in chalk on a tiny blackboard or in freckles on a subject's back. (Against some popular caricatures of the representationalist theory, see again Lycan, "The paradox of naming."

8. "Mental representation," *Erkenntnis* 13 (1978), 9–61.

9. See Vendler, *Res Cogitans* (Ithaca: Cornell Univ. Press, 1972), and Fodor, "Methodological solipsism."

10. "A puzzle about belief," in *Meaning and Use*, A. Margalit, ed. (Dordrecht: D. Reidel, 1979), 239–283.

11. Indeed, this is the line we took in "Who, me?" *Philosophical Review* 89 (1980), 427–466, as do Ruth Marcus in "A proposed solution to a puzzle about belief," *Midwest Studies in Philosophy* 6 (1981), 501–510) and Thomas McKay in "On proper names in belief ascriptions," *Philosophical Studies* 39 (1981), 287–303.

12. See the initial paragraph of section 4.

13. If names abbreviated descriptions in any semantical sense, this would be obvious, but names ubiquitously share the conceptual roles of descriptions *even though they do not abbreviate them*; see Lycan, "The paradox of naming."

14. At least one of us (WL) is inclined to think that denials of the "presuppositions" of questions do sometimes count semantically, though not illocutionarily, as answers to those questions; cf. our insistence in *The Myth of Semantic Presupposition* (sec. 4.1.1) on distinguishing semantic affirmation and denial from the speech acts of asserting and denying.

15. Note that our arguments here are compatible with the observation that a question intrinsically specifies an "answer space" in the sense of a partition of logical space. Cf. Elliott Sober, *Simplicity* (Oxford: Oxford Univ. Press, 1975); N. D. Belnap and T.B. Steel, *The Logic of Questions and Answers* (New Haven: Yale Univ. Press, 1976), and works cited therein.

16. For trenchant defense of such individuals, see G. Massey, "Tom, Dick and Harry, and All the King's Men," *American Philosophical Quarterly* 13 (1976), 89–107.

17. N. Goodman, *The Structure of Appearance*, second edition (Indianapolis: Bobbs-Merrill, 1966).

18. Hector-Neri Castaneda has posited a fairly dramatic interest-relativity in the concept of knowing per se, in "The theory of questions, epistemic powers, and the indexical theory of knowledge," in *Midwest Studies in Philosophy* 5 (1980), 193–237; see also our critique of Castaneda's view, in "Castaneda's theory of knowing," in *Profile: Hector-Neri Castaneda*, J. Tomberlin, ed. (Dordrecht: D. Reidel, 1985). Two different sorts of interest-relativity in knowing are touted in C. Kilgore and W. Lycan, "Epistemological relativity," unpublished.

19. We do not know whether such titles are syntactically fused. In colloquial speech people sometimes reach anaphorically into them, as in "The Moral Majority is neither"; but such constructions strike our ears as syntactic jokes or wordplay.

20. The point of our qualification "nonempty" is to provide for vacuous office terms T with respect to which $Q(T)$ is the empty set.

21. We would add (i) property-denoting singular terms, presumably lambda-abstracts of the sort employed in our semantical metalanguage; (ii) a binary predicate **INC**, denoting at an index I a relation that holds between a and b at I iff $a \in b$ and $b = Cl(Y)$ for some Y in the range of Q_I, and b is not a proper subset of any set c such that $c = Cl(X)$ for some X in the range of Q_I; and (iii) a binary predicate $\mathbf{IS}_{\text{def}}$ denoting at an index I a relation that holds between a and b at I iff $a = Cl(Y)$ for some Y in the range of Q_I, b is a subset of a, and a is not a proper subset of any set c such that $c = Cl(Z)$ for some Z in the range of Q_I. (Item (ii) provides for the notion of being a highest-level office to include a given power, and (iii) that of being a highest-level office to subsume a given office.) Thus, e.g.,

the "who" clauses in (21) and (22) might be represented respectively by $\hat{x}(\textbf{IS}_{\textbf{def}}(x, \textbf{THE Pope}))$ and $\hat{x}(\textbf{INC}(\lambda y(y \ \textbf{appoints Cardinals}), x))$.

Chapter 5

1. We also contend in chapter 6 that the two-scheme theory removes any mystery that may linger over attitudes *de se*, which we take to be only harmlessly special cases of the *de re*.

2. In *The Ways of Paradox and Other Essays* (New York: Random House, 1966), 183–194.

3. Recently, in "Intensions revisited" (in *Contemporary Perspectives in the Philosophy of Language*, P. A. French, T. E. Uehling and H. Wettstein, eds. (Minneapolis: Univ. of Minnesota Press, 1979), 268–274), Quine renounced the objectivity of this distinction and proclaimed it radically interest relative. See note 30 below about this renunciation.

4. Sosa, "Propositional attitudes *de dicto* and *de re*," *Journal of Philosophy* 67 (1970), 883–896; Pastin, "About *de re* belief," *Philosophy and Phenomenological Research* 34 (1974), 569–575; and Sosa and Pastin, "A rejoinder on actions and *de re* belief," *Canadian Journal of Philosophy* 11 (1981), 735–739. We believe that the term "latitudinarian" as it is used here is due to Roderick Chisholm in "Knowledge and belief: 'De dicto' and 'de re,'" *Philosophical Studies* 29 (1976), 1–20.

5. Latitudinarianism is further embarrassed by the following consequence (we adapt an example from Stephen Schiffer's "The basis of reference," *Erkenntnis* 13 (1978), 203–204): Suppose that Ralph believes, falsely, that he holds the world's record for eating the most spaghetti in a single sitting. In fact, Sister Angelica holds that record. Ralph also believes that his wife is completely faithful to him, and so, due to his false belief about the world record, he believes that the holder of the record is the only person who has ever slept with his wife. According to latitudinarianism, it follows from this last fact that Sister Angelica is believed by Ralph to be the only person who has ever slept with his wife. But, of course, Ralph himself is also believed by himself to be the only person who has done that, even though Ralph knows perfectly well that he and Sister Angelica are distinct. So we have two people, not only distinct but also known by Ralph to be distinct, both of whom are believed by Ralph to be the only person who has ever slept with his wife. Though far from fatal, this is indeed peculiar.

6. This was Russell's original idea, though the resulting view of *de re* ascriptions is so terribly restrictive that Russell's line has few if any adherents nowadays. (Stephen Schiffer flirted with it in "The basis of reference" (pp. 100–150), but has since recanted.) It is implausible that the truth of (8) should require John to be nose-to-nose with Tom.

7. This section overlaps in content with W. G. Lycan, "Thoughts about things," in *The Representation of Knowledge and Belief*, M. Brand and R. M. Harnish, eds. (Tucson: Univ. of Arizona Press, 1985). That paper also investigates the need for a notion of *de re* belief and its relevance to psychology.

8. See David Kaplan, "How to Russell a Frege-Church," *Journal of Philosophy* 72 (1975), 716–729.

9. Particularly in Boër and Lycan, "Knowing who," and in Boër and Lycan, "Who, me?"

10. "Demonstratives," unpublished.

11. "The Boethian compromise," *American Philosophical Quarterly* 15 (1978), 129–138.

12. "Quantifying in," in *Words and Objections*.

13. As we recall, this term is due to Robert Sleigh (University of Massachusetts, Amherst).

14. Cf. Michael Devitt, *Designation* (New York: Columbia Univ. Press, 1981). For a thorough discussion of the causal requirement as applied to natural-kind terms, see S. Boër,

"Substance and kind: Reflections on the new theory of reference," in *Analytical Philosophy in Comparative Perspective*, B. K. Matilal and J. L. Shaw, eds. (Dordrecht: D. Reidel, 1985), 103–150.

15. "Reference and definite descriptions," *Philosophical Review* 75 (1966), 285.

16. Saul Kripke, "Naming and necessity," and Kaplan, "Demonstratives."

17. In this same vein, John Wallace writes, "Our beliefs are a map; but a map of France which had Paris and Vezelay and Mont Blanc [*themselves*, not their names or dots] on it would *be* France" ("Response to Arnaud," *Nous* 9 (1975), 427).

18. Brian Loar speaks of distinguishing "vertical" from "horizontal" aspects of belief in *Mind and Meaning* (Cambridge: Cambridge Univ. Press, 1981).

19. For more detail, see Lycan, "The paradox of naming."

20. Donnellan ("Reference and definite descriptions") maintains that given suitable contextual cues, one can refer using a description to something that does not in fact satisfy that description. As a claim about speaker reference this is obvious, but as a claim about sentential semantics it is pretty clearly false; if one tokens a sentence containing a description, then even if the description is used rigidly, the *sentence* is a true sentence only if the item that satisfies the matrix of the description also satisfies the predicate attached to the description (see Kripke, "Speaker's reference and semantic reference") However, this truth-value determination is psychologically irrelevant; the speaker's description plays its characteristic computational role, regardless of its semantic mishap.

On the other hand, if "near miss" descriptions of Donnellan's sort can after all lose their normal sentential meanings and semantically denote their utterers' referents rather than the objects that satisfy their matrices, this is an even more dramatic example of grade-4 aboutness than are the standard cases of proper names and indexical pronouns.

21. "Individuation by acquaintance and by stipulation," *Philosophical Review* 92 (1983), sec. II. Cf. "Attitudes *de dicto* and *de se*," *Philosophical Review* 88 (1979), sec. 13.

22. See Sosa, "Propositional attitudes" and Adam Morton, "Because he thought he had insulted him," *Journal of Philosophy* 72 (1975), 5–15.

23. Schiffer took this austere line in "The basis of reference," but recanted it in "Indexicals and the theory of reference," *Synthese* 49 (1981), 43–100.

24. The possibility of direct reference to and belief *de* an object in the absence of any interesting knowledge about one's referent is well illustrated in some examples by Igal Kvart in "Quine and modalities *de re*: A way out?" *Journal of Philosophy* 79 (1982), 300–301.

25. Although we do tend to think reality has a joint here, we are by no means convinced that there is a fact of the matter as to which (if any) of our grades of aboutness is required for *real de re* belief. Both Myles Brand and Kent Bach have complained to us that they still think some epistemic condition is needed to capture *their* respective conceptions of the *de re*, but we are quite happy to write off this apparent disagreement as terminological. Our main aim in this section is to provide a useful taxonomy of the relevant conditions that sometimes obtain in the real world in such a way that as much remaining disagreement as possible *can* be written off as verbal.

In "Thoughts and their ascription" (*Midwest Studies in Philosophy* 9 (1984), 385–420), Michael Devitt complains justly that although distinctions of the sort we have drawn are real and important, one should not try to impose the labels "*de re*" and "*de dicto*" at any point unless a strict parallel can be drawn between this usage and the traditional alethic usage. He notes a prima facie disanalogy between necessity *de re* and *any* relevant notion of "belief *de re*": A case of believing involves a representation and its referential properties, whereas—unless a metalinguistic theory of modality should turn out to be right—a case of necessity does not; a *de re* belief involves a designational token of someone's language of thought, whereas an ordinary thing's having a property essentially does not (necessity is ostensibly subjectless, after all). This seems quite right, though perhaps it should make us consider more carefully the virtues of metalinguistic theories of modality. But there remain significant parallels between what we are calling grade-4 aboutness and traditional *de re* necessity: The singular-proposition/general-proposition distinction fits both cases nicely and works out formally; there is a clear sense in which a grade-4 belief is about a particular thing, whereas a belief of lesser grade is not, just as a *de re* modality is about a particular thing, whereas a general alethic fact is not; and in both cases the *res de* that belief or necessity obtains is intuitively felt to have a genuine property (being "suspected by Ralph" or being "necessarily human") that objects "involved" in merely grade-1 beliefs or *de dicto* necessities do not.

26. That thoughts and their ascription must be firmly and systematically distinguished is emphasized to excellent effect by Devitt in "Thoughts and their ascription."

27. Two qualifications here. First, there are certain sorts of cases in which latitudinarian quantification does sound quite natural. For example (cf. Sosa, "Propositional attitudes, 894–895), suppose that Ludwig is a successful arsonist. The police know that an arsonist is at work in the community, but Ludwig is so discreet that they have no clue whatever as to his identity. Nevertheless, they speculate that whoever set the fires is from out of town, since they do not suppose that any local boy would be clever enough to get away with it, and this conjecture is reported in the newspapers. Ludwig's wife reads her paper and says to him, "They think you are from out of town." This utterance of Ludwig's wife's does seem appropriate even though the police have no beliefs that are about him in any higher than grade 1 (let us suppose that the police have not read Kaplan or Plantinga and so have not rigidified their description). We are not sure what it is about this case and a few others like it that licenses the ascriber's use of a directly referential pronoun, when in standard cases the pronominal reference is quite out of place (try "Tatiana, every rational person who knows that there are spies is aware that you are a spy"). But notice that the plausibility of even the wife's ascription here evaporates if the speaker stresses the pronoun in a distinctively *de-re*-ish way, as in "They believe *of you* that you're from out of town," or "It is *you* they think is from out of town," or "They suspect *you*, Ludwig Flammenwerfer, of being from out of town."

Second, it may seem that in granting the interpretability of latitudinarian quantification we have posited an ambiguity in the quantificational construction or in the term "believe," for the quantifier characteristic of genuine *de re* belief is forbidden in the absence of an appropriate causal chain. We think that what is denied is rather the standard *de re voicing* and/or lexicalization of the bound variable—in particular, one may not preface the latitudinarian variable by the Quinean "of," as in "is an *x* such that … believes *of x*," and one may not use words such as "suspect" and "candidate," that presuppose genuine *de-re*-ness. Thus it seems that "quantifying in" is not per se the fundamental issue after all. (For a somewhat different defense of this last thesis, see Robert Kraut, "There are no *de dicto* attitudes," *Synthese* 54 (1983), 275–294.)

28. Some standard misconceptions have already been laid to rest by D. C. Dennett's "Beyond belief" and Kent Bach's "*De re* belief and methodological solipsism," both in *Thought and Object*, A. Woodfield, ed. (Oxford: Oxford Univ. Press, 1982), 1–95, 121–151.

29. Such identification has led to considerable confusion, as is evident. One victim is Hintikka; in addition to works already cited, see his "Answers to questions" and his argument against Quine on pp. 107–110 of "Quine on quantifying in: A dialogue." Another is Robert Kraut, in "Objects of affection," in *Emotion: Philosophical Studies*, G. Myers and K. D. Irani, eds. (New York: Haven, 1984).

30. Quine's reason for abandoning an objective *de re*/*de dicto* distinction in "Intensions

revisited" (cf. note 8 above) seems to be just that "knowing who" is interest relative. If our impending argument is correct, this reason is inadequate, though we continue to agree that the propriety of quantifying in *is* interest relative in its own narrower way.

31. For examples, see Dennett, "Beyond belief," sec. 5; John Searle, "Referential and attributive," *Monist* 62 (1979), 190–208; and S. Stich, *From Folk Psychology to Cognitive Science* (Cambridge: Bradford Books/MIT Press, 1983), chap. 6.

32. Several recent writers seem to have the idea that this *lexical* ambiguity claim is a popular view, or at least that it has been held by some respectable philosopher or another. So far as we are aware, it has never been held by anyone at all. It is briefly mentioned but immediately and rightly dismissed by Quine on p. 186 of "Quantifiers and propositional attitudes."

33. As Searle remarks in *Intentionality* ((Cambridge: Cambridge Univ. Press, 1983), 209), the phrase *"de dicto* belief" is redundant on this view.

34. *Journal of Philosophy* 74 (1977), 338–362.

35. Burge has made it clear in correspondence that he has no great disagreement with us over any matter of fact and in particular is not bent on denying that there are indexical dicta in the language of thought. His concern is for the question of whether a propositional attitude is fully characterizable and evaluatable in terms of its dictum alone, and his claim is that in the case of an indexical dictum this is not so. We naturally agree with that claim, since the truth condition of an indexical attitude is not determined by the intrinsic nature of its dictum. (But we would add that truth conditions are important only when our semantical individuation scheme is on the line; when computational role is all that matters, no extracalvarian characterization of the indexical dictum is required.)

36. He seems to argue ("Belief *de re*," 340) that "the grammatical distinction" is insufficient to capture "the intuitive *de re/de dicto* distinction" because even singular propositions are propositions and hence *dicta*. This would beg the question of whether the *de re* is a special case of the *de dicto*, for one who claims it is of course responds that a singular proposition is a special proposition in that it relates one who believes it directly to a thing in the world. But Burge informs us that he meant only to complain that one should not uncritically regard the grammatical distinction as settling more important issues in epistemology and the philosophy of mind—with which complaint we could hardly disagree.

37. Lycan, "The trouble with possible worlds," in *The Possible and the Actual*, M. Loux, ed. (Ithaca: Cornell Univ. Press, 1979), 313. See also W. Lycan and S. Shapiro, "Actuality and essence."

38. For example, Lewis, "General semantics"; and John Pollock, "Thinking about an object," in *Midwest Studies in Philosophy* 5 (1980), though it is clear that Pollock's initial conception *is* quite different from ours.

Chapter 6

1. Wayne Alt astutely explored the connection between "knowing who" and the cogito in *I Exist* (Ohio State Univ. Ph.D. dissertation, 1976). For an elegant expression of a similar intuition without any such effetely Cartesian basis, see Thomas Nagel, "The objective self," in *Knowledge and Mind: Essays in Honor of Norman Malcolm*, C. Ginet and S. Shoemaker, eds. (Ithaca: Cornell Univ. Press, 1983), 211–232.

2. Castaneda put just this sort of objection to Hintikka's theory of "knowing who" in "On the logic of attributions of self-knowledge to others."

3. Attention to these phenomena is due to Geach ("On belief about oneself," *Analysis* 18 (1957), 23–24) and especially to Castaneda ("'He': A study in the logic of self-

consciousness," *Ratio* 8 (1966), 130–157, and, to say the least, elsewhere). More recently the data have been vividly elaborated by John Perry ("Frege on demonstratives," *Philosophical Review* 86 (1977), 474–497, and "The problem of the essential indexical," *Nous* 13 (1979), 3–21) and David Lewis ("Attitudes *de dicto* and *de se*"); see also Roderick Chisholm, *The First Person* (Minneapolis: Univ. of Minnesota Press, 1981).

4. "Who, me?" 441–443. Castaneda replied to this component of our argument ("Philosophical refutations," in *Principles of Philosophical Reasoning*, J. Fetzer, ed. (New Jersey: Rowman and Allanheld, 1984), 249–256), pointing out correctly that our presentation of the sort of case we devised presupposes a view of singular reference and of the individuation of propositions, which he rejects. (On p. 254 he suggests that the question between us of sameness or difference of "proposition" is verbal, thus hinting laudably at the two-scheme theory.) We agree emphatically that our sort of case fell far short of *refuting* the irreducibility thesis; all we claimed for it at the time was that "intuition is not altogether on the side of the adverse party either" (p. 443). We would now reinterpret the examples in light of the two-scheme theory in any case, with results far more congenial to Castaneda's own position.

5. "Who, me?" 443–445.

6. "Who, Me?" sections 3 and 4.

7. Our position was almost exactly what Nagel (in "The objective self" characterizes as the "semantic response" to problems of first-person reference. His objection to this response is that "... even if it is right in denying that any further fact is involved [when I know or fail to know that *I am* TN], ... it leaves unexplained the content or apparent content of the philosophical thought that I am TN" (p. 216). We now think this is exactly half-, but importantly half-, right, and so we half-recant; see note 11 below.

8. The computational scheme is upheld at the expense of the semantical scheme by Hartry Field in "Mental Representation," 48, 51; Jerry Fodor in "Methodological solipsism," 67; and David Lewis in "What puzzling Pierre does not believe," 288–289. But the computational scheme is pooh-poohed in the name of semantics by Stephen Stich, "Autonomous psychology," 578, and by John Perry in a talk delivered to the University of Massachusetts' Sloan Workshop on Propositions, Propositional Attitudes, and Finite Representability (February, 1982).

9. The following account is lifted almost verbatim from Lycan, "Toward a homuncular theory of believing," 148–150.

10. Contrary to what is evidently presupposed by most earlier writers on this topic (see the references in note 8). But compare: Smith pats himself on the back. Brown walks over and pats Smith on the back. Did Smith and Brown perform *the same action*? Let us not start choosing up sides; it is hardly a factual question.

Perry's bifurcation also explains the evident absurdity, derided by D. C. Dennett in "Brain writing and mind reading" (in *Brainstorms* (Montgomery, Vermont: Bradford Books; Cambridge, Massachusetts: The MIT Press, 1978)), of the idea that politically motivated neurosurgeons might succeed in "cracking the cerebral code," examine your beliefs through a cerebroscope, and report you to the Thought Police. A cerebroscope scans only what is in the head, so it cannot scan one's belief *objects* and hence cannot reveal the propositions one believes.

11. And this is the sense that accounts for Nagel's entirely reasonable feeling, recorded in note 7 above, that a *thought* couched in the first person is a "quite different thought" from any of its third-person semantical equivalents. Such a thought is computationally (very) different and so is counted by the *computational role-individuation scheme* as being a (very) different thought; moreover the computational scheme is automatically put in play when one takes the first-person perspective, as Nagel is at pains to do.

Our present view combines our former "semantic response" with what Nagel calls the "epistemic response." Nagel objects to the latter, saying that a "causal behaviorist account" of an identity statement such as "I am TN" leaves that statement's "content" unexplained (p. 220). But we have argued that any notion of "content" must, in light of two-schemism, be disambiguated if not jettisoned; and either choice would destroy the objection as it presently stands.

12. Chapter 5 of *The Myth of Semantic Presupposition*; see also the overlapping chapter 5 of Lycan, *Logical Form in Natural Language*.

13. Pp. 455–459.

14. For example, Stephen L. White, "Partial character and the language of thought," *Pacific Philosophical Quarterly* 63 (1982), 347–365; Brian Loar, *Mind and Meaning*, and "Must beliefs be sentences?"

15. D. Kaplan, "On the logic of demonstratives," in *Contemporary Perspectives in the Philosophy of Language*, P. French, T. E. Uehling, and H. Wettstein eds. (Minneapolis: Univ. of Minnesota Press, 1979).

16. One reason for rejecting clause (iii), viz., the perennial temptation to assimilate "I" to "the owner of these [experiences]," should be resisted. Computationally, anyone's ·I am I·'s are axiomatic and trivial for that person (which, of course, is not to say that they express necessary truths). If the assimilation ploy worked, it would follow that a subject S could not fail to believe on a given occasion—whether occurrently or only dispositionally—that *he himself* uniquely owns such-and-such experiences, since this would just amount to his knowing-true a conceptually trivial ·I am I·. But S could perfectly well doubt or disbelieve this by virtue of doubting or disbelieving that there is a unique owner of those experiences. There is no reason why, e.g., S could not subscribe to a metaphysical theory of personhood according to which it is logically possible for distinct persons to "overlap" in their experience tokens. Indeed, there is even the possibility that S might regard a demonstrated sensation, e.g., a pain, as not "belonging" to *anyone*. This is not really as outrageous as it sounds. In the dissociative states produced by powerful neuroleptics, such as Droperidol, subjects point to regions of their bodies and sincerely say things like "There is a pain here" yet steadfastly deny *feeling* any pain. If owning a pain = being in pain, then it seems that S, suitably drugged, *could* coherently affirm both "This [pain] is such-and-such" and "No one owns/feels it."

17. This is not belied by our treatment of $\hat{x}_1$ ($x_1 = N$) as the logical form of "who N is," since, according to our theory, what X knows-true in knowing who N is is a sentence whose logical form plays the same conceptual or semantic role for X as a formula of the sort

(i) $(\exists x)[(y)(y = N \leftrightarrow y = x) \& G!(x)]$,

in which the essential work is done by the predication in the final conjunct. Expression (i) itself is "essentially predicative" in just the way that "Fido is a dog" would be even if the logical form of the latter were for theoretical reasons taken to be $(\exists x)(x = \textbf{Fido} \& \textbf{Dog} (x))$.

18. Actions that are *in* character but reaching unanticipated heights can have similar effects. Kingsley Amis describes Roger Micheldene (one of his protagonists) in the midst of sexual intercourse:

> He lost all interest in where he was and who he was with, in any part or aspect of the future. For perhaps a minute, though he himself could not have known how long, he came as close as he had ever done to being unaware of who he was. (*One Fat Englishman* (Harmondsworth, Middlesex: Penguin Books, 1966), 108)

19. As is noted by Brian O'Shaughnessy in *The Will: A Dual Aspect Theory*, vol. 2 (Cambridge: Cambridge Univ. Press, 1980), 32. Bruce Wilshire has made a similar observation, and other good points directly related to the themes of this section, in chapter 9 of *Role Playing and Identity* (Bloomington: Indiana Univ. Press, 1982).

20. For a related but slightly different view of alienation, see Andrew Oldenquist, "Loyalties," *Journal of Philosophy* 79 (1982), sec. 5.

21. That is, subjects undergoing "fugue states" of the sort commonly described in novels and in at least some standard clinical literature; see, e.g., J. C. Nemiah, "Dissociative amnesia: A clinical and theoretical reconsideration," in *Functional Disorders of Memory*, J. F. Kihlstrom and F. J. Evans, eds. (Hillsdale: Lawrence Erlbaum Associates, 1979), 303–323.

22.

> It should be noted ... that it is only the mental elements related to his personal identity that have disappeared. Basic functions such as language, general knowledge, and the skills of coping with the tasks of everyday living remain under his command, and there is no alteration in his state of consciousness of the new world of people and things around him. (Nemiah, "Dissociative amnesia," 307)

For related distinctions between various types of memory and between various memory disorders, see A. Mayes, ed., *Memory in Humans and Animals* (Wokingham, Berkshire: Van Nostrand Rineholt, 1983). We are indebted to Lynn Nadel (University of California, Irvine) for some references and for a useful conversation on this topic.

23. Consider, further, a dissociative amnesiac who has lived in his *second* identity for fifty years. When observers asked just after his initial trauma, "Does he know who he (himself) is?," the answer was "Yes and no." When we *now* ask that question, the answer is still "Yes and no," but it has a different sense in context; our theory explains that strongly felt difference.

24. Feminist writers sometimes contrast *relational* with *intrinsic* importance in this regard: "I am not who I am just in relation to my husband and children; I am important in and for myself." But "intrinsic" here cannot mean numerical identity as opposed to predication. Some of the predicates newly stressed by the liberated woman are relational even though nontraditionally so, such as her relations to her clients, to her hirelings, to her architectural products, etc.

25. Examples of the following sort were pointed out to us by Thomas E. Hill, Jr. (University of North Carolina).

26. See "Privacy, freedom and respect for persons," in *Privacy* (*Nomos*, vol. 13), J. Roland Pennock and John Chapman, eds. (New York: Atherton Press, 1971). In "Privacy, intimacy, and personhood" (*Philosophy and Public Affairs* 6 (1976), 26–44), Jeffrey H. Reiman criticized Benn's suggestion and proposed instead that privacy is a social ritual psychologically necessary for "the creation of *selves* ... , since a self is at least in part a human being who regards his existence—his thoughts, his body, his actions—as his own" (p. 39).

27. See, e.g., Jerome Neu, "What is wrong with incest?" *Inquiry* 19 (1976), 27–39. (Neu makes it clear that "identity" here means *important relation to the subject*; otherwise the definition would include any case of adultery under the heading of incest.)

28. Luisa in *The Fantasticks* remarks ruefully on her plurality of "me"'s. It is interesting to note that pronominal constructions that differ only slightly in their surface grammar or in their conventional deployment carry different suggestions about types of important properties. For example, to say of someone that he is "not himself" is to suggest that he is ill in some way that distorts his personality, whereas to exhort someone using the phrase "Be yourself" is normally to try to get that person to relinquish an affectation. We would say, "Be yourself, unless you are a jerk, in which case you would do better to be someone else."

29. A feminist childrens' record of the mid-1970s, starring Marlo Thomas, had that title. And a much better known popular oldie, starring that well-known feminist Frank Sinatra, had the title theme, "I've Got to Be Me."

30. Robert Kraut, "Objects of affection," and "Love *de re*," presented at the Seventeenth Chapel Hill Colloquium in Philosophy, October, 1982.

31. Perhaps human beings have noncontingent, essential properties other than haecceities. Yet on any plausible account of which properties these might be, they are hardly fit grounds for interpersonal regard. Suppose that Sandra has been dating Albert, a geneticist, on the sly. But Albert's interest in Sandra is entirely impersonal and technical: He has found that she has a genetic code that is of immense theoretical interest, and he is so obsessively devoted to his closely related research project that he revels in her genetic code to the point of committing various unnatural acts, giggling uncontrollably. On one plausible account of human essences, Sandra's genetic code is the one and only one property other than a haecceity that is uniquely essential to her; yet Albert is a *paradigm case* of a depersonalizing user who neither treats Sandra as a person nor loves her "for herself." "Herself" here can have nothing to do with what is *metaphysically* her individual essence.

32. This observation is also made by Robert Stalnaker in "Semantics for belief" (unpublished).

33. For example, consider the following truly perverse variant of a famous sentence of George Lakoff's: "I wish I were Raquel Welch and that I kissed me."

Chapter 7

1. A deliberately extreme version of "Kantianism" in this sense is sketched by Lawrence Blum in chapter 1 of *Friendship, Altruism and Morality* (London: Routledge and Kegan Paul, 1980). For a use of the notion of one's "moral self," which, incidentally, is nicely consonant with our view of identity, see Blum's chapter 8, particularly his remarks on *dissociation* (pp. 181–183).

2. It is noteworthy that in this sense of "impartialism," crass Act Utilitarianism is more strongly impartialist than are views based on respect for the separateness and autonomy of persons: For the Benthamite utilitarian, it does not *in any sense* matter who one is; equality in the sight of the moral law is *total*. Indeed, this is precisely what is deplored about utilitarianism by Kantians (in another sense) such as Rawls and Nozick, who complain that it obliterates the distinctness of persons and so ignores the crucial inviolability of individuals. (It is a double-edged truth that for the utilitarian, the moral law is no respecter of persons. For Kantians of this latter stripe, an agent must take account of who someone is in one sense, but ignore who someone is in another. Our own view is that every person, every individual human being, is a shining, sacred vessel, to be brim-filled with utility.

3. Russell made this point at least once, but it is surely older.

4. *Freedom and Reason* (Oxford: Oxford Univ. Press, 1963), chap. 6. Page references to this book are inserted parenthetically in the text.

5. For exposition of the "fanatic problem," see Fotion, "Gewirth and categorial consistency," *Philosophical Quarterly* 18 (1968), 262–264, and Lycan, "Hare, Singer and Gewirth on universalizability," *Philosophical Quarterly* 19 (1969), 136–137. (Gewirth replies to both papers in "Some Comments on Categorial Consistency," *Philosophical Quarterly* 20 (1970), 380–384.) The problem does not particularly bother Hare because he is a noncognitivist; for him, a willingly universalizing Nazi is not *wrong* but only unpleasant and dangerous to have around. But anyone who thinks that the Nazi's genocidal acts are immoral despite the Nazi's sincere willingness to march to the gas chamber himself should he turn out to have Jewish blood will find Hare's analysis of "putting oneself in another's place" no more satisfactory than that codified by the literal interpretation of the Golden Rule.

6. *A Theory of Justice* (Cambridge: Harvard Univ. Press, 1971).

7. Rawls argues here for a conservative maximin or worst-case scenario strategy rather than (say) a straight comparison of expected utilities (*Theory of Justice*, 154ff). Numerous commentators have challenged Rawls on the point and defended a less cautious principle of choice: R. M. Hare, "Rawls' theory of justice," *Philosophical Quarterly* 23 (1973), 144–155; Thomas Nagel, "Rawls on justice," *Philosophical Review* 82 (1973), 220–234; John C. Harsanyi, "Can the maximin principle serve as a basis for morality? A critique of John Rawls' theory," *American Political Science Review* 69 (1975), 594–606; Robert Paul Wolff, *Understanding Rawls* (Princeton: Princeton Univ. Press, 1977); Allen Buchanan, "A critical introduction to Rawls' theory of justice," in *John Rawls' Theory of Social Justice: An Introduction*, H. G. Blocker and E. H. Smith, eds. (Athens: Ohio Univ. Press, 1980), 5–41; and D. C. Hubin, "Minimizing maximum," *Philosophical Studies* 37 (1980), 363–372.

8. Pointed out by Nagel, "Rawls on justice"; Wolff, *Understanding Rawls*; and an unpublished note by Ben Overbey (United States Military Academy, West Point). We are grateful to Overbey for useful discussion of the present point.

9. In "Persons, character and morality" (in *The Identities of Persons*, A. Rorty, ed. (Berkeley and Los Angeles: Univ. of California Press, 1976)), Bernard Williams argues against impartialist moralities precisely on the ground that they can unrealistically and illegitimately force an agent to ingore the "projects," perhaps even the "ground" project or life plan, that gives meaning to his or her life. We discuss Williams' position later in the text.

10. Wolff (*Understanding Rawls*, 66–68) elaborates this complaint.

11. For similar reasons to those we have argued here, T. M. Scanlon urges a downplaying of empathetic thought experiments in moral reasoning ("Contractarianism and utilitarianism," in *Utilitarianism and Beyond*, A. Sen and B. Williams, eds. (Cambridge: Cambridge Univ. Press, 1982), 117, 122):

    [T]he thought experiment of changing places is only a rough guide. ... As Kant observed, our different individual points of view, taken as they are, may in general be simply irreconcilable. "Judgemental harmony" requires the construction of a genuinely interpersonal form of justification which is nonetheless something that each individual could argee to. From this interpersonal standpoint, a certain amount of how things look from another person's point of view, like a certain amount of how they look from my own, will be counted as bias.

12. Here and throughout, we allude to "empathy" in a perhaps misleadingly general way. In reality, a number of importantly distinct methods, positions, and attitudes are lumped under this heading. These range from *sympathy* in the warmest, runniest, most literal sense of actually bringing oneself to have the feelings and passions that another would have under such-and-such conditions, to the barest, chilliest attempt to forget one's own actual circumstances and preferences. Moreover, although "empathy" in one or another of these senses is normally proposed as an *implementation* of impartiality and/or "the moral point of view," the term may not stretch so far as to include just any deliberative calculation subject to formal conditions of impersonal abstraction, entirely irrespective of one's current psychological state. Probably no kind of empathy or empathizing strictly so-called is logically required for impartiality per se—Kant himself did not rely, to say the least, on anyone's human capacity for even hypothetically assuming any particular psychological state. Our argument in this section applies only to those impartialists whose positions essentially involve the notion of someone's identity or "place" in the world (we are indebted to Brad Goodman (University of North Carolina) for insisting on this clarification).

13. We here mean theories that are tied to empathetic thought experiments in the broad sense invoked above. The criticism does not apply to Act Utilitarianism, for example,

since that view (cf. note 2 above) is, so to speak, *too* uncompromisingly impartialist to raise worries about the merging of identities; it tells you exactly what the morally relevant facts are without leaving anything to empathy, imagination, contextual specification of teleological parameters, Kant, Jesus, autonomy, self-respect, human dignity, or sensitivity and caring.

14. We suppose that there is a chance that someone might come up with a worthwhile theory of morally relevant features that falls significantly short of being a fully normative ethics; obviously a normative ethics contains (by subtraction) a theory of morally relevant features as a logically proper part, but we find it hard to envisage a convincing defense or justification of the latter in the absence of the former.

15. In "Universality and treating persons as persons" (*Journal of Philosophy* 71 (1974), 57–71), Harry Silverstein raises a similar objection, more elegantly based on our original difficulty of deciding whose preferences to carry along into our hypothetical scenario.

16. See Gewirth, "Categorial consistency in ethics," *Philosophical Quarterly* 17 (1967), 289–299 (also, *Reason and Morality* (Chicago: Univ. of Chicago Press, 1978)), and Lycan, "Hare, Singer and Gewirth on universalizability."

17. Oxford: Oxford Univ. Press, 1970.

18. Here we are indebted to Andrew Oldenquist, "The possibility of selfishness," *American Philosophical Quarterly* 17 (1980), 25–33.

19. "Now, *that's* egoism," as Oldenquist observes ("Possibility of selfishness," 25).

20. As is argued by Blum, *Friendship, Altruism and Morality.*

21. Notice a difference in likelihood of reasons as between Hud, Ephraim, and the patriot. Real dyed-in-the-wool egoists are rare (between us we have met two, total), but if Hud is one, his reason for pushing to the head of the line almost certainly is the reflexive one (virtually no one holds egoism as a universalizable and unqualified moral theory). Ephraim's reason *most likely* is the reflexive one, but far from necessarily so; he may simply take domestic duties seriously. The patriot's reason could be any of the three. The explanation of this difference is presumably sociobiological, as Oldenquist has emphasized (see particularly "Loyalties"): The gene sees to it that family loyalties are in general stronger than national loyalties and that community loyalties are in general stronger than species loyalty or (God save us) loyalty to rational beings as such. Thus the patriot's sacrifice is less likely than is Ephraim's to be a gut reaction, and individual selfishness is far more likely to be visceral than to be based on an impersonal moral theory—though the gene also sees to it that a parent's gut reactions are well mixed as between self, spouse, and children, which is why there are so few genuine egoists in the first place. (Oldenquist speaks aptly of the shift from "me first" to "*mine* first" ("Loyalties," 176).)

It is significant that discussions of egoism and selfishness among laypersons and even among professional philosophers do not often feature cases of egoists' trampling their own families. Such cases do not often occur to people even though they occasionally happen in real life; and casual defenders of "egoism" in undergraduate classrooms would usually stick at antifamilial selfishness unless they caught themselves in time to make a philosophical point. We can think of three (mutually compatible) explanations for this otherwise puzzling doublethink: (i) The gene encourages agents to have such concern for their families' good that they do not often notice the frequency with which it conflicts with their own. (ii) A person's familial properties count by almost anyone's standards as important properties of that person, hence as partly constitutive of that person's "identity" (cf. Sandel, *Liberalism and the Limits of Justice:* "... we cannot regard ourselves as independent in this [Kantian] way without great cost to those loyalties and convictions whose moral force consists partly in the fact that living by them is inseparable from understanding ourselves as the particular persons we are" (p. 179)); in that way a benefit to one's family is fallaciously counted as a benefit to oneself. (iii) Egoism is thought of as the natural opponent of impartialism; so anyone who has instinctive doubts about impartialism will flirt with egoism unless he or she realizes that pure tribal loyalties are just as *unimpartial* as is genuine selfishness.

22. As Kraut ("Objects of affection") would have it, Ephraim's possible reasons can be distinguished by their intentional objects, the objects construed as world lines generated by Ephraim's behavior in counterfactual situations. Thus: Would he have saved Melinda herself in a world in which she was not his child, or would he have saved whatever child of his might have been in danger there? Would he save whatever child of his was in danger only at his deontic alternatives, or would he save such children everywhere?

23. "The possibility of selfishness." Oldenquist ties possession of a self-concept to the notion of *consciousness*, or vice versa; we think that is a significant (though for his purposes harmless) confusion.

24. Oldenquist, "Loyalties," and *Normative Behavior* (Washington D.C.: Univ. Press of America, 1983); Williams, "Persons, character and morality"; Michael Stocker, "The schizophrenia of modern ethical theories," *Journal of Philosophy* 73 (1976), 453–466; and Blum, *Friendship, Altruism and Morality*. See also Jesse Kalin, "Lies, secrets, and love," *Journal of Value Inquiry* 10 (1976), 253–265; John Kekes, "Morality and impartiality," *American Philosophical Quarterly* 18 (1981), 295–303; Susan Wolf, "Moral saints," *Journal of Philosophy* 79 (1982), 419–439; Michael Sandel, *Liberalism and the Limits of Justice*; and Peter Railton, "Alienation, consequentialism, and the demands of morality," *Philosophy and Public Affairs* 13 (1984), 134–172.

25. See, e.g., Williams, "Persons, character and morality," 210ff. In "Integrity and impartiality" (*Monist* 66 (1983), 242), Barbara Herman paraphrases Williams as maintaining that "you cannot ask a person to give up the activity constitutive of his being the person he is."

26. Alternatively, one might say (as Williams and Wolf tend to) that unrestricted universalizability is the mark of the moral, but that "moral" considerations in this sense neither do nor should always override other values. We prefer the first terminology.

27. "Persons, character and morality," 214.

28. Readers who are in the know will discern that "Mary Ann" is a clever portmanteau of "Mary" and "Ann."

29. Cf. also Stocker, "Schizophrenia," (*op. cit.*, 459):

> What is lacking ... is simply—or not so simply—the person. For, love, friendship, affection, fellow feeling, and community all require that the other person be an essential part of what is valued. The person—not merely the person's general values nor even the person-*qua*-producer-or-possessor-of-general-values—must be valued.

30. See, e.g., Brian Medlin, "Ultimate principles and ethical egoism," *Australasian Journal of Philosophy* 35 (1957), 111–118, and Kurt Baier, *The Moral Point of View* (Ithaca: Cornell Univ. Press, 1958), chap. 8.

31. The complaint is sometimes voiced that this (hardly original) "trying one's best" move does not capture the egoist's or tribal altruist's obligation; the obligation is to *succeed*, not just to try. If this is so, then a loser has still failed in his obligations even if we do not think harshly of him for it. We are unconvinced by this rejoinder but could not pursue the matter without an extensive look at the concept of obligation, with attention to the relevant questions in deontic logic.

32. Personally (so to speak), we still very much doubt that personalism itself is coherent when taken as a *moral view* rather than as a form of amoralism (which it cannot very well claim to be either), but the argument here is quite tricky to make.

33. Here again we are indebted to Brad Goodman.

34. To say that such actions violate "rights," in the absence of an articulate metaphysical theory of what "rights" are, is merely to repeat that there is something morally wrong with them in a way that is grounded in the inviolability of persons.

35. One further point about inviolability deserves mention. People who complain of being "used" or "treated as mere things" often express themselves as wanting others to regard them "for themselves" rather than "under a contingent description"; the vernacular of "using people as means" is tied to that of essences or haecceities versus depersonalizing extraneous properties. When a person's complaint is thus tied, it is misguided, for we have already seen that the latter distinction as applied in moral contexts is specious.

36. For generous help with this chapter we are grateful to Stephen Darwall, Thomas E. Hill, Jr., Andrew Oldenquist, Gerald Postema, and Larry Thomas.

Chapter 8

1. Since we take "K:SEM" and "K:CON" not as quasilogical operators but only as philosophically interesting predicates, we regard our subsequent remarks as contributing to epistemic *logic* only in the loose sense in which an axiomatic first-order theory whose logic is classical or free and which features "nonlogical" axioms involving certain implicitly defined predicates might be regarded as telling us something about the "logic" of those predicates.

2. For **L'** we envisage θ as a truth theory of the nearly homophonic sort presented by Tyler Burge in "Truth and singular terms," where **L** is regarded as governed by a free logic and where occurrences of iota-terms in **L** and **L'** are handled by having θ give denotation conditions for mentioned iota-terms of **L'** by using (distinct) iota-terms of $\mathbf{L} - \mathbf{L'}$ whose matrices embed a semantical vocabulary defined over **L'**.

3. See particular, "Quantified logic for knowledge statements," *Journal of Philosophy* 71 (1974), 127–140. Page references to this article are cited parenthetically in the text.

4. Stine, "Quantified logic for knowledge statements," 128. George Schumm has also reminded us that "dual" is a slight misnomer given that in Hintikka's system a quantifier has a new reading for every *iterated* epistemic operator in its scope.

5. For the main objections, see Castaneda's review of Hintikka's *Knowledge and Belief* (*Journal of Symbolic Logic* 24 (1964), 132–134 and "On the logic of self-knowledge," *Nous* 1 (1976), 9–21; Wilfrid Sellars, "Some problems about belief," in *Words and Objections: Essays on the Work of W. V. Quine*, D. Davidson and J. Hintikka, eds. (Dordrecht: D. Reidel, 1969), 186–205; R. Clark, "Comments," in *Perception and Personal Identity*, N. Care and R. Grimm, eds. (Cleveland: Case Western Univ. Press, 1969), 174–187; and Stine, "Quantified logic for knowledge statements." Robert Sleigh defused some of the objections in "Restricted range in epistemic logic," *Journal of Philosophy* 69 (1972), 67–77.

6. Stine too rejects the dual reading of the quantifiers by distinguishing between free variables and superficially singular terms; but her alternative treatment is marred, as we see it, by her acceptance of Hintikka's knowing-who requirement for quantifying in. For example, she is forced to understand "$(x)K_SFx$" as saying that every object x is *both known to S and* known by S to be F, even though the quantifier ranges over a universal domain; for some purposes at least, the italicized conjunct should not be forced on us by "$(x)K_SFx$."

7. "Restricted range in epistemic logic," 69.

8. Sleigh, "On quantifying into epistemic contexts," *Nous* 1 (1967), 23–31.

9. "Individuals, possible worlds, and epistemic logic," 56. Hintikka goes on to list a number of (C.ind $=$)'s additional virtues.

10. Hintikka ("Individuals, possible worlds, and epistemic logic," 59) expresses an inclination to deny that the ability to identify someone for such a limited purpose should be counted as *full-fledged* "knowing who." Harking ahead to his paper "On attributions of 'self-knowledge'" (*Journal of Philosophy* 67 (1970), 73–87), he might wish to require what he calls "individuation by acquaintance" for this stronger notion. But given a contrived enough perceptual setup, we think parallel counterexamples could be generated even when the subject has perceptual acquaintance (of two different sorts) with his victim.

11. However, if it were specified that the *truth-conditional* scheme is in force throughout, our suggested formalism could be made to yield an analog of (C.ind=) for our account of "knowing who," provided that we arrange for the provability of

(i) $\mathbf{K} : \mathrm{SEM}(a, \langle \ \rangle, \ulcorner \phi ! b \urcorner) \rightarrow \mathbf{K} : \mathrm{SEM}(a, \langle \ \rangle, \ulcorner b = \imath x \phi x \urcorner$,

since given the provability of (3), we could then derive "$\mathbf{K} : \mathrm{SEM}(a, \langle \ \rangle, \ulcorner b = c \urcorner)$" from the premises "$b = c$," "$(\exists \phi)[\mathrm{Imppred}(\phi, a, \mathrm{P}, \ulcorner b \urcorner)$ & $\mathbf{K} : \mathrm{SEM}(a, \langle \ \rangle, \ulcorner \phi ! b \urcorner)]$," and "$(\exists \phi)[\mathrm{Imppred}(\phi, a, \mathrm{P}, \ulcorner c \urcorner)$ & $\mathbf{K} : \mathrm{SEM}(a, \langle \ \rangle, \ulcorner \phi ! c \urcorner)]$." Personally, we find (i) plausible, but we will not pause to discuss the ways or the merits of implementing it, save to note that it would trivially follow from axioms expressing the closure of knowledge under deducibility, should anyone be moved to indulge in that particular idealization. Even given the analog of our formula for "CON," the derivation in question would presumably fail because (as we have repeated to the point of delirium since chapter 3) there is no analog of (3) for "CON." So it remains the case on our own account that (C.ind=) is not a correct principle when read without qualification as "If $b = c$ and S knows who b and c are [for purpose P], then S knows that $b = c$."

12. Cf. Stine, note 10, and Sleigh, "On a proposed system of epistemic logic," *Noûs* 2 (1968), 391–398.

13. Wolfgang Lenzen also urges Hintikka to drop his famous vernacular reading of "$(\exists x)\mathrm{K}_\mathrm{S}(x = a)$" in "Recent work in epistemic logic," *Acta Philosophica Fennica* 30 (1978), 110, 128.

14. Castaneda, "On the logic of self-knowledge" and "On the logic of attributions of self-knowledge to others," *Journal of Philosophy* 65 (1968), 439–456.

15. Elaboration of the war hero case would provide yet another counterexample to (C.ind=).

16. Hintikka, "Individuals, possible worlds, and epistemic logic," 49–54, and Castaneda, "On the logic of attributions of self-knowledge to others," 449–455.

17. "On attributions of 'self-knowledge'."

18. Richmond Thomason gave a similar but more detailed criticism of Hintikka's dichotomizing of modes of individuation in perceptual contexts ("Perception and individuation," in *Logic and Ontology*, M. Munitz, ed. (New York: New York Univ. Press, 1973)). Robert Kraut, in his criticism ("There are no *de dicto* attitudes"), stressed that there are not simply two determinate modes but a huge and variegated range of possible "methods of cross-identification" corresponding to different possible interests—and, we would add, to tests for "knowing who" generated by different purposes in our sense.

19.

> For any strictly third-person description, or name, D of a person, one can come to know who D applies to by satisfying purely third-person criteria, without in the least being required to take the additional step "and I am the one D refers to." ("On the logic of self-knowledge," 12)

This would apply, we take it, to any singular term save "I," "now," or perhaps the demonstrative name of a sense datum.

20. Review of *Knowledge and Belief*, 134.

21. "On the logic of attributions of self-knowledge to others," and elsewhere.

22. No wonder; recall our point in chapter 4 about irreducible indexicals' being a surd in semantics.

23. "On attributions of 'self-knowledge,'" 84–87.

24. In what follows we implement this idea within the framework of our own formalism, but we should also point out that it can be imported into Hintikka's original notation as well: Castaneda's own way will do so long as we can supplement it with appropriate and correct rules of inference as well as a semantics adequate to capture the difficult truth-theoretic behavior of dot or colon quotation.

    We can adopt Castaneda's original reflexive operator "s" and represent our target sentence "Jones knows that he himself is wise" as "Kj(s(j) is wise)," which clearly indicates both the singular proposition believed by Jones and the first-person element, which presents that proposition to him. Then it is easy to invoke (C.K), Hintikka's rule for inferring "p" from "K$_a p$," by stipulating that heretofore existing rules of inference ignore the operator "s." Likewise, "$a = j$" can be shown to follow from "($\exists x$)($x = a$ & K$_j$(s(j) $= a$))," and "$a = b$" from "K$_j$(s(j) $= a$)" and "K$_j$(s(j) $= b$)" jointly. The choice of a scheme of dot individuation obviously affects inferential properties, so complements of the epistemic operator in general have to be flagged for individuation scheme. (In particular, referential opacity for singular terms is still a sometime thing in the two-scheme theory.) When the reflexive operator s is present, however, the computational scheme is mandated, and particular inference rules can be stated without benefit of further flagging. For example, "K$_j$(Fs(j))," "K$_j$(s(j) $= a$)" $\vdash$ "K$_j$Fa" (note that this pattern does *not* remain valid if the reflexive operators are omitted, because of the transparency of the singular-term positions, unless the computational scheme is explicitly specified in some alternative way).

25. Castaneda, "On the logic of self-knowledge," 14–15, and Hintikka, "On attributions of 'self-knowledge,'" 87.

References

Alt, W., *I Exist*, Ohio State Univ., Ph.D. dissertation, 1976.

Arnaud, R., "Sentence, utterance, and samesayer," *Nous* 10 (1976), 69–96.

Bach, K., "*De Re* belief and methodological solipsism," in *Thought and Object*, A. Woodfield, ed. (Oxford: Oxford Univ. Press, 1982), 121–151.

Baier, K., *The Moral Point of View* (Ithaca: Cornell Univ. Press, 1958).

Baker, C. L., "Notes on the description of English questions," *Foundations of Language* 6 (1970), 197–219.

Belnap, N. D., and T. B. Steel, *The Logic of Questions and Answers* (New Haven: Yale Univ. Press, 1976).

Benn, S. I., "Privacy, freedom and respect for persons," in *Privacy*, J. Roland Pennock and John Chapman, eds. (*Nomos*, vol. 13) (New York: Atherton Press, 1971), 1–26.

Bertolet, R., "The semantic significance of Donnellan's distinction," *Philosophical Studies* 37 (1980), 281–288.

Blackburn, S., "The identity of propositions," in *Meaning, Reference, and Necessity*, S. Blackburn, ed. (Cambridge: Cambridge Univ. Press, 1975), 182–205.

Blum, L., *Friendship, Altruism and Morality* (London: Routledge and Kegan Paul, 1980).

Boër, S., "Attributive names," *Notre Dame Journal of Formal Logic* 19 (1978), 177–185.

Boër, S., "Names and attitudes," in *The Philosophy of Logical Mechanism: Essays in Honor of Arthur W. Burks*, M. Salmon, ed. (Dordrecht: D. Reidel, to be published).

Boër, S., "Substance and kind: Reflections on the new theory of reference," in *Analytical Philosophy in Comparative Perspective*, B. K. Matilal and J. L. Shaw, eds. (Dordrecht: D. Reidel, 1985), 103–150.

Boër, S., and W. Lycan, "Castañeda's theory of knowing," in *Profile: Hector-Neri Castaneda*, J. Tomberlin, ed. (Dordrecht: D. Reidel, 1985).

Boër, S., and W. Lycan, "Knowing who," *Philosophical Studies* 28 (1975), 299–344.

Boër, S., and W. Lycan, *The Myth of Semantic Presupposition* (Bloomington: Indiana Univ. Linguistics Club Publications, 1976).

Boër, S., and W. Lycan, "Who, me?" *Philosophical Review* 89 (1980), 427–466.

Buchanan, A., "A critical introduction to Rawls' theory of justice," in *John Rawls' Theory of Social Justice: An Introduction*, H. G. Blocker and E. H. Smith, eds. (Athens: Ohio Univ. Press, 1980), 5–41.

Burge, T., "Belief *de re*," *Journal of Philosophy* 74 (1977), 338–362.

Burge, T., "Truth and singular terms," *Nous* 8 (1974), 309–325.

Castaneda, H.-N., "'He': A study in the logic of self-consciousness," *Ratio* 8 (1966), 130–157.

Castaneda, H.-N., "On the logic of attributions of self-knowledge to others," *Journal of Philosophy* 65 (1968), 439–456.

Castaneda, H.-N., "On the logic of self-knowledge," *Nous* 1 (1967), 9–21.

Castaneda, H.-N., "Philosophical refutations," in *Principles of Philosophical Reasoning*, J. Fetzer, ed. (Totowa, NJ: Rowman and Allanheld, 1984), 227–258.

Castaneda, H.-N., Review of Hintikka's *Knowledge and Belief*, *Journal of Symbolic Logic* 24 (1964), 132–134.

Castaneda, H.-N., "The theory of questions, epistemic powers, and the indexical theory of knowledge," *Midwest Studies in Philosophy* 5 (1980), 193–237.

Chastain, C., "Reference and context," in *Minnesota Studies in the Philosophy of Science, Vol. 7: Language, Mind, and Knowledge*, K. Gunderson, ed. (Minneapolis: Univ. of Minnesota Press, 1975), 194–269.

Chisholm, R., *The First Person* (Minneapolis: Univ. of Minnesota Press, 1981).

Chisholm, R., "Knowledge and belief: 'De dicto' and 'de re,'" *Philosophical Studies* 29 (1976), 1–20.

Clark, R., "Comments," in *Perception and Personal Identity*, N. Care and R. Grimm, eds. (Cleveland: Case Western Univ. Press, 1969), 174–187.

Cooper, R., and T. Parsons, "Montague grammar, generative semantics and interpretive semantics," in *Montague Grammar*, B. Partee, ed. (New York: Academic Press, 1976), 311–362.

Cresswell, M. J., *Logics and Languages* (London: Methuen, 1973).

Cresswell, M. J., *Structured Meanings* (Cambridge: Bradford Books/MIT Press, 1985).

Davidson, D., "On saying that," in *Words and Objections: Essays on the Work of W. V. Quine*, D. Davidson and K. J. J. Hintikka, eds. (Dordrecht: D. Reidel, 1969), 158–174.

Davidson, D., "Truth and meaning," *Synthese* 17 (1967), 304–323.

Dennett, D. C., "Beyond belief," in *Thought and Object*, A. Woodfield, ed. (Oxford: Oxford Univ. Press, 1982), 1–95.

Dennett, D. C., "Brain writing and mind reading," in his *Brainstorms* (Montgomery, Vermont: Bradford Books; Cambridge, Mass.: MIT Press, 1978), 39–50.

Devitt, M., *Designation* (New York: Columbia Univ. Press, 1981).

Devitt, M., "Donnellan's distinction," *Midwest Studies in Philosophy* 6 (1981), 511–524.

Devitt, M., "Singular terms," *Journal of Philosophy* 71 (1974), 183–205.

Devitt, M., "Thoughts and their ascription," *Midwest Studies in Philosophy* 9 (1984), 385–420.

Donnellan, K., "Reference and definite descriptions," *Philosophical Review* 75 (1966), 281–304.

Dowty, D., *Word Meaning and Montague Grammar* (Dordrecht: D. Reidel, 1979).

Field, H., "Mental representation," *Erkenntnis* 13 (1978), 9–61.

Fodor, J. A., "Methodological solipsism considered as a research strategy in cognitive psychology," *Behavioral and Brain Sciences* (1980), 63–73.

Fotion, N., "Gewirth and categorial consistency," *Philosophical Quarterly* 18 (1968), 262–264.

Geach, P., "On belief about oneself," *Analysis* 18 (1957), 23–24.

Gewirth, A., "Categorial consistency in ethics," *Philosophical Quarterly* 17 (1967), 289–299.

Gewirth, A., *Reason and Morality* (Chicago: Univ. of Chicago Press, 1978).

Gewirth, A., "Some comments on categorial consistency," *Philosophical Quarterly* 20 (1970), 380–384.

Goodman, N., *The Structure of Appearance*, second edition (Indianapolis: Bobbs-Merrill, 1966).

Groenendijk, J., and M. Stokhof, "Semantic analysis of Wh—— complements," *Linguistics and Philosophy* 5 (1982), 175–234.

Hare, R. M., *Freedom and Reason* (Oxford: Oxford Univ. Press, 1963).

Hare, R. M., "Rawls' theory of justice," *Philosophical Quarterly* 23 (1973), 144–155.

Harman, G., "Nonsolipsistic conceptual role semantics," unpublished ms., Princeton Univ., 1984.

Harman, G., *Thought* (Princeton: Princeton Univ. Press, 1973).

Harsanyi, J. C., "Can the maximin principle serve as a basis for morality? A critique of John Rawls' theory," *American Political Science Review* 69 (1975), 594–606.

Herman, B., "Integrity and impartiality," *Monist* 66 (1983), 233–250.

Hintikka, K. J. J., "Answers to questions," in *The Intentions of Intentionality and Other New Models for Modalities* (Dordrecht: D. Reidel, 1975), 137–158.

Hintikka, K. J. J., "Individuals, possible worlds, and epistemic logic," *Nous* 1 (1967), 33–62.

Hintikka, K. J. J., *Knowledge and Belief* (Ithaca: Cornell Univ. Press, 1962).

Hintikka, K. J. J., "On attributions of 'self-knowledge,'" *Journal of Philosophy* 67 (1970), 73–87.

Hintikka, K. J. J., "On the proper treatment of quantifiers in Montague semantics," in *Logical Theory and Semantic Analysis*, S. Stenlund, ed. (Dordrecht: D. Reidel, 1974), 45–60.

Hintikka, K. J. J., "Quine on quantifying in: A dialogue," in *The Intentions of Intentionality and Other New Models for Modalities* (Dordrecht: D. Reidel, 1975), 102–136.

Hirschbühler, P., *The Syntax and Semantics of Wh—— Constructions* (Bloomington: Indiana Univ. Linguistics Club Publications, 1979).

Hubin, D. C., "Minimizing maximin," *Philosophical Studies* 37 (1980), 363–372.

Hull, R. D., "A semantics for superficial and embedded questions," in *Formal Semantics of Natural Language*, E. L. Keenan, ed. (Cambridge: Cambridge Univ. Press, 1975), 35–45.

Kalin, J., "Lies, secrets, and love" *Journal of Value Inquiry* 10 (1976), 253–265.

Kaplan, D., "Demonstratives," Unpublished ms., Univ. of California at Los Angeles, 1977.

Kaplan, D., "How to Russell a Frege-Church," *Journal of Philosophy* 72 (1975), 716–729.

Kaplan, D., "On the logic of demonstratives," in *Contemporary Perspectives in the Philosophy of Language*, P. French T. E. Uehling, and H. Wettstein, eds. (Minneapolis: Univ. of Minnesota Press, 1979), 401–412.

Kaplan, D., "Quantifying in," in *Words and Objections: Essays on the Work of W. V. Quine*, D. Davidson and J. Hintikka, eds. (Dordrecht: D. Reidel, 1969), 206–242. Reprinted in *Reference and Modality*, L. Linsky, ed. (Oxford: Oxford Univ. Press, 1971), 112–144.

Karttunen, L., "Syntax and semantics of questions," *Linguistics and Philosophy* 1 (1977), 3–44.

Kekes, J., "Morality and impartiality," *American Philosophical Quarterly* 18 (1981), 295–303.

Kenny, A., "Oratio obliqua," *Aristotelian Society Supplementary Volume* 37 (1963), 127–146.

Kilgore, C., and W. Lycan, "Epistemological relativity," unpublished ms., University of North Carolina, 1982.

Kraut, R., "Love *de re*," presented at the Seventeenth Chapel Hill Colloquium in Philosophy, October, 1982.

Kraut, R., "Objects of affection," in *Emotion: Philosophical Studies*, G. Myers and K. D. Irani, eds. (New York: Haven, 1984), 42–56.

Kraut, R., "There are no *de dicto* attitudes," *Synthese* 54 (1983), 275–294.

Kripke, S., "Naming and necessity," in *Semantics of Natural Language*, D. Davidson and G. Harman, eds. (Dordrecht: D. Reidel, 1972), 253–355.

Kripke, S., "A puzzle about belief," in *Meaning and Use*, A. Margalit, ed. (Dordrecht: D. Reidel, 1979), 239–283.

Kripke, S., "Speaker's reference and semantic reference," in *Contemporary Perspectives in the Philosophy of Language*, P. French, T. E. Uehling and H. Wettstein, eds. (Minneapolis: Univ. of Minnesota Press, 1979), 6–27.

Kvart, I., "Quine and modalities *de re*: A way out?" *Journal of Philosophy* 79 (1982), 295–318.

Lenzen, W., "Recent Work in Epistemic Logic," *Acta Philosophica Fennica* 30 (1978).

Lewis, D., "Attitudes *de dicto* and *de se*," *Philosophical Review* 88 (1979), 513–543.

Lewis, D., "General semantics," in *Semantics of Natural Language*, D. Davidson and G. Harman, eds. (Dordrecht: D. Reidel, 1972), 169–218.

Lewis, D., "Individuation by acquaintance and by stipulation," *Philosophical Review* 92 (1983), 3–32.

Lewis, D., "What Puzzling Pierre does not believe," *Australasian Journal of Philosophy* 59 (1981), 283–289.

Loar, B., *Mind and Meaning* (Cambridge: Cambridge Univ. Press, 1981).

Loar, B., "Must beliefs be sentences?" *PSA 1982*, vol. 2 (East Lansing: Philosophy of Science Association, 1982).

Lockwood, M., "Identity and reference," In *Identity and Individuation*, M. K. Munitz, ed. (New York: New York Univ. Press, 1971), 199–211.

Lycan, W., "Davidson on saying that," *Analysis* 33 (1972–1973), 138–139.

Lycan, W., "Hare, Singer and Gewirth on universalizability," *Philosophical Quarterly* 19 (1969), 135–144.

Lycan, W., *Logical Form in Natural Language* (Cambridge: Bradford Books/MIT Press, 1984).

Lycan, W., "The paradox of naming," in *Analytical Philosophy in Comparative Perspective*, B. K. Matilal and J. L. Shaw, eds. (Dordrecht: D. Reidel, 1985), 81–102.

Lycan, W., "Psychological laws," *Philosophical Topics* 12 (1981), 9–38.

Lycan, W., "Thoughts about things," in *The Representation of Knowledge and Belief*, M. Brand and R. M. Harnish, eds. (Tucson: Univ. of Arizona Press, 1985).

Lycan, W., "Toward a homuncular theory of believing," *Cognition and Brain Theory* 4 (1981), 139–159.

Lycan, W., "The trouble with possible worlds," in *The Possible and the Actual*, M. Loux, ed. (Ithaca: Cornell Univ. Press, 1979), 274–316.

Lycan, W., and S. Shapiro, "Actuality and essence," *Midwest Studies in Philosophy* 11 (to be published).

Marcus, R., "A proposed solution to a puzzle about belief," *Midwest Studies in Philosophy* 6 (1981), 501–510.

Massey, G., "Tom, Dick and Harry, and All the King's Men," *American Philosophical Quarterly* 13 (1976), 89–107.

Mayes, A., ed., *Memory in Humans and Animals* (Wokingham, Berkshire: Van Nostrand Rinehold, 1983).

McCawley, J., "A program for logic," in *Semantics of Natural Language*, D. Davidson and G. Harman, eds. (Dordrecht: D. Reidel, 1972), 498–544.

McDowell, J., "Quotation and saying that," in *Reference, Truth and Reality*, M. Platts, ed. (London: Routledge and Kegan Paul, 1980), 206–237.

McGinn, C., "A note on the Frege argument," *Mind* 85 (1976), 422–423.

McKay, T., "On proper names in belief ascriptions," *Philosophical Studies* 39 (1981), 287–303.

Medlin, B., "Ultimate principles and ethical egoism," *Australasian Journal of Philosophy* 35 (1957), 111–118.

Montague, R., *Formal Philosophy*, R. Thomason, ed. (New Haven: Yale Univ. Press, 1974).

Morton, A., "Because he thought he had insulted him," *Journal of Philosophy* 72 (1975), 5–15.

Munsat, S., "WH—— complementizers," *Linguistics and Philosophy* (to be published).

Nagel, T., "The objective self," in *Knowledge and Mind: Essays in Honor of Norman Malcolm*, C. Ginet and S. Shoemaker, eds. (Ithaca: Cornell Univ. Press, 1983), 211–232.

Nagel, T., *The Possibility of Altruism* (Oxford: Oxford Univ. Press, 1970).

Nagel, T., "Rawls on justice," *Philosophical Review* 82 (1973), 220–234.

Nemiah, J. C., "Dissociative amnesia: A clinical and theoretical reconsideration," in *Functional Disorders of Memory*, J. F. Kihlstrom and F. J. Evans, eds. (Hillsdale: Lawrence Erlbaum Associates, 1979), 303–323.

Neu, J., "What is wrong with incest?" *Inquiry* 19 (1976), 27–39.

Nozick, R., *Anarchy, State and Utopia* (Cambridge: Harvard Univ. Press, 1974).

Oldenquist, A., "Loyalties," *Journal of Philosophy* 79 (1982), 173–193.

Oldenquist, A., *Normative Behavior*, (Washington, D.C.: Univ. Press of America, 1983).

Oldenquist, A., "The possibility of selfishness," *American Philosophical Quarterly* 17 (1980), 25–33.

O'Shaughnessy, B., *The Will: A Dual Aspect Theory*, vol. 2 (Cambridge: Cambridge Univ. Press, 1980).

Pastin, M., "About *de re* belief," *Philosophy and Phenomenological Research* 34 (1974), 569–575.

Perry, J., "Frege on demonstratives," *Philosophical Review* 86 (1977), 474–497.

Perry, J., "The problem of the essential indexical," *Nous* 13 (1979), 3–21.

Plantinga, A., "The Boethian compromise," *American Philosophical Quarterly* 15 (1978), 129–138.

Platts, M., *Ways of Meaning* (London: Routledge and Kegan Paul, 1979).

Pollock, J., *Language and Thought* (Princeton: Princeton Univ. Press, 1982).

Pollock, J., "Thinking about an object," *Midwest Studies in Philosophy* 5 (1980), 487–499.

Prior, A., "Oratio obliqua," *Aristotelian Society Supplementary Volume* 37 (1963), 115–126.

Putnam, H., "The meaning of 'meaning.'" *Minnesota Studies in the Philosophy of Science, Vol. VII: Language, Mind, and Knowledge* (Minneapolis: Univ. of Minnesota Press, 1975), 131–193.

Putnam, H., "Philosophy of physics," in his *Mathematics, Matter and Method: Philosophical Papers*, vol. 1 (Cambridge: Cambridge Univ. Press, 1975), 79–92.

Quine, W. V., "Quantifiers and propositional attitudes," in his *The Ways of Paradox and Other Essays* (New York: Random House, 1966), 183–194.

Quine, W. V., "Intensions revisited," in *Contemporary Perspectives in the Philosophy of Language*, P. A. French, T. E. Uehling and H. Wettstein, eds. (Minneapolis: Univ. of Minnesota Press, 1979), 268–274.

Railton, P., "Alienation, consequentialism, and the demands of morality," *Philosophy and Public Affairs* 13 (1984), 134–172.

Rawls, J., *A Theory of Justice* (Cambridge: Harvard Univ. Press, 1971).

Reiman, J. H., "Privacy, intimacy, and personhood," *Philosophy and Public Affairs* 6 (1976), 26–44.

Sandel, M., *Liberalism and the Limits of Justice* (Cambridge: Cambridge Univ. Press, 1982).

Scanlon, T. M., "Contractarianism and utilitarianism," in *Utilitarianism and Beyond*, A. Sen and B. Williams, eds. (Cambridge: Cambridge Univ. Press, 1982), 103–128.

Schiffer, S., "The basis of reference," *Erkenntnis* 13 (1978), 171–206.

Schiffer, S., "Indexicals and the theory of reference," *Synthese* 49 (1981), 43–100.

Searle, J., *Intentionality* (Cambridge: Cambridge Univ. Press, 1983).

Searle, J., Referential and attributive," *Monist* 62 (1979), 190–208.

Sellars, W., "Some problems about belief," in *Words and Objections: Essays on the Work of W.V. Quine*, D. Davidson and J. Hintikka, eds. (Dordrecht: D. Reidel, 1969), 186–205.

Silverstein, H., "Universality and treating persons as persons" *Journal of Philosophy* 71 (1974), 57–71.

Sleigh, R. C., "On a proposed system of epistemic logic," *Nous* 2 (1968), 391–398.

Sleigh, R. C., "On quantifying into epistemic contexts," *Nous* 1 (1967), 23–31.

Sleigh, R. C., "Restricted range in epistemic logic," *Journal of Philosophy* 69 (1972), 67–77.

Sober, E., *Simplicity* (Oxford: Oxford Univ. Press, 1975).

Sosa, E., "Propositional attitudes *de dicto* and *de re*," *Journal of Philosophy* 67 (1970), 883–896.

Sosa, E., and M. Pastin, "A rejoinder on actions and *de re* belief," *Canadian Journal of Philosophy* 11 (1981), 735–739.

Stalnaker, R., "Semantics for belief," Unpublished ms., Cornell University, 1981.

Stampe, D., "Atributives and interrogatives," in *Semantics and Philosophy*, M. K. Munitz and P. K. Unger, eds. (New York: New York Univ. Press, 1974), 159–196.

Stich, S., "Autonomous psychology and the belief-desire thesis," *Monist* 61 (1978), 573–591.

Stich, S., *From Folk Psychology to Cognitive Science* (Cambridge: Bradford Books/MIT Press, 1983).

Stine, G., "Quantified logic for knowledge statements," *Journal of Philosophy* 71 (1974), 127–140.

Stocker, M., "The schizophrenia of modern ethical theories," *Journal of Philosophy* 73 (1976), 453–466.

Thomason, R., "Perception and individuation," in *Logic and Ontology*, M. Munitz, ed. (New York: New York Univ. Press, 1973), 261–285.

van Inwagen, P., "Creatures of fiction," *American Philosophical Quarterly* 14 (1977), 299–308.

Vendler, Z., *Res Cogitans* (Ithaca: Cornell Univ. Press, 1972).

Wallace, J., "Response to Arnaud," *Nous* 9 (1975), 427–428.

White, S. L., "Partial character and the language of thought," *Pacific Philosophical Quarterly* 63 (1982), 347–365.

Williams, B., "Person, character and morality," in *The Identities of Persons*, A. Rorty, ed. (Berkeley and Los Angeles: Univ. of California Press, 1976), 197–216.

Wilshire, B., *Role Playing and Identity* (Bloomington: Indiana Univ. Press, 1982).

Wolf, S., "Moral saints," *Journal of Philosophy* 79 (1982), 419–439.

Wolff, R. P., *Understanding Rawls* (Princeton: Princeton Univ. Press, 1977).

Index

⊒Ⴑ Bradford Books

Natalie Abrams and Michael D. Buckner, editors. MEDICAL ETHICS.

Peter Achinstein and Owen Hannaway, editors. OBSERVATION, EXPERIMENT, AND HYPOTHESIS IN MODERN PHYSICAL SCIENCE.

Jon Barwise and John Perry. SITUATIONS AND ATTITUDES.

Ned J. Block, editor. IMAGERY.

Steven Boër and William G. Lycan. KNOWING WHO.

Myles Brand. INTENDING AND ACTING.

Robert N. Brandon and Richard M. Burian, editors. GENES, ORGANISMS, POPULATIONS.

Paul M. Churchland. MATTER AND CONSCIOUSNESS.

Robert Cummins. THE NATURE OF PSYCHOLOGICAL EXPLANATION.

Daniel C. Dennett. BRAINSTORMS.

Daniel C. Dennett. ELBOW ROOM.

Fred I. Dretske. KNOWLEDGE AND THE FLOW OF INFORMATION.

Hubert L. Dreyfus, editor, in collaboration with Harrison Hall. HUSSERL, INTENTIONALITY, AND COGNITIVE SCIENCE.

K. Anders Ericsson and Herbert A. Simon. PROTOCOL ANALYSIS.

Owen J. Flanagan, Jr. THE SCIENCE OF THE MIND.

Jerry A. Fodor. REPRESENTATIONS.

Jerry A. Fodor. THE MODULARITY OF MIND.

Morris Halle and George N. Clements. PROBLEM BOOK IN PHONOLOGY.

Gilbert Harman. CHANGE IN VIEW: PRINCIPLES OF REASONING.

John Haugeland, editor. MIND DESIGN.

Norbert Hornstein. LOGIC AS GRAMMAR.

William G. Lycan. LOGICAL FORM IN NATURAL LANGUAGE.

Earl R. Mac Cormac. A COGNITIVE THEORY OF METAPHOR.

John Macnamara. NAMES FOR THINGS.

Charles E. Marks. COMMISSUROTOMY, CONSCIOUSNESS, AND UNITY OF MIND.

Izchak Miller. HUSSERL, PERCEPTION, AND TEMPORAL AWARENESS.

Zenon W. Pylyshyn. COMPUTATION AND COGNITION.

W. V. Quine. THE TIME OF MY LIFE.

Irvin Rock. THE LOGIC OF PERCEPTION.

George D. Romanos. QUINE AND ANALYTIC PHILOSOPHY.

George Santayana. PERSONS AND PLACES.

Roger N. Shepard and Lynn A. Cooper. MENTAL IMAGES AND THEIR TRANSFORMATIONS.

Elliott Sober, editor. CONCEPTUAL ISSUES IN EVOLUTIONARY BIOLOGY.

Elliott Sober, THE NATURE OF SELECTION.

Robert C. Stalnaker. INQUIRY.

Stephen P. Stich. FROM FOLK PSYCHOLOGY TO COGNITIVE SCIENCE.

Joseph M. Tonkonogy. VASCULAR APHASIA.

Hao Wang. BEYOND ANALYTIC PHILOSOPHY.